IRAN IN WORLD POLITICS

ARSHIN ADIB-MOGHADDAM

Iran in World Politics

The Question of the Islamic Republic

Columbia University Press
New York

Columbia University Press
Publishers Since 1893
New York

Paperback edition, 2010

Library of Congress Cataloging-in-Publication Data

Adib-Moghaddam, Arshin.
Iran in world politics : the question of the Islamic republic / Arshin Adib-Moghaddam.
p. cm.
Includes bibliographical references and index.
ISBN 978-0-231-70046-7 (cloth: alk. paper)
ISBN 978-0-231-70047-4 (pbk: alk. paper)
1. Iran--Politics and government--1997- 2. Iran--Politics and government--1979-1997. 3. Iran--Foreign relations--1997- 4. Iran--Foreign relations--1979-1997. 5. Political culture--Iran. 6. Islam and politics--Iran. I. Title.
DS318.83.A35 2008
327.55—dc22

2010026387

Columbia University Press books are printed on permanent and durable acid-free paper.
This book is printed on paper with recycled content.
Printed in India by Imprint Digital

c 10 9 8 7 6 5 4 3 2 1
p 10 9 8 7 6 5 4 3 2 1

CONTENTS

They inscribed their humiliations, their hatred for the regime, and their resolve to overthrow it at the bounds of heaven and earth, in an envisioned history that was religious just as much as it was political.

—*Michel Foucault on the Islamic revolution in Iran*

PREFACE

Iran in World Politics is very much a book reflecting on the tumultuous political processes surrounding contemporary Iran and the wider West Asian region. The introduction explains the ways Iran has been interpreted both within and outside the country over the periods before and after the Islamic revolution in 1979. The argument is that history is produced by men and women, just as it can be invented and reinvented in order to market a particular image of the Islamic Republic. What is needed, to guard ourselves from identifying with one particular opinion on Iran is a critical attitude towards world politics in general and Iranian affairs in particular. The question of the Islamic Republic can only be sufficiently addressed, it is argued, if we pluralize our understanding of post-revolutionary Iran.

I call for 'critical Iranian studies' as a means to challenge thoroughly positivistic accounts of Iranian affairs, which are too often written with polemical intent or, worse still, out of ideological conviction. Whilst each part of the book is an essay, and each essay contains a self-contained discussion of a particular issue, they follow a clear ambition: to emphasize that contemporary Iran is a complex subject, that we cannot rely on one opinion about the country, that we need to explore the political frameworks into which a particular image of Iran is incorporated, that we cannot trust our politicians to 'enlighten' us, and that the international media are equally unreliable. Ideally, the reader will start reading the book with a particular understanding of what Iran 'is' or what the Islamic Republic stands for, and finish it with a totally new understanding of the country. So one of the primary purposes of this book is to create discontinuities in the way we think about Iran and world politics more generally.

My ambition to attempt to pluralize the meaning of Iran evolved out of a passage in Ibn Sina's *Mantiq al-mashraqiyyin* (The Logic of the Orientals) written in the eleventh century AD, out of his self-criticism that—as I read the passage—questioned all the familiar certitudes of my own understanding of history, theory, method and methodology. In this particular passage Ibn Sina (Avicenna) describes how the overbearing authoritative narrative of the Greek Peripatetics determined how he viewed the world and said he would now like to distance himself from that system of thought. 'Since those who were the people of learning were strongly in favour of the Greek Peripatetics,' he admits ,'we did not find it appropriate to separate ourselves and speak differently from everyone else.' He thus felt compelled to 'take their sides', lamenting that 'with those philosophers who were more fanatical than any of the Greek sects' he too became fanatical. Ibn Sina criticised himself for overlooking their faults and providing a leader and tutor for them while he was 'aware of their errors'. If he revealed some opposition to the guild philosophers, 'It was only in matters in which no patience was possible'.[1]

What I found particularly striking in this passage is that Ibn-Sina was ready to dismiss his own position (including his vast corpus of earlier writings) in order to distance himself from the system of thought dominating his 'discipline' and age. He was thus not afraid to take on the uncertainties of 'anti-foundational' knowledge, of leaving the solitudes of a familiar territory, and was ready to sacrifice his reputation amongst his peers in order to question the status quo. In this early manifestation of the powers of negation engendered by critical thinking, the issue that I have taken on, what reveals—by means of Ibn-Sina's self-critique—the dangers of teleological knowledge is the relativity of my own understanding of my subject matter. This made it impossible for me to position the present study within a predefined, all-encompassing narrative. I am not attempting to make the case in favour or against the Islamic Republic. The horizon of this book is not ideology, I am not prostituting myself for a political cause. To some readers the book may thus appear 'controversial'. Not that it was written in order to cause controversy, but without an explicit chronology, without an iron-clad argument that either dismisses or acknowledges the Islamic Republic, without a school of thought or theoretical disposition that could be called in order to defend it, without the 'elegance' of a descriptive account of Iranian affairs, the present study opens itself up to criticism from many sides.

Moreover, any inquiry that emphasizes the importance of invented norms, ideas, values, institutions and other cultural artefacts, which are quite naturally the subject of differing opinions, is *ipso facto* 'controversial'. But until the day when we may 'cut and paste' Iran into the laboratories of the natural sciences, where action A causes a reaction B, and where Iran can be formulaically defined, where the country can be reduced to a set of mathematical mnemonics that we can all agree upon, I retain my emphasis on the way cultural 'facts' are invented, socially engineered and internalized only to be challenged by a competing counter-culture. In my opinion, only with an emphasis on these inventions can our use of the terms 'Iran' and 'Iranians', and the peoples, cultures, dialects, politics, ethics, morals and histories to which these vastly abstract words refer, be adequately explored. The following essays are my first steps towards that beginning and they therefore cut through many disciplines and 'schools of thought', from social psychology, neurophysiology, cultural studies, critical theory, and post-colonial studies to sociology, political science, International Relations (IR), 'Middle Eastern' studies, and post-modernism. I hope that upon engaging with this book, the reader will appreciate the utility of these disciplines for our understanding of the political world surrounding us.

I am conscious that some of the theoretical material may appear 'grey', to use Goethe's famous metaphor. But I would claim that the reader will reappear strengthened and equipped with the tools necessary to foster a critical attitude, whenever he or she dares to enter some of the theoretical 'tunnels' underlying the structure of this book. Ultimately, I hope to recompense the cost of entering them, with the pleasure of giving access to another 'reality' or truth configuration. I would go as far as saying that *everything* surrounding us is theorized reality. I feel thus obliged to place myself within it in order to break out of its confines, to extend my knowledge about the way invented abstractions violate us. In short, this book attempts to fill the vast parenthesis that should follow simplifications such as Iran, Islam, Shiism, Arab, East, West; it claims to extend our understanding of them, to open them up for investigation, rather than to accept their conventional 'definitions' all too readily.

I have been teaching and writing about world politics for some time now, but this book is the product of two distinct phases of my academic endeavours. The first was the period immediately after my PhD at Cambridge University in 2004, when I lived, studied, lectured (and eventually married) in Tehran; the second, my tenure as the first Jarvis Doctorow research Fellow and faculty member at, respectively, St Edmund Hall and the Department of Politics and International Relations, Oxford University from October 2005 until September 2007. I have researched and worked between England and Iran ever since and I have thus accumulated debts of gratitude to friends and colleagues in both places. I would like to thank Louise Fawcett, James Piscatori, Sir Adam Roberts, Ali-Reza Sheikholeslami and Philip Robins for their comments on earlier versions of chapter four. Reza and James are mentors and friends, and their intellectual honesty has made a profound impact on me. Among those others who have supported my research along the way, I would like to mention Charles Jones and Yezid Sayigh. Farid Marjai, Mehdi Zakerian, and Davoud Gharayagh-Zandi have helped me to introduce my writings to a Persian-speaking audience and I am thankful for their guidance. I would also like to express my gratitude to Michael Dwyer of Hurst & Co. whose dedication and integrity I found admirable. Tat Yan Kong, the head of my current port of call—the Department of Politics and International Studies at SOAS, London University—was very helpful in supporting my application for a book grant. I am grateful to his guidance and the support of my colleagues Charles Tripp and Laleh Khalili to that end. My wife Elham, a 'product' of Iran's post-revolutionary society, supported me a great deal with translations of Iranian literature and poetry and her ideas for the cover of this book. I would like to apologize to her for the vast intrusions into our private life that this project caused and I am forever grateful for her patience with me and my work.

Parts One and Two are based on essays that have appeared in *Critique: Critical Middle Eastern Studies*[2] and *Middle East Report*,[3] and Parts Three and Four on essays which were published in *Third World Quarterly*[4] and the *International Studies Journal*.[5] I would like to thank the editors of these journals, Eric Hooglund, Chris Toensing, Shahid Qadir and Mehdi Zakerian respectively, for their editorial comments and for granting permission to incorporate those essays as a part of those chapters.

Tehran, April 2007 Arshin Adib-Moghaddam

INTRODUCTION
THE QUESTION OF THE ISLAMIC REPUBLIC

Once the noble Ibrahim, as he sat on his throne,
Heard a clamour and noise of cries on the roof,
Also heavy footsteps on the roof of his palace.
He said to himself, 'Whose heavy feet are these?'
He shouted from the window, 'Who goes there?'
The guards, filled with confusion, bowed their heads , saying,
'It is we, going the rounds in search.'
He said, 'What seek ye?' They said, 'Our Camels.'
He said, 'Who ever searched for camels on a housetop?'
They said, 'We follow thy example,
Who seekest union with God, while sitting on a throne

— Jalaledin Rumi (Mowlana)

Not east
not west
not north
not south
only this spot I am standing on now.

— Abbas Kiarostami

At the same time as I was writing *The International Politics of the Persian Gulf* which was published in 2006, I began to reflect more specifically on post-revolutionary Iran: on the country's foreign relations and domestic politics and on the way Iran is represented. The paragraphs that follow are the results of this process and they are in many ways an extension of the argument of my previous book. My object there was to inquire into, and where necessary challenge, some of the mainstream analyses of international politics in the Persian Gulf, and my object here is to do the same with regard to contemporary Iran. That the 'field' of Iranian studies is a field of general change doesn't make my task easier. It has become a truism that almost everyone has something to say about Iran, whether on the Achaemenid kings, the legend of Sheherzade, Persepolis, the Peacock Throne, the splendour of Isfahan, or, more recently, Ayatollah Khomeini and the Islamic revolution. Personalities that have become part of the historical self-understanding of the country—Zoroaster, Cyrus, Xerxes, Rumi, Hafiz, Khayyam, Sa'adi, Ferdowsi, Avicenna, Razes—have largely survived the 'onslaught' of the cultural reputation of contemporary Iran, even in the 'Western' worlds. Yet ironically, because these personalities have such a prominent presence in world culture, in their distance from anything associated with the revolution and the Islamic Republic, they also indicate how contested is our knowledge of contemporary Persia (itself a contested term), which after all, has a life independent of our representations.[1] Thus I feel that one of my purposes in this book must be to describe and analyse the complexity of the country, rather than to reduce the meaning of it to a set of easily digestible headlines. For what I see in the modern history of Iran, in its foundational myths and ideological content, is a diverse and wide movement in thought and meaning.

Ideally, this book equips you, the reader, with the necessary tools to widen and fill the gaps between the lines next time you read a newspaper article about Iran in particular and the political world in general. It is as much a book about Iran as it is about critical reading. My point is that facts are made by humans, that they are not God-given, not inevitable. It is our responsibility to investigate how politicians, the media, and other agents invent and perpetuate them. If we are equipped with the tools to think critically, it would be far more difficult to lure us into another war; it would certainly make us rather more alert about what politicians and some media pundits say. At the time of writing there is a systematic and aggressive campaign to castigate Iran for many things, from the civil war in Iraq to the Hamas takeover in Gaza. Here, it does not come as a surprise that the advocates of war against Iran are the same people who supported the invasion of Iraq: Con Coughlin of the *Daily Telegraph* (UK), Charles Krauthammer of *The Washington Post*, Michael Ledeen, Joshua Muravchik of the American Enterprise Institute and a long list of right-wing politicians from Joseph Lieberman and Charles Tannock to Dick Cheney, Rudi Giuliani and John McCain (the latter joked about bombing Iran at a campaign appearance in April 2007).[2] My idea in this book is to employ critical theory in order to place Iran out of the reach of their awesome propaganda, to place the country more firmly within a new intellectual discourse, to find alternatives to the bursts of polemical insouciance that have paved the way for so many wars in the region. Here lies the normative ambition of this study. The struggle for sustainable peace in Iraq, Palestine, Afghanistan, Lebanon and elsewhere can only evolve out of a new intellectualism, a critical consciousness that fosters protests against the crimes of governments and their enforcers amongst us. My focus on the Islamic Republic in this book is in many ways a contribution to this new type of radical critique.

Some are going to object that by focusing on the Islamic Republic I am undervaluing Iran's historical continuity as one of the 'few relatively permanent political entities' or 'historic nations' of the world.[3] They will recall that owing to this historical continuity, Persia has repeatedly attracted the attention of thinkers, historians, poets and conquerors from Aeschylus, Herodotus, Alexander and Genghis Khan to Marco Polo, Machiavelli, Goethe, Schlegel, Massignon, Renan, de Sacy and others. They will argue that in the twentieth century, owing to the discovery of the first commercially viable oil fields in Masjed-e Soleiman in 1908, imperial interests became more intense, and that commercial empires like the Reuters news agency and British Petroleum (BP) would not exist without the profitable 'rent' extracted from Iranian oilfields. They will say that all these factors are part of the historical consciousness of Iranians, and they are right. But there is no escaping the fact that the Islamic revolution in 1979 fundamentally changed the way Iran was approximated as an abstraction and an absolute, and that the revolution radically questioned Iran's historical consciousness, the country's self awareness and *jahanbini* (world-view).[4] Suddenly, for many in the 'West' and in Iran itself, the country was more Semitic than Aryan, more Iran than Persia, more Oriental than Indo-European, more black than white, more Third World than emerging economy, more Eastern than Western. Indeed, the historical consciousness on which analysts of Iran have prided themselves may be little more than a reflection of these invented images of the country. Ultimately, it is possible to view that historical consciousness as a specific prejudice of an author who claims to know Iran and who artificially substantiates the presumed superiority of one specific image and understanding of the Islamic Republic over another.

In the present study I do not attempt to put forward a singular argument about the politics of Iran. I do, however, intend to contribute to a new, critical perspective on the way Iran is approximated as a subject matter. One way to do this is to find the different possible theories by which a particular image of the country is justified. Edward Said provides a point of reference here. According to him, Iran's changing image in the 'West' has been due to the ideological connection between the representation of Islam in the 'Western' media and perceptions of the Islamic revolution in 1979. He links reactions to what took place during the revolution to the 'longstanding attitude to Islam, the Arabs and the Orient' which have been implanted continuously into the 'public's subliminal consciousness' by the 'culture industry:'[5]

For whether one looked at such recent critically acclaimed fiction as V.S. Naipaul's *A Bend in the River* and John Updike's *The Coup*, or at grade-school history textbooks, comic strips, television serials, films, and cartoons, the iconography of Islam was uniform, was uniformly ubiquitous, and drew its material from the same time-honoured view of Islam: hence the frequent caricatures of Muslims as oil suppliers, as terrorists, and more recently, as bloodthirsty mobs. Conversely, there has been very little place either in the culture generally or in discourse about non-Westerners in particular to speak or even to think about, much less to portray, Islam or anything Islamic sympathetically. … And to judge from the various in-depth media studies and interviews on the Iranian revolution during the spring of 1979, there has been little inclination to accept the revolution itself as much more than a defeat for the United States (which in a very specific sense, of course, it was), or a victory of dark and light.[6]

This does not mean, of course, that since the revolution only politically biased material has been produced about Iran. I do not say that and I don't think Said implied that. But prominent strata of particular societies have had the motivation and power to portray Iran in a particular way, and this image has therefore become more widely disseminated and acceptable. Ultimately, Iranians themselves have felt the discriminatory effects of that process. A recent report on the attitudes of Iranian scientists shows, for instance, that for them being Iranian 'means being regarded suspiciously; at best they are viewed as insignificant; at worst they are seen as "terrorists" or as belonging to non-respectable networks.'[7] The report also refers to one scientist who mentioned that 'he could not say publicly in international scientific meetings that he worked on "explosions," because he might be treated as contributing to terrorism.'[8] From the perspective of another one 'being

Iranian was considered a negative feature by Western colleagues: in a letter of support his tutor wrote, "Although Mr. X is an Iranian, he is still one of the best in his branch".'[9]

Few Iranians would doubt that after the Islamic revolution negative images of Iran have become more prevalent than balanced ones. These images do not correspond to what Iran 'is', of course, but to what powerful strata of a particular society take it to be. Those individuals—primarily in the 'West', not so much in the Third Worlds—use their position to advocate a particular (largely perverted) image of the country, and this image therefore has become more accepted. I think that my emphasis on individuals in the 'West' is qualified here because on average person A in Miami has disproportionately more quantitative and qualitative access to communication channels than person B in Zahedan. Likewise, the former US Secretary of State Henry Kissinger has more opportunities at his disposal to influence international public discourse on Iran than the former Iranian foreign minister Ibrahim Yazdi has. Indeed, because of his prominent position within the political culture of the US, analyzing the attitudes of the former provides a good starting point to explore the kind of engineering of the meaning of Iran that I am referring to. 'The single most important factor in the Shah's collapse,' Kissinger writes in his autobiography,

> was the policy he learned from the West: the modernisation of a feudal, Islamic society … Western liberal maxims caused the Shah to build a secular, modern state in the reformist mould of Kemal Atatürk and to force-feed industrialisation to a population that had barely left the feudal age. … The modernising cultural influences from the West, flooding over the broken dam of Iran's cultural isolation, overwhelmed Iran's religious and social traditions. The rootless, the newly powerful, the orthodox, and the spiritually dispossessed came together with disparate, often conflicting motives and swept away the Shah's rule in an orgy of retribution and vengefulness.

> But retribution for what? To be sure, there was corruption at the Shah's court, though not unusually so by the standards of the region or even by the standards of the regime that followed. ... However, his accumulated failures were almost certainly less severe than the practices of other nations in the Persian Gulf or among the nonaligned that have not been exposed to opprobrium. And nothing that happened can compare with the witch trials, executions, terrorism, and lunacy that followed, reminiscent in bloodiness and judicial hypocrisy of the worst excesses of Robespierre.[10]

In analyzing this passage we must not ignore, as Edward Said reminds us, that this type of discourse is essentially ideological, unscholarly and polemical.[11] Nor, as Noam Chomsky emphasizes, should we dismiss the point that it expresses the power discrepancy between the 'West' and the Third World.[12] And, as some post-colonial theorists understand, we must not underestimate the way revolutions in the Third World are portrayed from without.[13] Yet what we also must appreciate before all else, in my opinion, is that the Third Worlds are not merely products of 'Western' colonialism, that they *do* have a life independent of Orientalist representations.[14] It is important, in other words, to understand that statements like the one made by Kissinger do not only advocate or affirm a certain political bias expressed by the author, that they are not merely part of a larger imperial attitude; they are reactions to a reality that is remote and not immediately controllable. Kissinger, and other ideologically minded authors, feel compelled to counter this 'alien' reality, because it threatens the status quo and because it challenges the familiar order of things. Consider Kissinger's reference to Robespierre in this context. The same comparison was made by the British press to describe Mohammad Mossadegh, the 'Robespierre fanatic' and 'tragic Frankenstein', who was 'obsessed with the xenophobic idea' to nationalize the Anglo-Iranian Oil Company in 1951. Moreover Kissinger's emphasis on Iran's 'pre-modern' societal structure is very close to N. Marbury Efimenco's interpretation of Iranian society in the 1950s as essentially 'medieval and fragmented' and hence unable 'to fit the democratic mould'.[15] In all these instances the authors reacted to events that were happening in another, parallel reality that could not be easily controlled. Hence the attempt—not entirely unsuccessful—to deny their audiences access to an 'independent' historical reality in which the unfolding events could be assessed from a non-manipulative perspective. What was emphasized instead was a counter-reality that could be superimposed on the unfolding events, a reality that was more amendable to 'Western' interests. Politics, in this case, revealed itself as the most distinguished art of 'reality production'.

The efforts to manipulate Iranian history are not restricted to these examples, of course. In order to organise the coup d'état in 1953, there were also very direct efforts to misrepresent what was happening in Iran. To that end, the Iran desk of the US State Department was able to plant a CIA study in *Newsweek* 'using the normal channel of desk officer to journalist'. The article was one of several planted press reports that, when reprinted in Tehran, fed the 'war of nerves' against the democratically elected government of Mohammad Mossadegh.[16] We may further extend the empirical scope of this discussion by focusing on the efforts of historians to portray the coup d'état as a triumph of the Shah, which was in line with the CIA/MI6 version of the events. In an article published in the *International Journal of Middle East Studies (IJMES)* in 1972, for instance, Roger M. Savory claimed that the 'warmth and spontaneity of the Shah's welcome by the people when he returned to Iran on 22 August 1953 ... should not have occasioned any surprise to the student of Persian history',[17] reassuring the reader that there 'is no reason ... to attach any special significance to the virulence of the anti-Shah feeling among Iranian students in foreign countries.'[18] 'The Shah's good intentions,' George Lenczowski concurred in the same year, 'were thwarted by the onrush of emotional nationalism which resulted in the ... standstill of oil operations.'[19] 'Seen in perspective' the policy of reinstalling the Shah 'could be considered successful: Iran's independence was preserved and America's security frontier was more firmly established.'[20] Stanford Shaw, the editor of *IJMES* in 1972, reconfirmed the 'scholarly' consensus:[21]

Roger M. Savory, Professor of Persian at the University of Toronto, Canada, stresses the inbred tendency of Persian society to remain unchanged ('homeostatis'), regardless of efforts to reform it, and points out the importance of the Persian monarchy, as typified by Shah Mohammad Reza Shah, as the sole element of Persian society strong enough to overcome this tendency and introduce significant reforms despite the powerful opposition of those with vested interests in the old order. Dr Savory describes how the opposition to the Shah today, led by a segment of the Persian intelligentsia, particularly Persian students outside the country, is based largely on the same romantic views of contemporary Iran which led Mohammad Mossadiq and others in the Iranian national movement to disrupt reform and so join the opposition led by the great landowners, the *ulama*, and others who successfully frustrated reform until the Shah himself took the lead in the famous 'white revolution'. Dr Savory points out how the Shah has gained the support of the mass of the people benefiting from his reforms, particularly the peasants, and also the army and the younger civil servants.[22]

Kissinger, Efimenco, Savory, Lenczowski and Shaw all attach a particular meaning to Iran in order to manipulate the reader's understanding of the reality in the country. Their misrepresentations of Iranian history are by no means inconsequential. Apart from their legitimation of the Shah's dictatorial rule and the US support for his regime, they also had a very direct impact on the way Iranian history has been taught until the present day. The fifth edition of a widely distributed US high school textbook entitled *America: Pathways to the Present*, for instance, refers to Mohammad Mossadegh as a 'pro-Communist leader'.[23] A concerned parent wrote to the authors in April 2001 indicating that he did 'not think this kind of historical alteration comes from a miss print, especially in a textbook.' It appears odd, he maintained, 'to see how reality can be changed—not by a journalist or radio/TV show—but a professor of the department of history!'[24] What started in the minds of a few intelligence officials, embedded academics and politicians was passed on all the way down to the history books taught at US high schools. Such is the power and longevity of ideological inventions.

So the authors mentioned above were, alas, not entirely unsuccessful in their efforts to misrepresent what was happening in Iran. From a critical perspective, this kind of historical engineering must be treated as ideological reactions to the very real events unfolding 'on the ground', which were 'real' irrespective of their representations. Similarly, the argument that Iranians should be content with the dictatorship of the Shah was made in order to persuade us that revolution and national independence movements are intrinsically irrational, even unreal. With regard to Pahlavi Iran, that rationale has also been central to the writings of Marvis Zonis, James A. Bill and Leonard Binder, who all employed their prominent position at US universities to explain 'academically' the 'benevolent' rule of the Shah.[25] For Binder, writing in 1964, it was quite necessary to look forward to 'the establishment of a government with which Iranians might identify themselves'. But at the same time Iranians were told it was better to achieve 'such a desirable end through the patient working of the present [Pahlavi] system than by violently overthrowing it.'[26] James A. Bill and Carl Leiden had similar calculations in mind when they wrote in 1974 that it 'would be a serious mistake to underestimate the importance and effect of the Shah-sponsored reforms.'[27] Marvin Zonis agreed, concluding one year later that the Shah's 'control over the internal situation is at its zenith'. For him it was 'undoubtedly true that no Iranian ruler … commanded as responsive a political system as does Mohammed Reza Pahlavi' which put the Shah and the political elite of the country in an 'enviable situation'.[28] Moreover, if we interpret these statements on Iran in conjunction with the following passage taken from a conversation in the Oval Office (8 April 1971) among the political contemporaries of the aforementioned authors—Richard Nixon, Alexander Haig and Douglas MacArthur II—our understanding of 'where they are coming from' gets even clearer. Eight years before the Islamic revolution in 1979, Nixon observes that

Iran's the only thing there. The Philippines is a can of worms, as you know. Taiwan, curiously enough, is a pretty strong little place, but it lives in sufferance. Malaysia and Singapore are at each other's throats. [Singapore Prime Minister] Lee Kuan Yew, the socialist, being probably the ablest leader in the region. The Indonesians are beginning to come back, but they're 20 years away. ... It's one friend there. Iran is not of either world, really [Christian or Arab?]. By God, if we can go with them, if we can have them strong, and they're in the centre of it, and a friend of the United States, uh, I couldn't agree more, 'cause you look around there, it's [Gen. George] Patton who said, 'Who else do we have, except for Europe?' ... The southern Mediterranean is all gone. [Morocco's King] Hassan will be there, he's a nice fellow, but Morocco, Christ, they can't last. Morocco, Tunisia, Libya, uh, Algeria, Sudan, naturally, the UAR [Egypt], all those little miserable countries around Jordan, and Lebanon, the rest, they're like, they'd go down like tenpins, just like that. ... Let's look at Africa, generally. This country [Iran] at least has got some degree of civilization in its history, but those Africans, you know, are only about 50 to 75 years from out of the trees, some of 'em. But did you know, in all of Africa, of all those new countries, there is not one country that has a so-called parliamentary democracy that meets even the standards that we would happily insist on for Vietnam? Happily! ... But you see ... we've just got to be, not tolerant, not tolerant of violation of principles that we feel and believe in very deeply, not supporting the idea that there ought to be a dictatorship to replace democracy or some sort of thing, not saying that dictatorship of the left is wrong but that dictatorship of the right is right but, having in mind one solemn fact: That people in the world are in different states of development and they are different, and that each needs a system that fits its own. ... Japan, for example—sure they have elections and all that sort of thing, but you know damn well that a business oligarchy runs Japan. Right? You were there, huh? And it's the way it has to be![29]

A singular statement like the one made by Kissinger is not confined to the imagination of the author and it cannot therefore be analyzed in isolation. If that were the case we wouldn't have to 'worry' because his statement would be pre-systematic—that is, it wouldn't be part of a wider, 'reality producing' cultural system. But the preceding quotations show that beyond the visible façade of Kissinger's representation of Iran, there is a whole systematic political culture that is both uncompromisingly hostile towards everything that is considered non-Western—for example, Iran was considered a 'quasi-friend' before the revolution because it was considered to be of 'neither world' and hence susceptible to be drawn into the 'Western' narrative—and at times insidiously racist (e.g. Nixon's comments on Africa). Thus Kissinger's statement becomes structural and hence of analytical value only if it is pasted into the epistemology of US representations of the 'other', into the cultural apparatus that has been able to take the 'West' (embodied by 'America') as a starting point for—and *Endziel* of—civilisation.

I think those uniformly negative statements on the Islamic revolution in Iran, especially in the US, could only be successfully nurtured within that cultural habitat. How else could we trace how they 'travel' horizontally between Kissinger's contemporaries in US politics and 'academia', and vertically, e.g. back and forth from the 'low culture' of international politics and 'Middle Eastern' studies to the 'high culture' of the literary world? Consider in that regard this diary entry by John Fowles dated 14 February 1989 and written with reference to the Rushdie crisis: 'Everyone falls over themselves to avoid the truth that most Muslims are very primitive people and can't be treated as sophisticated ones. If you endlessly prod a tiger, of course its claws will flash out.'[30] Consider also V.S. Naipaul's best-selling book *Among the Believers: An Islamic Journey*, where he expresses a similarly unsympathetic view of Islam in general and Iran's Islamic revolution in particular describing both as anarchic, medieval, archaic, and ultimately irrational.[31] This image, in turn, is very close to the one imagined by the late Polish intellectual Ryszard Kapuscinski:

[T]he Iranian revolution … emerged as a reaction to the optimistic efforts for development. … The rapid importation of technology into Iran, for example, was also perceived by Iranians as a humiliation for a people with such a long, traditional culture. Because they were not able to learn the technology, they felt ashamed. This humiliation caused a very strong reaction. … The emotional and religious movements we see in reaction today across the Islamic world are only the beginning. The Iranian revolution opened a new period in Third World countries—the period of cultural decolonisation. But this counter-revolution cannot succeed. It is not creative, but defensive. It remains defined by what it resists. It leads to paralysis. Meanwhile, America moves on at relative light speed.[32]

Without contestation, now that we have pasted it into a wider narrative, the initial statement quoted from Kissinger's autobiography would threaten to assume the threshold of objectivity, it would appear 'real'. Certainly, it would no longer be an autonomous, singular, pre-systematic argument. Rather, without criticism, it would slowly claim 'an inert objectivity available to all, with a significance conceived of as belonging to it intrinsically rather than as expressive of something else.'[33] In the absence of critique, in a matter of a few pages, Kissinger's initial statement could thus have been *reified*; it could claim the status of 'reality'. Consequently, if it is read in conjunction with the other very pronounced anti-Muslim, not entirely non-'racist' quotations, it could have claimed 'a thing-like facticity separated from its human source', which, *ab initio*, entails the de-humanization of the object,[34] i.e. in our case the de-humanization of Iranians in particular and Third World 'natives' in general. To render useful an argument Gramsci makes in *The Modern Prince* here: 'Reality is a product of the application of human will to the society of things,' and since also 'everything is political, even philosophy and philosophies,' we are obliged to understand that in the realm of ideas each statement exists not only to occupy a place for itself, but to contain or prevent competing realities from emerging.[35] If four pages could have triggered such a process, one can only imagine with awe the impact of the multifarious, global reification processes on our perceptions of Iranians, Muslims and other non-'Western' peoples.

I hope that even the most sceptical reader will agree that the revolution gave impetus to an almost immutable, emotionally charged struggle for the meaning of modern Iran. The question of the Islamic Republic which concerns us here emerges out of this struggle. On the one side, there is the Iran whose 'cultural essence' is considered 'Persian', in which the country's ancient, pre-Islamic civilisation and the poetry of Hafiz, Rumi and Khayyam is artificially divorced from contemporary life in the country. This is the Iran favoured in the 'West'. It is the picture of Iran that continues to have a 'celebrated', if distorted presence in mass-culture fed by Hollywood productions such as Oliver Stone's or Robert Rossen's *Alexander the Great*, Raoul Walsh's *Esther and the King*, international bestsellers such as Tom Holland's *Persian Fire* or Deepak Chopra's *The Love Poems of Rumi* and videogames such as *The Prince of Persia*.[36] On the other side, there is the Iran whose Islamic and revolutionary identities are in conflict with those representations. This is 'Hussein's Iran', the land of sacrifice in the name of Islam, the birthplace of the 'party of God' (Hezbollah), the country that celebrates Ashura with immense cultural sincerity, the place where Muhammad, Jesus and Moses become revolutionary figures in an eternal struggle for justice and spiritual atavism. These emotive ideas, at least, are central to the way the Islamic Republic wishes to portray itself.

Those cultural tensions between the self-perception of post-revolutionary Iran and the representation of the country from without are central to the following sections. Even though the main theoretical claims and empirical hypotheses will be obvious to the reader engaging with this book, a few underlying themes are worth re-emphasizing at this stage. One of the arguments I make here is that there is an almost unbridgeable difference between the way Iran is translated to us by the international media, political functionaries and academics and the reality on the ground, the complex existence of the post-revolutionary Iranian polity. In the current period when millions of US dollars are spent on 'democracy projects' all over West Asia, intellectuals can hardly remain ignorant that an insidiously close relationship exists between power and knowledge—especially when it comes to such contested subjects as the Islamic Republic.[37] One of the immediate consequences of this relationship is that discourse on Iran is saturated with policy-relevant, think-tank-type analyses, which are too often designed to reify the caricature of Iran as a monolithic, unchangeable, eternally anarchic place.[38] These types of analyses fail to recognize, sometimes deliberately, that since the Islamic revolution in 1979, and in many ways before then, Iran has been in the middle of a complex transformation process that affects the country in an irregular fashion. It will become immediately obvious that I am arguing against 'positivistic' readings of Iranian politics that have dominated our understanding of Iran for quite some time now. I am referring to those studies that are devoid of questions about the way history is invented, those that neglect focusing on the way reality is wilfully engineered. Indeed, a subtitle of this book might have been 'In Opposition to Orthodoxy'. If there is one common theme that lies behind the following essays, it is the denial of the presumption that Iranian politics (and world politics in general for that matter) are conducted in a mono-causal, linear, unilaterally defined mode.[39]

So intransigent is scholarly positivism on Iran that our understanding of the country has been shielded almost entirely from questions of epistemology, methodology and theory. These approaches continue to hold up well, owing no doubt to disciplinary and paradigmatic boundaries. Most scholars of 'Middle Eastern' studies simply do not care much for theory, and political theorists have not done much to extend their empirical scope to the domestic and international politics of West Asia.[40] At a time when nearly all the social sciences experiment with critical theories, when questions about the social engineering of politics have become central, when the cultural constitution of states is scrutinised, when mono-causalities are revealed, when 'problem-solving theories' are abandoned in favour of 'critical theory', students of contemporary Iran have not felt compelled to follow suit.[41] I think the political economy surrounding the subject area is part of the problem. There is a scarcity of discursive analysis, interpretive approaches and critical ideas on Iran. This is not necessarily because there is no demand for such approaches. Rather, it is because many think-tank pundits, journalists, political activists, writers and others who are not 'regulated' by academic standards have cashed in on the Iran business, giving their consumers the self-assurance that they have understood Iran, that they know the Islamic Republic, that they can explain the country, its ancient history, diverse peoples, powerful revolutions, indeed the collective reality of its 70 million inhabitants—without at the same time intimating to the reader that a great deal in their analyses is based on one-dimensional empirical material, aestheticized narration or anecdotal journalistic description. It is this market for 'Iranian pop studies' that allows some to become 'experts' on the country by writing a travelogue, without footnotes or quoting a few newspaper sources at best. Indeed, the higher quantity of these populist studies, especially in the US, indicates that discussion of contemporary Iran, far from undergoing a process of scholarly rationalization, on the contrary continues to be subjected to intransigent politico-emotional incitement.[42]

That the techniques of biased discourse exercised over Iran in some circles have not been subdued, and that the will to know the complexities of the country's current transformation has been compromised, is of course primarily due to the intellectual climate in the Islamic Republic itself. Iran's cultural revolution in 1981-82 ensured a process of artificial 'monopolization' of the academic curricula under an Islamicized meta-narrative that marginalized competing views, to such an extent that we continue to have a whole armada of poets, writers, political analysts and philosophers who think about Iran either under duress within the country or from the confines of exile. I do not at all want to suggest that this situation is all-encompassing, nor to claim that there are no grey zones that need to be taken into consideration.[43] All I am saying is that the intransigent attempts to mobilize scholarly activity by the state, before and after the revolution in 1979, have hampered the establishment of decentralized, democratic academic structures, and that the immediate presence of the state 'on campus' stymied the growth of disinterested human studies (especially with regard to the social and political sciences and philosophy).[44] Most Iranian intellectuals, both in the Diaspora and within Iran, would probably agree that in the face of these intrusions into academia, the '*reconquista*' of Iran's vast intellectual archives has remained unaccomplished.[45]

But it seems to me that the absence of critical Iranian studies is not due merely to that political economy of the field, but rather, as I have implied, to the ideological commitment to positivism—the idea that Iran is 'simply there', that there is no genealogy of Iran's national interests, that Iranian society is undifferentiated, that the processes of change are decisively halted by the forces of an authoritarian state.[46] The central question confronting us then is: have the alternatives for students of Iranian politics been narrowed down either to formulaic analyses presented by embedded pundits,[47] or to semi-scholarly analyses catered for the mainstream reader (or the new breed of writers in exile whose representation of Iranian culture is tailored to the literary preferences of consumers in New York, London and Paris for that matter)?[48] The answer is no, of course; fortunately, there is a range of alternative material out there. Among others, I am thinking of Ali Rahnema's perceptive political biography of Ali Shariati;[49] the eminent philosophical treatise of Daryush Shayegan;[50] the anthropological study of cultural preferences in contemporary Iran by Fariba Adelkhah;[51] the exploration of modern Shia political thought by the late Hamid Enayat;[52] the important annotated translations of Ali Shariati's and Ayatollah Khomeini's manifestos by Hamid Algar;[53] or the encyclopaedic volumes on Islamic philosophy and its impact on Iran by Seyyed Hossein Nasr.[54]

The distinctively compelling strength of studies like these is that they situate specific periods of Iranian history within a political, philosophical, socio-economic and/or cultural context.[55] If we accept with the German philosopher and Heidelberg Professor Hans-Georg Gadamer that 'the historian usually chooses concepts to describe the historical particularity of his objects without expressly reflecting on their origin and justification';[56] if we concur that he 'simply follows his interest in the material and takes no account of the fact that the descriptive concepts he chooses can be highly detrimental to his proper purpose if they assimilate what is historically different to what is familiar and thus, despite all impartiality, subordinate the alien being of the object to his own preconception'; if it is true that 'despite his scientific method, he behaves like everyone else', then the scholars mentioned above write in opposition to teleological history.[57] They accept, in short, the epistemological contention that truth is context-bound. I am conscious that I am abstracting from a vast amount of material, but it is perhaps true to say that their moral and analytical disposition depends very greatly upon that insight, which is a form of critical interpretation, treating knowledge as relative, questionable, conditioned.

Critical practice is of course not reducible to a school of thought, it is no paradigm in the Kuhnian sense,[58] there is no headquarters where its proponents can gather and unify their methodological and theoretical standpoint. It is, rather, connected by an implicit consensus, a 'theorem of relativity': the understanding that representing someone or something is a complex and subversive endeavour filled with uncertainty. With regard to Iran this means that critical theorists cannot give themselves over to the mainstream contention that an Archimedean point exists outside the contexts they are exploring, or that disparate objects of analyses can be captured by one inclusive methodology independent of the concrete historical circumstances from which our understanding of Iran derives and from which we draw sustenance. A critical theory of Iranian affairs implies that we do not search for absolute truths. It alerts us to the fact that critique does not open up formal structures, does not contribute to the almost impenetrable canon of established truths about Iran. Rather the reverse—a critical theory of the Islamic Republic stands in opposition to universal objectivity. It suggests exploring the dialectics that have led us to constitute 'ourselves' and to recognize 'ourselves' as Iranians, the events that have led to 'our' dispersion across domestic, regional and international boundaries, 'our' reification, objectification and internalization as a people, 'our' common fate as a nation-state in world politics.[59] Criticism understood in this sense, in short, differentiates between the material that has made us who we are, our representation, and prescriptions of who we should be.[60]

Exploring the Iranian self and its corresponding 'other' has been a constant theme in the modern intellectual discourse of Iran.[61] The question *ma cheguneh ma shodim?* (How have we become who we are?), revisited in the post-revolutionary context by the prominent Tehran University Professor Sadeq Zibakalam,[62] has occupied the paradigms of most modern intellectual 'godfathers' of the country,[63] from Khalil Maleki (1901-1969) and Ahmad

Kasravi (1890-1946) to Jalal Al-e Ahmad (1923-1969) and Ali Shariati (1933-1977, differences notwithstanding).[64] Consider Al-e Ahmad's fierce assault on the 'culturally inauthentic status' of Pahlavi Iran in the 1960s, his critique of Iran's 'Westtoxification' or *Gharbzadegi*, to him 'a characteristic of an era in which we haven't yet obtained machines and don't understand the mysteries of their structure and construction.[65] Consider also Ali Shariati's succinct but dense narration of the cultural constitution of 1970s Iran and the country's perceived assimilation into 'Western' modernity which he deemed synonymous with the demise of Iran's native culture; his struggle with the 'particular pains, sufferings, emotions and sensitivities that have been caused by a different spirit, a different past, a different background and a different material and economic society';[66] and his self-interrogation and inevitable self-admission that the pressures exercised by that 'alien machine' eliminate

> my culture from my mind and then replace it with another culture that is suited to another time and stage of development, another history, another economic level and structure, and another system of social and political relations. And then when I want to recognise my self, I feel another culture's culture in place of my own. I complain of sufferings which are not even my own, and lament the pessimism that is not suited for my cultural, philosophical, and societal realities, and I discover aims, ideals and sufferings which are natural for that other society ... but which do not pertain to my society.[67]

The impulse to flee the present reality in reverence for the past found its radical form in the narratives of *Bazgasht beh khish* (return to oneself) and *Gharbzadegi* which were central to intellectual life in 1960s and 1970s Iran. 'Iranian romanticism' condemned the materialism of Pahlavi Iran and transplanted the intellectual himself into the struggle for an idealized future. Its agents advocated respect for origins, for authenticity; Iranian romanticism placed a special value on the past, and revered the great heroes of Islamic civilization, especially the persona of Imam Hussein, who was celebrated as the eponymous hero of the evolving revolutionary play.

Yet I consider it a feature of Iran's *post*-revolutionary intellectual landscape that the very self of Iran's identity discourse, appropriated and interrogated in the pre-revolutionary period, is in the process of being deconstructed all the way down to the 'traces' of the country's ideational archives: to the arcane *ghazzal* permeating the poems of Jalaledin Rumi (Mowlana) and Hafiz, the epic tales of Rostam and Sohrab compiled in the *Shahnameh* of Ferdowsi, the esoteric mysticism of Omar Khayyam's *rubayyat* (quatrains), the political treatise of Abu Nasr Farabi, the *Avesta* (Fundamental Utterance) of Zoroaster, the dialectical musings of the Mu'tazillah and the Shia imamate. Indeed, I do not think it an exaggeration to say that Iran's critical current, the intellectual *hejra* away from the solitudes of imagining Iran within one authentic, exclusive identity, is nurtured by two major institutions of Iran's intellectual heritage: on the one side Islamic philosophy, the dialectic imperative intrinsic to the writings of Farabi, Tusi, Razes, Avicenna and others;[68] on the other side Persian poetry, the enduring relevance of Attar, Hafiz, Khayyam, Sa'adi and Rumi.

In a short introduction like this, one can scarcely begin to cover the ideas of these thinkers and poets; nor, for that matter, can one expect to present an intellectual historiography of contemporary Iran. Suffice it to say that all social and political research, in a certain mimetic sense, is a reinterpretation of something; originality in our trade, as opposed to the natural sciences, is really to go beyond the *given*. Not only do intellectuals act within a given culture which shapes their thoughts, but they also work on the basis of pre-existing knowledge that can never really be discarded in total. Again, I know I am simplifying, but isn't it true to say that Iran's contemporary intelligentsia thinks within the ideational genealogy of Iran, conscious of its suspicion toward ontological certainty (*yaquin*), normative assent (*tasdiq*), methodological conception (*tasawwur*) and empirical definition (*hadd*)?[69] Haven't Iranian intellectuals moved away from authority and towards individual freedom, away from self-objectification and toward an independent self, away from the secure fixities of the status quo and towards the drama of the spiritual, away from hierarchy and towards the sovereignty of the people, away from utilitarianism and towards transcendence? And aren't these movements central to the 'School of Love' and especially to Hafiz's poetry which gained him the title 'Tongue of the Unseen' (*lisan al-ghaib*), a translator of the other-worldly?

I think that as students of Iran, we need to be aware that contemporary debates between Iranian intellectuals cannot be detached from the overall ideational archives of the country. On the one side, many of the arguments that are floating around cannot be divorced from the philosophical engagements between *Akhbaris* and *Usulis*, *Asharites* and *Mu'tazillah*, *Kalam* and *Falsafah*, *Mashasha'i* and *Ishraqi*, *Urafa* and *Irfani*. On the other side, they cannot be analyzed in isolation from the Iranian passion for the transcendental, the propensity for poetic romanticism, which is embedded in the Persian language. Don't get me wrong—we shouldn't indulge ourselves in the practice of wilful abstraction in order to make self-interested use of the past. But there is some merit in trying to attain to a higher level of critical historical consciousness, where the problem of bridging the gap between past and present is apprehended as a problem in itself—that is, a problem whose solution is not to be found by pushing Iranian history into a confined space, Islamic, Persian, Shia or otherwise. Indeed one tends to agree with Foucault that the 'more History attempts to transcend its own rootedness in historicity, and the greater the efforts it makes to attain, beyond the historical relativity of its origins and its choices, the sphere of universality',

> the more clearly it bears the marks of its historical birth, and the more evidently there appears through it the history of which it is itself a part;

… inversely, the more it accepts its relativity, and the more deeply it sinks into the movement it shares with what it is recounting, then the more it tends to the slenderness of the narrative, and all the positive content it obtained for itself through the human sciences is dissipated.[70]

Iran's emerging critical historical consciousness arises in the impulse to break up the past, not in order to idealize it; not as a means to 'deify' Iran's status quo, but to interrogate it in order to show its genealogy. This critical consciousness departs from the positivism intrinsic to the narratives of *Gharbzadegi* and *Bazgasht beh khish* and the rhetoric of the Iranian state, which all work within totalities that are rendered a-historical (e.g. Occident vs. Orient, Islam vs. *shirk*, oppressed vs. oppressors, East vs. West). In their anti-foundational, relativist project, Iran's 'prototypical' post-revolutionary intellectuals may be positioned within a long tradition of critical thought in Iran. We may trace this tradition back at least to the tenth-century Muslim philosopher Abu Nasr Farabi who spoke of the impermissibility of universal judgement, and who agreed that reality is structured, differentiated, relative, that our surrounding world cannot be essentialized along a set of variables:

You must know that drawing universal judgements from the perception of particulars is certainly part of the nature of things, which do not abandon it, and cannot be free from it or dispense with it in sciences, opinions, and beliefs or in the reasons for rules and religious laws, or in civil associations and relationships. In physics, this is exemplified by our judgement that every stone sinks in water, but perhaps some stones float; that every plant burns in fire, but some plants do not burn in fire; that the universal body is finite, but perhaps it is infinite. In religious matters, this is exemplified by our judgement that whoever manifests good deeds on the whole is therefore just and of sound testimony in many things, though that is not observed in all cases. In civil associations, this is exemplified by our judgement that calmness and tranquillity in our souls are confined [*hadduhuma fi anfusina mahdud*], yet from those definitions there are only general conclusions [*istidlatat*] without their being observed under all of their conditions.

Since the condition of universal judgement is as we have described it—it takes hold and captures the natures of things—how can the mind determine a link between Plato and Aristotle, in spite of imagining and grasping the universal difference between them, when the two of them emerged with apparent differences between them in terms of their lives, actions, and many statements?[71]

Whereas the narratives of *Bazgasht beh khish* and *Gharbzadegi* were creative when they reminded Iranians of their 'authentic' past, they were destructive when they made of the 'fallen' present of Pahlavi Iran *nothing but* a consequence of deviation from Iran's idealized self. By contrast, interrogating that very self equips post-revolutionary Iranian intellectuals with the power to penetrate the myths of a coherent past, to move away from universal certainty towards relative judgement as Farabi demanded. From that perspective the meaning of Iran is in the making: the historical archives of Iran are the *a prioris* of what can be expressed about the Islamic Republic. This means, in less abstract terms, that the country has not stopped in order to look back and develop a retrospective view with universal and all-encompassing validity—quite a futile endeavour, one must add, because fragments of Iran's heritage continue to be excavated in the vast archaeological sites of Iranian-Azerbaijan, Kurdistan, Lorestan, Khorrasan, Khuzestan and Fars province almost on a weekly basis.[72] Iran's 'prototypical' post-revolutionary intellectual thus admits that we are the effects of previous generations, that we cannot escape from their passions, crimes and errors, that although we may think that we can transcend the past we cannot escape the fact that we spring from it. Such an intellectual may be searching for what Nietzsche termed a 'second nature that withers the first', but I think that he or she is conscious that this is 'an attempt to gain a past *a posteriori* from which we might spring', that reinventing history is 'always a dangerous attempt, as it is difficult to find a limit to the denial of the past, and [that] the second natures are generally weaker than the first.'[73]

The salutary turn towards critical reflection on the contested, historically engineered meaning of Iran has been spearheaded by—amongst others—'revisionist' clerics such as Mohsen Kadivar, Abdollah Nouri and Hasan Yousefi Eshkevari and opposition intellectuals such as Abdolkarim Soroush and Hashem Aghajari. If there is one common denominator between these thinkers, it is their concern for dispensing with one-dimensional verities about Iran in general and the Islamic Republic in particular. What they intend to do is to thread the laws governing Iranian perceptions of politics, society, culture and Islam, appreciating—to quote Eshkevari—that an 'idea, a thought, a religion, a religious school always first has a truth, a message, which then unfolds, evolves and changes in the course of historical development.'[74] Although Iran's critical thinkers have no real methodological, theoretical or epistemological headquarters and only a few tolerated outlets to express their thoughts, their anti-foundational ideas continue to extract themselves across the vast spaces of Iran's contemporary intellectual landscape. They have thus created 'liberated territories' for intellectual activism in the Islamic Republic, making a form of pluralism possible with regard to scholarly work and Iran's political status quo alike.[75]

That is the intellectual juncture at which I have positioned *Iran in World Politics*, the present study being at the same time an introduction to critical Iranian studies and my first attempt to find a critical attitude towards politics more generally. To that end, four areas of interest are investigated. Part One elaborates on the way culture is invented, reified, and internalized by political elites, with a particular emphasis on the foreign policy culture of the Islamic Republic. I try to present here insights into the 'mindset' of Iran's foreign policy elites, charting the changes that have occurred in the post-revolutionary process. This part of the book is addressed to all those who want to understand Iran's attitude towards the world, weapons of mass destruction and itself. It ends with self-criticism that discusses the theoretical and methodological arguments made, in relation to the disciplines of Middle Eastern Studies and International Relations (IR).

The second part switches the reader's attention to the devastating legacies of the Iran-Iraq war (1980-88). Currently, bookhops in the US and elsewhere are filled with literature about the invasion of Iraq in 2003, the wider 'Middle Eastern question', Islam etc. Most of them bear sensationalist headlines about an inescapable stand-off between Shia and Sunni, Islam and America or Persian and Arab. I argue against this 'neo-Orientalist' vogue, investigating the way Saddam Hussein invented the 'Persian menace' in order to sustain his rule and organize Arab states behind him during the first Gulf War. In an extension of the argument presented in *The International Politics of the Persian Gulf*, I dissect the impressive amount of empirical material on the 'West's' assistance to Saddam Hussein's war efforts, with a particular emphasis on his WMD infrastructure. There is no such thing as a historically determined enmity between Arabs and Iranians, I conclude, and Iran's evolving political, economic and cultural relations with post-Saddam Iraq may be a strong indicator of this.

Employing and reinterpreting the ideas of the German philosopher Hans-Georg Gadamer and the Muslim thinker Abu Nasr Farabi, Part Three presents an analysis of the contemporary dynamics of Iranian-American relations with a special focus on the impact of neoconservative ideology. Without a well organized campaign to demonize the target country, it is argued, no war can occur. Neoconservatives in the US, together with some of their allies in Israel, are constantly producing the image of Iran as an international pariah. This campaign, which is ongoing at the time of writing, has had its impact on the foreign policy of the US to the detriment of better relations between the two countries. I intend to reveal the myths and the outright lies about Iran that have found their way into the mainstream press and the way they are employed in order to produce and legitimate war.

Part Four establishes how a critical attitude towards Iranian domestic politics switches the focus away from analysis of the state, the primacy of which is a particular bias of the 'Western' social sciences. Rather than working our way merely through governmental declarations, elite politics, presidential campaigns etc., it may be rather more useful to show how Iranian civil society functions, how the multifarious discourses permeating the Islamic Republic affect state-society relations, how the emerging political economy of the country feeds into that process, and how the new intellectual paradigms proposed by Eshkevari, Kadivar, Soroush and others have recoded Iran's intellectual culture. The 'pluralistic momentum' emanating from Iran's burgeoning civil society, it is suggested, will continue to drive the democratization of Iran. The point I am trying to make is that a tremendous post-revolutionary battle continues in the Islamic Republic, occurring at the same time as we are reading yet another article about the ways it is fought by the state.

In Part Five, I attempt to anticipate the criticisms of my theoretical, methodological, and epistemological suggestions. I reiterate my case against wilful, ideologically motivated abstraction, the kind of simplified view of world politics in general and West Asia in particular that a few functionaries, pseudo-intellectuals, academics and media pundits have disseminated. Their nihilistic world-view habituates us to war and destruction and much of the terrorist blowback that we are currently facing all over the world can be linked to this type of thinking. Even worse, education itself—both institutional education within the University and other education—is threatened by the new nationalist and religious orthodoxies disseminated by all too powerful media conglomerates and functionaries as they produce deceptive continua about the way we see the world. In this final part of the book, I try to make a number of suggestions that I found useful for guarding against that type of politics.

What I am interested in more generally is individualizing what is being said about Iran within different empirical frameworks, not in order to provide immediate access to objective truths, but to capture the plurality of meanings attached to Iran's Islamic project from within the country and without. Whilst each part of the book is a relatively freestanding discussion of a particular issue affecting the Islamic Republic and the wider West Asian region, there is a common *methodical* concern binding them together: the ambition to put contemporary Iran in context, to provide alternative paths of explanation, to imbibe in a preliminary manner the ontological traces that allow us to formulate a set of arguments about the politics of contemporary Persia. The book has thus both a *de*scriptive and *pre*scriptive ambition: on the one side it presents 'case-studies' focusing on Iran's international relations and domestic politics, on the other it proposes ways to study Iran and the wider West Asian region from a critical perspective. Both ambitions fit into my overall research agenda, into my project to pluralize the way I perceive the political world in general and international life in particular.

Ultimately, this book explores the case of a country which has been at the centre of world attention at least since the Islamic revolution in 1979, a state which has been self-consciously detaching itself from superpower politics, which speaks of its sense of identity with immense authority; a society which has been affected by two major revolutions,[76] a political elite that is fractured and a governmental leadership that is increasingly differentiated. In each of the following sections, I will investigate not only the ideas permeating contemporary Iran, but also the political cultures sustaining them and the political dynamics affecting them. The questions that guide me then are not, how can I explain the Islamic Republic *in toto*, how can I subsume the international relations and domestic politics affecting my subject matter under a set of easily digestible headlines? I am not interested in reducing Iran in that way. The issues that I will analyze are approached from a rather different angle. I am interested in dissecting instances of Iran's political representation since the Islamic revolution in 1979, not only from the perspective of Iran itself, but also from 'without', from the external discourses implanting images of the Islamic Republic in our minds. The questions that guide me then are: how is Iran represented in international affairs and domestic politics, how is the country appropriated by political agents (Iranian reformers and traditionalists, American neoconservatives, Arab ultra-nationalists etc.)? How is the ideological map of the Islamic Republic relocated? The question of the Islamic Republic is therefore dialectical; it denotes, on the one side, how Iran 'enacts' itself domestically and in world politics (internal dialectic); and, on the other side, how Iran is 'enacted' from without (external dialectic). The question of the Islamic Republic represents, in short, my first attempt to explore instances of Iran's past, present and future during a period that is definitive for the country's post-revolutionary generation, regional peace and the very existence of the Islamic Republic itself.

PART I
ISLAMIC UTOPIAN ROMANTICISM AND THE FOREIGN POLICY CULTURE OF IRAN

On account of his dualistic and contradictory nature, man, this dialectical phenomenon, is compelled to be always in motion. ... How disgraceful, then, are all fixed standards. Who can ever fix a standard? Man is a "choice," a struggle, a constant becoming. He is an infinite migration, a migration within himself, from clay to God; he is a migrant within his own soul.

—Ali Shariati, *On the Sociology of Islam*

The disappearance of utopia brings about a static state of affairs in which man himself becomes no more than a thing. ... Thus, after a long tortuous, but heroic development, just at the highest stage of awareness, when history is ceasing to be blind fate, and is becoming more and more man's own creation, with the relinquishment of utopias, man would lose his will to shape history and therewith his ability to understand it.

—Karl Mannheim, *Ideology and Utopia*

Dialectics of Iran's international affairs

During the winter of 1978-79, Michel Foucault cogitated about the Iranian revolution in a series of reports for *Corriere della Sera* describing the protests as a revolt against the 'planetary system,' inspired by a 'religion of combat and sacrifice', a counter-hegemonic mass movement that could bring about the 'transfiguration' of the world. Witnessing the departure of Iran's last Shah, few analysts doubted that the demise of the Pahlavi dynasty was one of the central events of the twentieth century.[1] Like Iranians themselves, Foucault perhaps underestimated the authoritarian moment of Iran's Islamic enterprise, whilst overestimating its potential, but his reports adequately captured the universal claim and 'libidinous' idealism intrinsic to the revolutionary process. Like the French, Russians, Chinese and Cubans before them, Iranians believed in the imminence of change, brought about by an Islamic international that would shatter the status quo. Their political and spiritual guide, Ayatollah Rouhollah Khomeini, who made it unmistakably clear that the Islamic Revolution did not belong exclusively to Iran, nurtured this idealism, declaring that 'Islam [was] revealed for mankind and the Muslims. ... An Islamic movement, therefore, cannot limit itself to any particular country, not even to the Islamic countries; it is the continuation of the revolution by the prophets.'[2]

In this part of the book I will explore how the revolutionary reality of late 1970s Iran transmuted into a new identity for the Iranian state and how core principles of the revolution—radical cultural and political independence, economic autarky, diplomatic and ideological mobilisation against Zionism and resistance against US interference in regional and domestic affairs—guide the country's foreign policy elites. My argument is that Iran continues to challenge the international system in general and the US state as its most dominant power in particular, because of a 'utopian-romantic' meta-narrative permeating the Iranian foreign policy culture. The way the phrase 'foreign policy culture' is used here does not refer merely to cognitive filters through which impulses from the international system are processed.[3] Reverting to ideas developed by critical theorists and historical sociologists, I contend that analytical autonomy can be attributed to foreign policy culture as a structured system populated by intersubjective knowledge, e.g. ideologies, norms, identities, institutions, and other cultural artefacts. Foreign policy culture is thus conceived as a systemic phenomenon that transcends the concrete minds of its agents. It is the cultural expression of the dominant *Weltanschauungen* carried by elites. It is these world-views, I argue, that give meaning to power and content to interest. This part of the book seeks to dissect this culture and to establish how it informed the grand foreign policy preferences of the Islamic Republic. To that end, it is divided into two sections, one theoretical-abstract, the other empirical-descriptive.

The first section explains a 'four-dimensional dialectic' of culture and foreign policy preferences. 'Dialectic,' write Adorno and Horkheimer, 'interprets every image as writing. It shows how the admission of its falsity is to be read in the lines of its features—a confession that deprives it of its power and appropriates it for truth'.[4] Gadamer has a comparable understanding of the term: 'Dialectic consists not in trying to discover the weakness of what is said,' he explains, 'but in bringing out its real strength. It is not the art of arguing (which can make a strong case out of a weak one) but the art of thinking (which can strengthen objections by referring to the subject matter).'[5] This view of dialectical analysis as critical analysis is quite obviously different from the Hegelian dialectic which is based on the final reconciliation of opposites. As it is understood here dialectical analysis does not look for finitude, I do not attempt to give an absolute overview of Iran's international affairs; I am not proposing a universal method that can be applied indiscriminately to any of Iran's foreign policies. Instead, I attempt to enact a form of pluralism with regard to Iran's strategic preferences, extending our understanding about the way they emerge culturally. I am aware that some readers will find this part of the argument too abstract, too 'theoretical'. But I found it necessary to trace the *Herkunft* of culture to its 'base'—human invention—in order to avoid the perils of cultural reductionism that have sometimes infested 'Orientalist' discourse on our subject matter. I found such a 'genealogical' approach toward culture helpful to show that cognitive beliefs about the world are neither predetermined ontologically nor eternally valid. As it is pursued here, analysis of culture is 'not an experimental science in search of law but an interpretative one in search of meaning.'[6]

Moreover, a genealogical approach focuses as much as possible on the manufacturing, reification, theorization, and institutionalization of (political) culture. How is culture produced, reproduced, legitimated, contested and changed? How is the meaning of culture fixed or stabilized historically via theory and political practice? How does culture affect strategic preferences? Framing the empirical analysis with a four-dimensional dialectic is helpful to trace historically the life-cycle of cultural constructs and their corresponding effects upon collective action. My method is essentially to sketch the 'functioning' of culture in relation to strategic preferences of the modern Iranian state; I am trying to charter the way Iranian foreign policy elites perceive the outside world. What I contend about Iran's foreign policy culture is that it is not only a set of ideas but also a mentality, a *Geist*, a systemic phenomenon that is strong enough to penetrate the strategic thinking of Iran's foreign policy elites to its core. Thus, it is claimed, culture has both an internal consistency and a highly articulated set of relationships to its agents. My analyses consequently try to show the ideational shape of culture as pertinent to Iran's grand strategic preferences, which requires some discussion about the emergence, perseverance, and transformation of culture.

The second part focuses on the content of Iran's foreign policies. Primarily, it is addressed to those readers who wonder why Iran is repeatedly challenging central tenets of international society.[7] It demonstrates how utopian-romantic ideals formulated during the revolutionary years, and institutionalized as central norms of the Islamic Republic, inform the contemporary grand strategic preferences of the Iranian state. By arguing that the Islamic Republic has not discarded certain core principles formulated during the revolutionary period, I question interpretations of Iranian foreign policies as thoroughly status-quo oriented, pragmatist or 'realist'.[8] It is not at all obvious that challenging the international status quo and the US as its dominant guardian is considered 'irrational' from the perspective of Iranian political elites. Nor is it clear that Iran has discarded the export of the Islamic republican model. Like other revolutionary entities—China, Cuba, France—the Iranian state and Iranians themselves have a nostalgic self-perception about the role of their country in world affairs. While the means and rhetoric to advocate Iran's international agenda fluctuate (e.g. from Khatami's dialogue amongst civilization policy to Ahmadinejad's populism), the motivational drives toward challenging international realities continue to be strong.

Where does culture come from?

If we aspire to look over the shoulders of decision-makers, as Hans Morgenthau so famously advocated,[9] we have to strengthen our empathetic understanding of the 'mindset' of decision makers, we need to know where their ideas come from. This in turn requires going through the pains of exploring the cultural fabric producing that mindset. In contrast to 'political realists' like Morgenthau himself, who tend to take existing social structures for granted, cultural and sociological theorists agree that the essential factor of the social world that humans create is socially engineered meaning.[10] Depending on how they order their environment, humans infuse their own meanings or interpretations into reality. Hence, the surrounding social order is not preordained or biologically given. It is an 'ongoing human production. It is produced by man in the course of his ongoing externalisation.'[11]

Marx and Hegel in the Western worlds and Farabi and Ibn-Sina in the Islamic worlds agree that human externalization, that is the ongoing outpouring of human activity in society, is an act of anthropological necessity. We all need to make sense of our surrounding world and in order to do this, we interact with it. A comparable dialectic may be established between the nation-state and international society. In order to give meaning to the external, international world, nation-states constitute themselves *in relation to* international society, and more specifically in relation to other members of that society. Nation A can only be a superpower *relative to* nation B which does not command the same resources. Moreover, nation-states interact with other countries economically, politically, diplomatically whilst defining themselves in relation to them. They constantly inject their ideas, cultures, mores, attitudes into the very fabric of international society. Thus, like man who is not merely *Homo socius* but also *Homo faber/Homo pictor*, the nation-state is both world and culture maker. In this sense international society exists only as a human product and—by extension—as a product of the nation-state (itself a product of individual action).[12]

In a second dialectic between man and society, sociological theory suggests that socially constructed meaning attains the status of objective reality. 'Human expressivity,' Berger and Luckmann explain, 'is capable of objectivication, that is, it manifests itself in products of human activity that are available both to their producers and to other men as elements of a common world.'[13] The most obvious signs and symbols of the objectivated world surrounding us are norms, values, traditions or institutions and other cultural artefacts. Ultimately, they tell us what is good and bad and sometimes even who we are. They are *there*, external to us, invented by history (or by our parents), but nonetheless claiming factual validity, commanding a persistence that is beyond our control. This goes to the heart of what Marx meant when he observed that 'Men make their own history ... not under circumstances they themselves have chosen but under the given and inherited circumstances with which they are directly confronted.'[14] It also points towards a comparable dialectic in our international world. Both the nation-state and its product, international society, are objectivated human activity; they are made 'real' through individual action. The nation-state, the producer, and international society, the product, exist *only* as human objectivity, they are there because we reproduce them via our actions. Their meaning, importance, legitimacy, indeed their very existence is mediated to us via their cultures—norms, institutions, traditions, values, etc. These cultural artefacts define subjectively plausible representations of reality, morally sanctioned codes of collective behaviour, rules of social discourse and a general plot for the conduct of the day-to-day affairs of the state. Culture in this sense functions as shared, 'factualized' ideational patterns that permit the nation-state to interpret its relationship with the external environment (alter, or international society) and to order the internal self (ego, or self-identity). Hence, for ourselves and the nation-state, culture is a 'sense-building device.'

The social construction of cultural systems

It has been suggested that through the process of externalisation a structured cultural system is constructed that is experienced as an intersubjectively shared object of reality in common with others. Let me take this argument one step further now and open up another dialectic of culture. To understand culture as externalized, objectivated systems of knowledge is close to Wilhelm Dilthey's observations regarding the relationship between cultural system and the individual. According to Dilthey:

> The individual slant which colours the personal knowledge of life is corrected and enlarged by the common experience. By this I mean the shared beliefs emerging in any coherent circle of people. These are assertions about the passage of life, judgements of value, rules of conduct, definition of goals and of what is good. It is characteristic of them that they are the products of the common life. They apply as much to the life of individuals as to that of communities. As custom, tradition and public opinion they influence individuals and their experience; because the community has the weight of numbers behind it and outlasts the individual, this power usually proves superior to his will.[15]

The last sentence is crucial and introduces the third moment of the dialectic between culture and individual. Dilthey discerns that culture emerges as aggregations of meaning which are the product of human experience. Once externalized, objectivated as custom, tradition and values, the cultural structure reacts back on the individual, exercising a power that 'proves superior to his will'. If we attribute structural qualities to interaction, the cultural system under focus develops *emergent* properties that may have causal impacts on its constituent agents. This is rather consequential. To say that a cultural system has emergent properties refers to a paradox in the dialectic between culture and individual. The cultural system, having emerged as an externalized, objectivated human product, is experienced by us as something other than our own invention. Once externalized through our actions and objectivated through reification and institutionalization, culture appears as an externalized product, which implies that it has acquired a measure of distinctiveness from us (it has acquired systemic qualities).[16] As an external cultural system, it exercises a certain degree of hegemony over the culture bearer, which at times is overwhelming, at times reformed through consistent resistance, and at times overthrown *in toto* by revolutionary force. Culture conceived in this sense is objectified as a facticity external to its creators, and hence is experienced as an outer objective reality in common with others.[17] Sociologist Margaret Archer argues in a comparable vein:

As an emergent entity the Cultural System has an objective existence and autonomous relations amongst its components ... At any moment the CS [Cultural System] is the product of historical Socio-Cultural interaction, but having emerged (emergence being a continuous process) then *qua* product, it has properties of its own. Like structure, culture is man-made but escapes its makers to act back upon them.[18]

Archer speaks of an objectively existing cultural system that is the product of interaction and acts upon its constituent parts. This idea not only corresponds to my argument about the relative autonomy of the cultural system as an external, objectified reality transcending its makers, but also with my second proposal regarding the social construction of culture. If the cultural system is produced, reproduced, and reified in interaction with others, as Archer argues, the formation of culture is an intrinsically social process. Individuals and nation-states do not retain integrity as they engage in interaction; they do not 'function' in encapsulated habitats. They have a myriad relationships with the international world, with other nation-states, and with other actors in world politics. This 'sociality' suggests two central characteristics of cultural systems: it is through externalization of socially produced knowledge that culture is a product of individuals; and it is through objectification that culture becomes a reality *sui generis*. What needs to be provided in a third step is the link between that cultural system and the emergence of preferences and interests. We need to find out, in other words, the ways that culture affects our behaviour.

Foreign policy culture and strategic preferences

If externalization produces a cultural system and objectification makes it appear as reality, it should follow that this objectivated world is reabsorbed by us, who are the addressees of the reflexive reality. This process is termed 'internalization' in sociological theory. It is something we do on an everyday basis, when we adopt certain lifestyles, religions, political viewpoints etc. Sociologists argue that we internalize culture through the process of socialisation—a continuous process whereby the contents and meanings of culture are mediated. This process habituates us to accept the ideational attributes of that cultural system (e.g. identities, roles, norms, institutions). Relating our argument back to the findings in the previous section, this would mean that the third dimension of the production and workings of culture has 'reactive' qualities: first, it is through externalization that culture is a human product; secondly, it is through objectification that culture becomes a reality *sui generis*; and thirdly, it is through internalisation that agents are products of culture. The behavioural component—intrinsic to all three moments of this cultural dialectic—manifests itself most forcefully in internalization through socialization in culture, because it is there that external structures affect the subjective structures of the consciousness of the agent itself, not only transcending the external-internal divide, but also transposing the outer cultural system into the inner self. It is this moment of the cultural process that transforms us from culture *maker* to culture *taker*.

If the cultural systems we have created react back on us, we may talk about a process of 'introjection', in the way the progressive Frankfurt School theorist Herbert Marcuse employed the term. In a provocative form, this quality of culture reveals that socialization in cultural systems not only has mediating or quasi-causal impacts, but also *constitutive* effects. According to Marcuse:

> The efficiency of the system blunts the individuals' recognition that it contains no facts which do not communicate the repressive power of the whole. If the individuals find themselves in the things which shape their life, they do so, not by giving, but by accepting the law of things—not the law of physics but the law of their society. … This identification is

not illusion but reality. However, the reality constitutes a more progressive stage of alienation. The latter has become entirely objective; the subject which is alienated is swallowed up by its alienated existence. There is only one dimension, and it is everywhere and in all forms. The achievements of progress defy ideological indictment as well as justification; before their tribunal, the "false consciousness" of their rationality becomes the true consciousness.[19]

Reinterpreted, Marcuse's dramatic argument about the deterministic impact of society on man may be transferred to our cultural milieu. By its very constitution, as both shared 'reality' and formally institutionalized and codified fact, culture not only penetrates us but also 'introjects' us with objectivated meanings (fundamentally through language).[20] The invented artefacts of the culture—norms, values, institutions—are maintained not simply by their coercive ability but by implicit and sometimes formally explicit claims to legitimacy.[21] They possess a degree of historically legitimated moral authority which signals that conforming to the dominant culture is morally right and dissent is morally wrong. Socialized in such an authoritative, yet invented cultural milieu, we are violated 'all the way down', shaped to take on the roles and attitudes communicated by the dominant cultural system surrounding us.[22] 'By a complicated process of indoctrination, rewards, punishments, and fitting ideology ... most people believe [that] they are following their own will,' Erich Fromm remarks. Yet they are 'unaware that their will itself is conditioned and manipulated.'[23] Culture thus introjects us whenever we accept and vigorously defend a certain viewpoint, issue or ordinance as part of our identity. Soldiers, for instance, may be considered to have one of the highest degrees of introjection, because they are made to believe whole-heartedly in the justness of their cause; they are introjected with the idea that the nation is worth dying for.

Our journey into the making of 'reality' does not end here. Following the symbolic-interactionist school of social psychology in the tradition of George Herbert Mead, one further may assert that social roles have particular identities (or an identity set) attached to them.[24] These *role identities* are socially constructed representations of the Self (ego), which by implication require representation of an Other (alter): 'By taking a particular role identity Ego is at the same time "casting" Alter in a corresponding counter-role that makes Ego's identity meaningful. One cannot be a trader without someone to trade with, a proselytiser without a convert, or a conqueror without a conquest.'[25] Culture in this sense functions as a source for identity, it differentiates 'us' from 'them'. Boundaries of identity expressed by abstract 'typologies' that differentiate the 'in-group' from the 'out-group' would not make sense without reference to shared knowledge or culture. The self-depicted identities would not be recognizable if individuals or states did not constantly act out, reproduce, and legitimate them. Once cognitively internalized and formally institutionalized, the cultural system represents our preferred self-identification or identity in relation to the Other, guiding us in relation to both *goal oriented preferences* (interest) and *strategy* (means). Reconfigured for our understanding of foreign policy culture, a four-dimensional dialectic emerges: (1) it is through externalization that culture is a human product; (2) it is through objectification that culture becomes a reality *sui generis*; (3) it is through internalization that we are products of culture; and (4) it is through introjection that culture constitutes our identities, interests and preferences. These are, of course, ideal-typical categorizations that are not meant to define separable positions in a causal transmission belt. Here and elsewhere, there is no suggestion that there are benchmarks which would define the transformation of one dialectic into another. What has been presented here is a preliminary four-dimensional dialectic of culture that may offer mnemonic (yet ephemeral) value for the relationship between agents (individuals, nation-states) and cultural systems (society, the international system). Culture conceived in this sense is 'not a power, something to which social events, behaviors, institutions, or processes can be attributed causally; it is a context, something within which they can be intelligibly—that is, thickly—described.'[26]

The making of Iranian foreign policies

Now that we have endured the difficulties of theoretical abstraction, we may indulge ourselves in finding out how the suggested genealogy affects the relationship between culture, identity and the definition of goal-oriented preferences. In our case, we are dealing with a specific manifestation of culture, attempting to address the relationship of one specific agent (Iran) with its external environment (international society). To that end, it makes sense to commence by exploring the emergence of ideas, institutions, and norms as pertinent to the contemporary strategic preferences of the Iranian state. But how do we specify their location? Where do we 'look' for the production and reproduction of shared knowledge? I suggest two interdependent sources of Iran's foreign policy culture: 'cognitive', referring to the intellectual production and processing of categories of the self and the other; and 'institutional', denoting the formalization of cultural artefacts as authoritative narratives of the state. Both moments of cultural production and reproduction claim the quality of objectiveness, resisting attempts to be altered. Both are interdependent, i.e., they 'inhabit' the same foreign policy culture. Both are legitimated by authoritative narratives of discourse, wielding mechanisms of social control to enforce their reality. However, both also are under permanent pressure from competing and oppositional ideas, which may succeed in transforming the prevalent culture altogether.

Cognitive sources

The introjection of masses by intellectuals has figured prominently in discourse about the workings of culture. According to Max Weber, intellectuals are a group of people 'who by virtue of their peculiarity have special access to certain achievements considered to be "culture values" [*Kulturwerte*] and who therefore usurp the leadership of a "culture community" [*Kulturgemeinschaft*].'[27] It was Antonio Gramsci, of course, who highlighted the hegemonic fulcrum of culture, observing that intellectually produced and legitimated ideologies are particularly deterministic and functional in perpetuating and reproducing the dominant social system. 'The intellectuals,' Gramsci observed, 'are the dominant group's "deputies" exercising the subaltern functions of social hegemony and political government.'[28] The hegemony of the dominant ideas articulated by intellectuals is not, however, unalterable. With the formation of a revolutionary cadre of 'organic' intellectuals, Gramsci argued, a counter-hegemonic movement may succeed in spreading ideas that organize the masses against the exploitation of the ruling groups. From Gramsci's perspective then, intellectuals are manufacturers, re-manufacturers *and* inventors of culture.

Whereas followers of Gramsci might emphasize the function of intellectually sanctioned culture primarily as a servant of power, I focus on the formative and inventive moment of the intellectual engineering of ideational systems. In pre-revolutionary Iran, it was the 'inventive manufacturer' of intellectual ideas who was instrumental in producing a counter-hegemonic political culture that ushered in the revolution in 1979.[29] Whereas the Pahlavi state adhered to the representation of the monarchy and Iran as the heir of pre-Islamic Persian empires, heading for revival of a 'great civilization' (*tamadon-e bozorg*), the opposition to the metaphysics propagated by the Pahlavi state reverted to Shia-Islamic anti-imperialist imageries as the dominant narrative of the Iranian self.

The actual existing and ongoing order of the Pahlavi state ('topia'), was counteracted with 'wish-images' suitable as a counter-hegemonic rallying call for the opposition (utopias).[30] Romanticizing, yet frugal in their exaltations of the millenarian cause, erudite, yet bellicose in their manifestos for political emancipation, opprobrious, yet sanctimonious in their language of protest, and passionate, yet myopic in their promises about a better future, Iranian intellectuals managed to organize the population around powerful ideas, advocating not only revolutionary domestic change but also transformation of the identity of the Iranian state from a monarchic-nationalistic status quo power to a revolutionary-universal people's movement, perceived to be in the vanguard of the fight for a new, equitable world order. This utopian-romantic, even hubristic self-perception (in the sense that the frail nation-state is elevated to the status of a vehicle of divine substance), is central to the foreign policy culture of contemporary Iran. The following paragraphs investigate both the cognitive sources of this disposition, and its institutional manifestations.

Carried by a cadre of revolutionary visionaries equipped with a range of counter-hegemonic utopias (Marxist, Communist, Maoist, Islamist, etc.), the political culture of Iran experienced a radical change during the 1960s. While the domestic aspect of this cultural shift that led to the revolution in 1979 is well documented, the consequences for Iran's strategic preferences have not been studied rigorously.[31] Nevertheless, the protests against the Pahlavi state did not reflect dissatisfaction only with domestic issues. The revolutionary-internationalist ethos of the Iranian movement transcended the nation-state, creating the dynamism that propelled it to spiral out of the Iranian context. Opposition activists and intellectuals not only protested against the institution of monarchy, they also demanded redefinition of the country's identity and redirection of relations with the whole world;

Iranians wanted to reinvent both themselves and the way they saw the outside world. As Ayatollah Mottahari argued:

If it is decided that [the] basis in determining the limits of the Iranian nation is the Aryan factor, the ultimate end of that is proclivity toward the Western world. But this proclivity in our national and political mission involves submissions and consequences, the most serious being a severance with neighbouring Islamic nations that are not Aryan and an attachment to Europe and the West. ... [I]f we [would choose as] the foundation of our nation our intellectual, behavioural and social heritage over the past fourteen centuries, [however,] we would have a different mission and other costs ... Therein, Arab, Turk, Indian, Indonesian and [Chinese] would become our friends, even kinsmen.[32]

In order to legitimate the monarchy, the Pahlavi state emphasized the ancient, pre-Islamic Persian heritage of Iran. Moreover, both Mohammad Reza Shah (r. 1941-79) and his father Reza Shah Pahlavi (r. 1925-41) nurtured the idea of 'Persianism'. They embedded the Iranian self in the romantic discourse about a superior 'Aryan' nation (*mellat-e aryan*), married to Indo-European heritage because of common linguistic roots and hence different from the 'Arab-Semitic other'.[33] Golnar Mehran, a professor at Al-Zahra University in Tehran, argues in a similar vein: 'The self presented during the late Pahlavi period was mostly Aryan, taking pride in Iran's "superior" civilisation, language, and culture, and filled with a sense of supremacy toward neighbouring nations and cultures. What was important,' she elaborates, 'was Iraniyat. Thus, government sponsored schoolbooks, especially history and Persian-language textbooks, instilled a sense of Iranianness, Iranian spirit, and Iranian identity among the young.' Conversely, in the textbooks of the Islamic Republic, there is a 'shift to the Irano-Islamic identity, as opposed to the solely Iranian one. The *national-religious* identity', in short, 'replaced the exclusive emphasis on *national* identity.'[34]

Indeed, if we think with the late Edward Said that 'Orientalists' such as Louis Massignon found an Iranian mystic 'more intrepid than an Arab one, partly because he was Aryan',[35] then Iran's late nineteenth century ultra-nationalists, such as Mirza Fath Ali Akhunzadeh, Jalaledin Mirza or Mirza Aqa Khan Kermani, demonstrate close affinity with Orientalist views about the supremacy of the Indo-European peoples and the mediocrity of the 'Semitic race' characteristic of the writings of Ernest Renan and others.[36] 'Like Akhunzadeh,' Firoozeh Kashani-Sabet observes, 'Kermani seemed to subscribe indirectly to the European bifurcation of Semitic and Aryan languages and cultures—a position that privileged Iran's Indo-European roots over its subsequent arabized culture.'[37] Ultimately, these ideas, which were not unaffected by European fascism, were the forerunners of the metaphysical myth of racially coded Iranian supremacy advocated by the Pahlavi state and secular intellectuals. The Shah's adoption of the title *Aryamehr* (light of the Aryans), his celebration of 2,500 years of Persian empire in Persepolis in 1971, and his decision to abandon the Islamic solar *hegra* calendar in favour of an imperial one exemplify his adherence to the *Iraniyat* topia. The identification with the kings of pre-Islamic Persian empires, especially with Cyrus, was quite explicit. The author of a US 'Scope Paper' of 1968, for instance, described the Shah as 'motivated by the desire to be recorded in history as one of the greatest Shahs in the 2500 years of the Persian monarchy. ... While in any conversation with him it is helpful to inject some humour,' the author also advised, 'the Shah should be treated at all times with the utmost respect and dignity.'[38]

Nurtured by the dream of reviving ancient Persian grandeur and establishing the ultimate 'great civilization' (*tamadon-e bozorg*), divorcing the Muslim identity of Iran from the Persian-Aryan self was meant to rationalize the Pahlavi claim to 'natural' affinity with the 'Western' world. In her examination of the image of Arabs in modern Persian literature, Joya Blondel Saad reaches a similar conclusion. She argues that for 'some Iranian nationalists, the Other has been not so much the West, but the Arabs and Islam.'[39] Indeed, 'the restoration of Iran's ancient inheritance, which was emphasised at various gatherings such as the Ramsar Educational Conference (1966-7) and the International Congress of Iranologists (1966-7),' Mahmood Davari agrees,

> possessed two important social functions for the Pahlavi dynasty (1920-1979) and thus gave them two political achievements. First, sanctity was conferred upon the monarchy as an institution deeply rooted in the country's history with the Pahlavis as the legal and legitimate heirs to the throne. Second, the Arab invasion, with its introduction of Islam, was presented as the ultimate cause of the downfall of the splendid and magnificent ancient empire of Persia and consequently was responsible for the lack of progress and the social problems characteristic of present Persian society. Therefore, these nationalist events implicitly created suspicion as to the sincerity and truth of present religious movements, thus hindering the latter's growth and influence.[40]

In turn, the Shah's identity politics provoked criticism by those strata of society who remained loyal to Iran's Muslim identity, namely by progressive clerics of the Islamic left such as Ayatollah Mottahari:

> We, as followers of a spiritual path and ideology named Islam, in which race and nationalism are non-existent, cannot be neutral towards certain movements which are opposed to this ideology and practise under the headings of nationalism and ethnicism. We all know that in recent years a widespread struggle has been generated in opposition to Islam, under the pretext of the defence of Iranian nationalism and ethnicism, insulting the sanctity of Islam in the name of anti-Arabism. The reports of this conflict [with Islam] which we observe in Persian books, newspapers, journals and so forth, point out that this struggle is not of an accidental or occasional nature but rather a component of an overall plan, with a clearly defined purpose. The growth of Zoroastrianism which is becoming more and more fashionable, is an organised political activity. Everybody knows that the present Iranian people will never return to Zoroas-

trianism. Al Muqann'a, Sandbad, Babak Khurramdin and Maziyar can never replace Ali ibn Abi-Talib, Husain ibn Ali or even Salman. Everybody is aware of these facts. However, these may stimulate the ethnic, racial and national prejudices and the emotions of naïve, ignorant young people who may then, as a result, cut their relations with Islam.[41]

At the heart of the revolutionary process, then, was a relentless battle for the ideational fabric of modern Persia. If the Pahlavi state attempted to externalize the Arab-Semitic other from the Iranian-Aryan self in order to position Iran more firmly in the 'Western' camp, opposition intellectuals constructed the narrative of 'Westtoxification' to protest against the 'Westernization' of Iran. The particular strength of Jalal Al-e Ahmad's influential book, which was published in the autumn of 1962 under the Persian title *Gharbzadegi*, was its focus on dissonance, the articulation of an increasing gap between what was considered to be the authentic self of Iran and the 'distortions' caused by 'Western' modernity. Employing a medical analogy, Al-e Ahmad deprecated the decadent, mediocre and unauthentic status of Pahlavi Iran. If left untreated, he argued, the spread of the disease-like present would lead to the demise of the country's cultural, political and economic independence, because society was made susceptible to 'Western' penetration.[42] Moving beyond the Iranian context, Al-e Ahmad saw the struggle against *Gharbzadegi* (West-toxification, occidentosis or Westitis) in terms of a conflict between the 'Occidental West' and the 'Oriental East'.[43] Reverting to the metaphor of 'the machine', he argued that while the 'West' had learned to master the 'technology of modernity', the mediocre 'East' was kept in a state of political and economic dependency. The definition of this milieu of subjugation and power was dramatized as a means to alert the 'Eastern mind' to the creeping intrusion of 'West-toxification' and its corrupting effect on societies programmed to be subservient to their imperialist masters:

So the time is now past when we divided the world into two 'blocs', the two blocs of East and West, or communist and non-communist. Although the first articles of most of the constitutions of the governments of the world still contain that huge twentieth-century sham, the flirtation between the United States and Soviet Russia (the two supposedly unrivalled leaders of those blocs) over the Suez Canal and Cuba showed how the owners of two neighbouring villages can sit down together comfortably at the same table ... Behind the scenes at every riot, *coup d'état*, or uprising in Zanzibar, Syria, or Uruguay, one must look to see what plot by what colonialists company or government backing it, lies hidden. ... These days any schoolchild not only sees the expansionist aims of mechanised industry on both sides of the dispute at work behind the scenes in the Second World War, but also sees the things that were happening in Cuba, the Congo, the Suez Canal, and Algeria were disputes over sugar, diamonds, and oil. The bloodshed in Cyprus, Zanzibar, Aden and Vietnam was for achieving a bridgehead to protect trade routes, which are the first determinant of the policy of governments.[44]

The second dominant narrative that had an impact on Iran's shifting self-perception and its relationship to the 'West' emerged from the writings of Ali Shariati. With reference to the anti-dependency theory of Al-e Ahmad and the Islamic-reformist writings of Mehdi Bazargan, Ayatollah Mottahari and others, Shariati developed a comparably critical position towards imperialism and cultural, political and socio-economic dependency on the 'West'. During his education at the Sorbonne in Paris, Shariati was in contact with figures of the French left whose political outlook and intellectual paradigms were influential in his later writings. Those included the Catholic Islamologist Louis Massignon to whom he was a research assistant between 1960 and 1962, the Jewish-Russian émigré George Gurvitch who was his professor of sociology, the Islamologist Jacques Berque whose class on the 'Sociology of Islam' Shariati attended in 1963-64, Frantz Fanon whose seminal *The Wretched of the Earth* he translated (in collaboration with others) into Persian, and Jean-Paul Sartre whose attempt to reconcile existentialism with Marxism and humanism had an important influence on Shariati's own attempt to synthesize social scientific concepts with Shia-Islamic political thought.[45]

In one of his main publications, entitled *Bazgasht beh-khhish* (Return to oneself), which appeared as serialized articles in the Iranian daily *Kayhan* between 22 April and 22 June 1976, Shariati juxtaposed what he considered as the perfectly true and authentic identity of Iran as a nation, whose inner structure is expressed in the epic of Imam Hussein's *shahadat* (martyrdom), with the unauthentic status of the fallen present under the Pahlavi Shahs, whose inner structure made Iran susceptible to the corrupting influences of 'Western' culture. For Shariati, the former is rectitude and totality, the latter disintegration and inadequacy:

In the nineteenth century I would have felt as an Iranian that I was attached to the great civilisation of the fourth, fifth, sixth, seventh and eighth Islamic centuries ... I would have felt attached to a culture that was more than two thousand years old, which has created in various ways new intellectuality, literature and art in the world of humanity. ... I would have felt attached to an Islam that created the most beautiful spirits and the most sublime faces of humanity. And I would have been able to feel, as a human, a human personality in relation to the world and all the people. So how could they change such an 'I' into a tool whose only worth is to consume new merchandise?

They must empty him of his personality. They negate the 'I' that he feels within himself. And they compel him to believe that he is attached to a weaker civilisation, culture and way of life. He must believe that European civilisation, Western civilisation and race are superior. An African must believe that he has been wild in order to create the temptation in him to become civilised. ... Even their medical doctors and biologists have proved (!!) that the Westerner's brain has an additional grey layer which is not found in Eastern man or negroes, and which assists in the intelligence and the sensitivity of Western man. They have also proved that the Western man's brain has an additional part (which the Easterner lacks) that is the reason for his greater talent and intelligence.[46]

The romantic dimension of Shariati's world-view, that is the emotionally charged assertion of the self and the value of the individual together with the sense of the infinite and transcendental, can be attributed to his interest in Sufism (or 'Islamic mysticism') and the role he allocated to it in the political arena. The trajectory of his intellectual thought makes it difficult to discern a genuine Sufi tendency. But one might argue that he presented elements of Sufism as a revolutionary and libertarian programme, suitable to challenge the status quo in Pahlavi Iran. As Ali Rahnema argues in his perceptive political biography of him:

> In a way Shari'ati argued that an individual's gnostic experience was an educational process which paved the way for the meaningful dedication of one's life to the cause of the people. By the time the Sufi wayfarer is free of all worldly chains including his love for life and ready to be accepted by Him, he has acquired all the attributes of a true warrior for the cause of God. ... Thus Shari'ati replaces the Sufi concept of self-annihilation and subsequent assimilation or living in God with self-annihilation and subsequent assimilation of living in 'the people.' This is certainly a novel interpretation. According to it, Che Guevara becomes an armed and socially responsible reincarnation of Hallaj and 'Ayn al-Quzat Hamadani [two Persian Sufis executed on charges of heresy]. They are both selfless martyrs of love.[47]

The narratives of *Bazgasht beh-khish* and *Gharbzadegi* represented the apotheosis of the socialist, 'third-worldist' and revolutionary-Islamic *Zeitgeist* dominating Iranian society during the 1970s. The agents of that political culture engineered situationally transcendent ideas that promised to succeed *de facto* in the realization of their projected contents. 'Only those orientations transcending reality,' Karl Mannheim argues, 'will be referred to ... as utopian which, when they pass over into conduct, tend to shatter, either partially or wholly, the order of things prevailing at the time.'[48] According to Mannheim, such 'chiliastic' utopias are expressions of the ideal that is attainable in the here and now. 'For the real Chiliast,' he elaborates, 'the present becomes the breach through which what was previously inward bursts out suddenly, takes hold of the outer world and transforms it.'[49] Paul Ricoeur argues in a similar vein, elaborating that chiliasm 'has the idea of a millennial kingdom coming from heaven. ... [it] assumes a transcendent point of departure for a social revolution based on religious motives.'[50]

The concept of chiliastic utopianism is immediately relevant to the events in Iran. Once the religiously framed, anti-imperialist discourse was codified as a revolutionary narrative, it developed a dynamism of its own, 'shattering the order of things' not only in Iran, but also beyond. As lay religious intellectuals whose ideas appealed to the disillusioned urban youth in 1970s Iran, Shariati and Al-e Ahmad introduced Islamic-revolutionary ideas to a wide audience outside the religious seminaries. This interaction gave impetus to the emergence of a systematic, Islamic culture of revolt. Translated by the organized political movements into revolutionary action, the force of this systemic movement transcended the powers of both its makers and its agents—it engendered its own dynamism, its own 'utopian reality' rendered transcendent by its intoxicating claim. Introjected with such a powerful, authoritative discourse, Iranians were driven by the belief that the revolution *was* a revolt against the *mostakbaran* (oppressors), that the Shah *was* the incarnation of Yazid, that Iran *was* the battlefield where the party of God (*hezb'allah)* was struggling against the Greater and Lesser Satan, that Imam Khomeini *was* the messianic chaperone guiding the slave revolt in its mission to smash the idols (*bot*) of the imperial masters. This revolutionary reality penetrated Iranian thinking to its core, and not only the mindset of Iranians. Even Michel Foucault and others in the 'West' such as Oriana Fallaci, Peter Scholl-Latour and *The Independent*'s foreign affairs correspondent Robert Fisk could not escape its 'awesome' force. 'When I first saw Yassir Arafat—admittedly he was no Khomeini—I was mesmerized by his eyes,' writes the latter symptomatically.

What big eyes you have, I wanted to say. When I first met Hafez al-Assad of Syria, I was captivated by the absolute flatness of the back of his head, so straight I could have set a ruler against it without a crack showing. I spent an evening at dinner with King Hussein, perpetually astonished at how small he was, irritated that I couldn't get him to stop playing with the box of cigarettes that lay on the table between us. And now here was one of the titans of the twentieth century, whose name would be in every history book for a thousand years, the scourge of America, the Savonarola of Tehran, the 'twelfth' Imam, an apostle of Islam. And I searched his face and noted the two small spots on his cheek and the vast fluffy eyebrows, the bags under his eyes, the neat white beard, his right hand lying on his knee, his left arm buried in his robe. ... We were the foreign consuls arriving at the oriental court, waiting to hear the word of the oracle.[51]

Even Oriana Fallaci, who is not known for her sympathies for Muslims in general and Islamic politics in particular, could not escape the gnomic appeal of revolutionary Iran in that winter of 1978-79. Fallaci found Khomeini intelligent, and 'the most handsome old man I had ever met in my life. He resembled the "Moses" sculpted by Michelangelo.' Khomeini was

not a puppet like Arafat or Qaddafi or the many other dictators I met in the Islamic world. He was a sort of Pope, a sort of king—a real leader. And it did not take long to realise that in spite of his quiet appearance he represented the Robespierre or the Lenin of something which would go very far and would poison the world. People loved him too much. They saw in him another Prophet. Worse: a God.[52]

So it was not only Iran's revolutionary generation that was caught up in the powerful reality of late 1970s Iran: the revolutionary momentum engendered trans-cultural reactions. Thus it should not come as a surprise that after toppling the Shah, the Islamic Republic institutionalized the revolutionary utopias as central ideological precepts of the state. Ultimately, it was this process that established Iran as a revisionist power in international affairs.

Institutional structure

What gave Iran's revolutionary narrative its force was its religious passion. The revolutionary reality transmuted the paradigms of *Gharbzadegi* and *Bazgasht beh-khish* into a radical counter-culture that succeeded in destroying one of the most powerful states in the Persian Gulf. Glorifying the symbols of Iranian and Shia romanticism—the aesthetics of *shahadat* (martyrdom), the sufferings of Imam Hussein, the just age of the Imam Mahdi—they extracted, channelled, and dispersed the emotional energy onto the receptive revolutionary masses.[53] Once internalized, this emergent culture appeared as an objectified reality to its agents. This aestheticized political reality had its own structure, meaning, symbols and imagery. Hence the *Shuhada* (martyrs) were not merely freedom fighters giving their lives for the revolutionary cause. The revolutionary reality represented them as the 'candles of society [who] burn themselves out and illuminate society.'[54] Martyrdom was not a loss, it was a choice 'whereby the warrior sacrifices himself on the threshold of the temple of freedom and the altar of love and is victorious.'[55] Likewise, Imam Hussein—the exalted, almost eponymous hero of the revolutionary play—was not merely a religious-political personality among others: 'He was that individual who negated himself with absolute sincerity, with the utmost magnificence within human power.'[56] This 'ideal man,' Shariati contended,

> holds the sword of Caesar in his hand and he has the heart of Jesus in his breast. He thinks with the brain of Socrates and loves God with the heart of Hallaj. ... Like the Buddha, he is delivered from the dungeon of pleasure-seeking and egoism; Like Lao Tse, he reflects on the profundity of his primordial nature; ... [l]ike Spartacus, he is a rebel against slave owners ... and like Moses, he is the messenger of jihad and deliverance.[57]

After the triumph of the revolution, the newly created Islamic Republic fused the revolutionary energies and channelled them into politics, transforming the self-attribution of Iran from a systematically legitimated status quo power to an internationalist Islamic movement. The Iranian state thus equipped itself with the transnational mandate for the export of the revolution (*sudur-e enghelab*). How was this abstract self-identification institutionalized, and how did it shape Iran's grand strategic preferences?

Owing to his charismatic appeal and his institutionalised position as the leader of the revolution (*rahbar-e enghelab*) and supreme jurisprudent (*vali-e faqih*),[58] Ayatollah Khomeini commanded the resources necessary to translate Iran's self-bestowed revolutionary mandate into the new disposition of the Islamic state. The imagery of the millenarian struggle between the 'oppressed' and the 'oppressors', Khomeini's Manichean *mostazafan-mostakbaran* dichotomy, was central to this task. It should be kept in mind here that Khomeini himself emerged out of a particular intellectual and political culture. Hence his emphasis on the anti-imperialist terminology of the Iranian left which linked what was happening in Iran with the struggle of liberation movements all over the world, in particular to those in Palestine and Latin America.[59] Hence also his reference to a wider global battle, not only between the forces of 'arrogance' and the 'dispossessed' but also between justice and injustice, which he inherited from the political philosophy of Abu-Ala Mawdudi and Ayatollah Baqir al-Sadr. According to that ideological dualism, the ongoing clash between the 'oppressed', who have been deprived of their political, cultural, natural and economic resources, and the 'oppressors,' who have subjugated the 'disinherited', is zero-sum in nature. Expressing thoughts somewhat resembling Gramsci's ideas about the functions of organic intellectuals in society, and here especially their responsibility to create awareness among different social strata, Khomeini urged Muslim scholars 'to struggle against all attempts by the oppressors to establish a monopoly over the sources of wealth or to make illicit use of them. They must not allow the masses to remain hungry and deprived' h declared, 'while plundering oppressors usurp the sources of wealth and live in opulence.' This mission was closely related to the Shia Imamate, and here especially to the life of Imam Ali, the Commander of the Faithful (*amir-ol momenin*), whose role was reinterpreted as thoroughly revolutionary:

> The Commander of the Faithful (upon whom be peace) says: 'I have accepted the task of government because God Exalted and Almighty, has exacted from the scholars of Islam a pledge not to sit silent and idle in the face of the gluttony and plundering of the oppressors, on the one hand, and the hunger and deprivation of the oppressed, on the other.'
>
> Here is the full text of the passage we refer to: 'I swear by Him Who causes the seed to open and creates the souls of all living things that were it not for the presence of those who have come to swear allegiance to me, were it not for the obligation of rulership now imposed upon me by the availability of aid and support, and were it not for the pledge that God has taken from the scholars of Islam not to remain silent in the face of the gluttony and plundering of the oppressors, on the one hand, and the harrowing hunger and deprivation of the oppressed, on the other hand—were it not for all of this, then I would abandon the reins of government and in no way seek it. You would see that this world of yours, with all of its position and rank, is less in my eyes than the moisture that comes from the sneeze of a goat.'[60]

'Khomeinism' elevated the Iranian nation-state to the status of a vehicle of divine substance. Inevitably, the Islamic Republic felt destined to change what was perceived to be an overbearingly hierarchical world order. This was by no means merely an abstract self-perception. It was formalized, inscribed in the current Constitution of Iran which declares that the revolution aims to bring about the triumph of the *mostazafan* against the *mostakbaran*, that it 'provides the necessary basis for ensuring the continuation of the Revolution at home and abroad.' Illustrated in accordance with the Quranic verse 'This your nation is a single nation, and I am your Lord, so worship Me (21:92)', it is further declared that the Constitution 'will strive, in concert with other Islamic and popular movements, to prepare the way for the formation of a single world community.'[61]

Islamic utopian romanticism and the challenge to world order

True, other sections of the Iranian Constitution emphasize abstention from 'aggressive intervention in the internal affairs of other nations' (see, for example, Article 154), and the Islamic Republic adopted an overall anti-militaristic, if rhetorically confrontational, posture during the early days of the revolution. But Khomeini also explicitly endorsed the export of the revolutionary idea, whilst cautioning against applying force. On the one side he proclaimed that

> we have set as our goal the world-wide spread of the influence of Islam and the suppression of the rule of the world conquerors ... We wish to cause the corrupt roots of Zionism, capitalism and Communism to wither throughout the world. We wish, as does God almighty, to destroy the systems which are based on these three foundations, and to promote the Islamic order of the Prophet ... in the world of arrogance.[62]

On the other side, he also cautioned that this 'does not mean that we intend to export it by the bayonet. We want to call [*dawat*] everyone to Islam [and to] send our calling everywhere.'[63] Although covert backing for 'liberation movements' in Afghanistan, Iraq, Lebanon, Latin America, Africa and Palestine was sometimes justified openly, exporting the *idea* of the Islamic Republic without military aggrandisement was rather more central.[64] Reliance on *dawat* (calling) and *tabligh* (propagation, advertisement, dissemination) was hence substituted for the militaristic coercion periodically characteristic of the Shah's reign. In accordance with that attitude, the Islamic Republic cancelled the Shah's multi-billion dollars defence contracts with the United States and Western

Europe and abandoned Iranian military installations in Oman. Revolutionary Iran thus felt very self-conscious about the appeal of the Islamic-republican model to the Muslim worlds in particular and the Third Worlds in general. Caught in the momentum of religious intoxication, the revolutionaries relied on their ideological power, transmitted by the charisma of Ayatollah Khomeini and transplanted by sympathizing movements in the region and beyond, rather than military force.[65] It was this self-confidence about the justness of the revolutionary cause and the spiritual superiority of religious values that motivated Khomeini to write a letter to the Soviet leader Mikhail Gorbachev in January 1989, attempting to persuade him to consider religion in general and Islam in particular as an alternative to the materialism of capitalist societies. He argued in a similar vein in his response to a letter from Pope John Paul II (in the midst of the hostage crisis) in May 1980:

> I ask His Honor to warn the U.S. government of the consequences of its oppressions, cruelties and plunders, and advise Mr. Carter, who is doomed to defeat, to treat nations desiring absolute independence of global powers on the basis of humanitarian principles. He should be advised to observe the guidelines of Jesus Christ and not to expose himself and the U.S. Administration to defamation.[66]

A similar belief in the justness of the Islamic revolution, together with suspicion towards the US government, motivated the *daneshjuan-e musalmanan-e piramun-e khatt-e imam* (Muslim Students following the line of the Imam) to occupy the US embassy in Tehran in November 1979.[67] There was a very immediate political rationale behind the occupation: it was meant to demonstrate that this Iranian generation would not accept another 'Operation Boot/Ajax', another CIA/MI6 engineered coup d'état that would reinstall the Shah. Hojjatoleslam Mousavi Khoeiniha, who acted as the spiritual guide of the *khatt-e imam* student movement, would write in retrospect that the historical memory of the Iranian nation, and in particular the revolutionaries, of the United States-inspired coup of August 1953, that resulted in the overthrow of the government of Dr. Mohammad Mossadegh, needs an honest appraisal. That event resulted in the return of Shah Mohammad-Reza Pahlavi to Iran and the continuation of his dictatorial regime. When all the implications of this tragic episode in our history are taken into consideration, an unbiased arbiter would surely judge the students' action as having been the only real avenue for seeking justice from the American government.[68]

A letter by the Iranian Ministry of Foreign Affairs to its counterpart in Panama (21 December 1979), which had acquiesced to demands by the US Government to admit the Shah, is equally revealing of Iranian perceptions of world politics during that period:

In demanding the extradition of Mohammad Reza Pahlavi, the Iranian people do not seek to quench a thirst for vengeance, but legitimately desire that the deposed Shah answer to his crimes and unmask all the plots which enabled him, during 25 years, to establish a veritable organised terror and to smother the voice of the people in the sombre prisons of Savak.

In demanding this extradition, the Iranian people wish to demonstrate that oppressed nations of the world will no longer allow imperialist powers to play with their destiny, scorn their national pride, forge coup d'état at the whim of their interests or impose upon helpless people tyrants servilely [sic] devoted to foreign orders.

In this anti-imperialist struggle, all oppressed peoples should be united, and we hope that the people and the government of Panama will understand the true direction of this fight and will refuse to submit to the diktats of the United States of America.[69]

Bruce Laingen, then US Ambassador to Iran, understood that prevalent mood in the newly established Islamic Republic. In July 1979, that is three months before the Shah was admitted to the United States for medical treatment and four months before the

US embassy was occupied, he advised then US Secretary of State Cyrus Vance that giving

> refuge to the Shah would almost certainly trigger massive demonstrations against our embassy. With luck, they may stop at that, without a physical assault of the kind we experienced last February. But there could be no assurance of that, since Iran's regular military and police force remain largely demoralised and cannot yet be relied on to apply force that might be needed to prevent violence against us.[70]

There was then a general consensus among those immediately involved in the political process in Iran, that the revolution had engendered its own self-fulfilling prophecies, its own truth conditions, its own objectified reality, its own introjective force. Didn't this emergent culture empower the revolutionaries to reject one of the central pillars of international society, and here especially the institutions of international law which were deemed to be mere instruments in the hands of the 'hegemonic' superpowers? It appears to me that the *khatt-e imam* (the Imam's line) students did sincerely believe in their cause; they were convinced that denying diplomatic immunity to 52 American embassy personnel would symbolise the revolution's protest against imperialism, and here specifically the US, which was perceived to be the guardian of an increasingly unjust world order. The 'hitherto prevailing conventions of diplomatic immunity and representation' were considered 'worthy of attack' because of the legitimating force of revolution.[71] The revolutionary culture was determining, it constituted a whole new reality in Iran, and it was this, rather than the statutes of the international community, that guided the action of the proponents of the Islamic republic. Their decisions, which were governed not by crude, short-term cost-benefit calculations but rather by the correlation of international justice and Iran's revolutionary momentum, led very quickly to abstraction and idealism. Thus pragmatic judgement was overridden by generalizations as, for example, in descriptions of the 'Islamic Revolution of Iran [as] a new achievement in the ongoing struggle between the peoples and the oppressive superpowers.'[72]

Moreover, the revolutionary quasi-state supervised by Ayatollah Khomeini, and here especially the *khatt-e imam* revolutionary wing of the Iranian factions, condoned the occupation as a means to reiterate Iran's break with the past and, not least, to encourage a process of internal radicalization and subdue their liberal-left competitors organized around Prime Minister Mehdi Bazargan.[73] The preferred state identity espoused by that faction was to be offensive, revolutionary, and idealistic, rather than conservative, accommodating, and status quo oriented. As the closest manifestation of the omnipotence of the US, whose government was deemed to be the prime agent of anti-Iranian conspiracies, occupying the 'den of spies' (*lane-ye jasusan*), as the US embassy was called, was meant to reiterate the anti-imperialistic character of the Iranian movement. For those involved, the occupation of the embassy thus symbolized

the last years of the bipolar international system that emerged from World War II. Direct and indirect intervention by the two superpowers—the U.S.A. and the U.S.S.R—were commonplace throughout what once was called the "Third World." But the Islamic Revolution in Iran transformed a once-devoted ally of the West into a "rogue state" that insisted on taking orders from none other than God.

In those circumstances, safeguarding the revolution and thwarting efforts to undermine it was the only possible approach. We looked on with amusement as the international agreements and conventions that had given the green light to the oppression of the Iranian nation were seen critically only after the students detained 52 Americans. From our point of view, the double standard we had exposed was reason enough for the action we took. ... We owe our independence and freedom today to those moments of clarity during the takeover and resistance against the West, and during the war against the aggressors, and also to the perseverance Iranians have demonstrated as they rebuilt the nation and set out to restore a civil society.[74]

The point of Iran's revolutionary generation was not merely rhetorical or metaphysical, confined to their minds and not exercised in practice. The *mostazafan-mostakbaran* dichotomy was not merely part of a suggestive analogy, it described what was perceived to be reality. One immediate result of this kind of internalization can be seen in the persistent attempts to challenge the international status quo. If you get into the habit of thinking that a hierarchical world order produces injustice in a causal way, then you are likely to think that an Islamic republic must foster a just world order, also in a causal way. It must follow from this state of mind that denying the very basis of the 'Westphalian nation-state system'—whereby the citizens of a sovereign state are only subject to the jurisdiction of territorial state law and, where applicable, to secular international law—becomes almost obligatory. This logic is what motivated Ayatollah Khomeini to issue a religious verdict (*fatwa*) against Salman Rushdie and the publishers of *The Satanic Verses*. From Khomeini's perspective, the extension of *sharia* law to someone who used to be part of the *umma*, had become an 'apostate' member of the Islamic community, and had insulted the Qur'an and the Prophet Muhammad was not only legitimate, but also an obligation.[75] The international system, considered as nothing but a field of hypocrisy, war and destruction, was thus opened up to penetration by the 'wretched of the earth'. Positioning divine law above secular international law during periods when safeguarding the *maslahat* (interest) of the Islamic state and—by extension—the Muslim *umma* demanded radical political action was immediately related to a culture and a *Geist* which apprehended both its present reality and its future in dichotomous terms: revolution vs. orthodoxy, Hussein vs. Yazid, Islam vs. hypocrisy, justice vs. oppression, commanding good vs. forbidding evil, authenticity vs. Westtoxification, and so on. Ayatollah Khomeini and his followers apprehended the international system as the negative, oppressive side of those dichotomies, while the ideal and dominant side, that by which the world is given its meaning and identity, is conceived to exist in another, yet to be approximated, utopian reality. Thus, far from recognizing the overbearing injustice of the present, Iran's revolution was meant to strive for the transcendence of all the tensions between utopia and reality which those dichotomies opened up. No wonder then that the more international society turned against Iran, the more this reaction confirmed the self-perception of the Iranian state as the leader of an 'oppressed' nation, facing the overwhelming force of the 'arrogant' powers. The revolutionary state closely related this imagery to the sufferings of Shias at the hands of unjust rulers and the martyrdom (*shahadat*) of the Shia Imam Hussein during the Battle of Karbala against the Umayyad monarch Yazid in 680 AD:

> Imam Husayn was not to be killed again. Thus, he defeated Yazid [i.e. the Shah] in Iran last year. Imam Husayn, who is now leading a battle against a greater Yazid [i.e. imperialism], will also triumph, God willing. The revolutionary Imam Husayn in Iran, who is fighting imperialism, is not alone now. In addition to some 35,000,000 Iranians who bravely and devotedly rally around him, there are billions of Muslims and non-Muslims everywhere in Syria, Libya, Algeria, Lebanon, Palestine, Pakistan, Africa, the Omani liberation front, Eritrea, the Chilean resistance, the Chadian liberation movement, the Canary Islands' liberation movement, the Futami liberation movement, Spain, Korea and many other places as well as the entire Islamic world, and the oppressed all over the world, who all support Iran, the revolution and Imam Husayn, represented in leader Imam Ayatollah Khomeini.[76]

The anti-imperialist norm advocated by Al-e Ahmad and Shariati, translated into reality by Iran's revolutionary generation and an element constituting the Islamic state, became a dominant institution in Iran. The country's foreign policy culture, Iran's perception of international affairs and its role in world politics were being transformed. This driving agency, which commanded its own reality, soon broke the boundaries between political idiom and political action. In agreement with the concepts of the

Muslim left, encroachment on the Islamic world by 'corrupting' 'Western' concepts was deemed poisonous for the evolution of a just society and the emergence of the ultimate *Homo Islamicus*. In theory, regaining authenticity—returning to the self (*Bazgasht beh-khish*), as Shariati put it—and retaining independence required detachment from the bipolar international system that was perceived as 'dangerous for humanity'.[77] Scholars of Iran's modern intellectual history agree, when they explain that the question of authenticity has been central to the country's political culture, and that 'this has translated into a rejection of the apish imitation of the West on the grounds that mimicry and submission are fraudulent and counterfeit states of being. As a result,' it is argued correctly, 'precarious policies (i.e., hostage taking, export of revolution, the death sentence against Salman Rushdie) should not come as a surprise.'[78]

No wonder also, then, that Iran was reluctant to retreat from its ideological positions after it had been invaded by Saddam Hussein's Iraq in 1980. For the hundred of thousands of Iranian volunteers, the war was a re-enactment of the eternal battle between absolute evil, represented by Saddam Hussein, and absolute justness, represented by Ayatollah Khomeini. Thus, when the Iraqi army entered Iran, it accentuated the interaction between the identity of the Islamic Republic and that of the nationalistic, largely secular Ba'thist state in Iraq. This antagonistic interaction engendered the notion among Iranian soldiers that they were fighting in order to defend the Islamic order, not only in Iran, but globally. Shia Islam's holy places, Karbala and Najaf, were to be liberated from the 'Pharaoh of the age', even if it meant that a whole generation of Iranians would perish in the war trenches. For them the conflict had nothing to do with 'revenge' or power politics. Rather, it was perceived to be a war for 'Islam, country and honour'.[79] The metaphysics, symbolism and imagery that engendered the 'reality' that Iranians were fighting for a transcendental cause was consciously engineered by Khomeini and the newly established Islamic state. In turn, for many of the people receiving the message among the receptive revolutionary generation, this 'reality' was synonymous with an 'age whose every moment is light and illumination, wisdom and perfection … Yes my brothers,' reads a will by one of the soldiers who died in the war, 'we have witnessed Islam, its Prophet and his valuable traditions, and the innocent Imams; in a short span of time we have felt, with all our existence, the rich history of Islam which [previously] we had only read or heard about.'[80] Now that Iranians were entrenched by this reality it seemed that the legendary story of Imam Hussein was repeating itself, 'in the matter of guardianship and leadership, in the [presence of] sincere disciples and companions of falsity, in belief, sacrifice and martyrdom, in blasphemy, belligerence and dissension, in the expansion of Islam and the multiplicity of enemies.'[81] In this dichotic order, Imam Khomeini was perceived to represent 'the spirit of God. [W]e have made a compact with you, heard your words and endeavoured to implement them', it is proclaimed in another will.

> [W]e have written your message onto the face of history with our blood saying: In our time, we were with our Imam, and if we were not in Karbala to assist Hossein, we have added his child and this way our duty. Oh Imam! I have understood your command when you stated: The present war is a conflict between truth and falsehood and since truth is the victor, we are victorious. Since I wished to join the ranks of the combatants of truth, I entered the scene and this was my message…[82]

The Islamic Republic, as many Iranians saw it during the revolutionary period, existed in a severed, schismatic condition: on the one side of the Atlantic the 'great Satan', the United States, on the other the atheist Leviathan, the Soviet Union (and in between other, lesser enemies such as Apartheid South Africa, Israel and Saddam Hussein). Having completed its diagnosis of Iranian and Islamic civilization, and its prognosis that revolutionary action would bring about the renewal of both, Iran's revolutionary generation was introjected with the idea that radical independence from both superpowers would start a process, at the end of which the existing world order would be transformed. Hence the emergence of the *na sharghi na gharbi, jomhur-e eslami* norm (neither Eastern nor Western, only the Islamic Republic). Hence the country's decision to end its membership of Cold War institutions such as the Central Treaty Organization (CENTO). Hence the prolonged war with Iraq, which was seen as a part of an international conspiracy to subdue the revolution (which in many ways it was, of course—see the following part of this book). Hence the Islamic Republic's immediate support for the PLO (Yassir Arafat was the first major foreign political leader to visit Iran, where he received the keys to what had ceased to be the Israeli embassy in Tehran) and sympathy with leftist movements all over the world, especially in Latin America. Hence the Islamic Republic's decision to sever ties with Apartheid South Africa. Hence, also, Iran's enduring antagonism toward the policies of the United States. The costs of these changes to the country's identity were accepted, even if that meant that it would be isolated and labelled as a 'rogue' or 'outlaw' state by prominent members of the international community.

The realist influx: Iran's changing domestic regime

It has been argued that Iran's contemporary foreign policy culture is rooted in the revolutionary paradigms formulated in the 1970s, and that this cultural system informed the country's grand strategic preferences. Revolutionary utopias were institutionalized as central narratives of the state, and the Islamic Republic followed them at the level of interest as well as behaviour. In other words, the radical wing that took over the Iranian state did not see a contradiction between the revolutionary ideals and 'the' national interest of the country. On the contrary, from their perspective, realizing those ideals *was* in the national interest of the Islamic Republic and—by implication—the Muslim *umma*. Iranian foreign policy elites were aware that the appeal of the revolution in the Muslim world (and in some other parts of the Third World) would be enhanced greatly if the counter-hegemonic rhetoric were to be backed up by action. If the US was the 'Great Satan', conquering the moral high ground in world politics required confrontation. If the Islamic Republic wanted to propagate its revolutionary claim, it needed to confront real and perceived imperialism both at home and abroad. If the revolution was to act as a model for other Third World countries, it had to assert its legitimacy, if necessary through violent action. In the Iranian case, then, as elsewhere, utopia offered both 'a vantage point from which to perceive the given, the already constituted' and, more importantly, 'new possibilities above and beyond the given'.[83]

The composition of Iran's contemporary foreign policy culture shows both residual elements of the revolutionary utopias and signs of an emergent 'counter-culture' that signals loyalty to the country's commitment to a rather more equitable world order, but using less 'raucous' methods to achieve that goal.[84] In the Iranian context, as elsewhere, culture does not appear as a monolithic system resistant to changes from below. 'The reality of any hegemony', Raymond Williams notes, 'is that, while by definition it is always dominant, it is never either total or exclusive. At any time, forms of alternative or directly oppositional politics and culture exist as significant elements in the society.'[85] One needs only to consider the speeches of women activists such as Shirin Ebadi, Shahla Habibi or Zahra Rahnavard, and intellectual paradigms developed by oppositional figures such as Mohammad Shabestari, Mohsen Kadivar, Akbar Ganji and Abdolkarim Soroush (or even watch the films of the internationally acclaimed directors Jafar Panahi, Niki Karimi, Abbas Kiarostami, Majid Majidi, Mohsen Makhmalbaf and his daughter Samira) to conclude that Iran's post-revolutionary cultural order (yesterday's utopia turned today's topia) is undergoing rapid transformations.[86] Undeniably, this emergent counter-culture—which has manifested itself in a multi-dimensional movement for a pluralistic democracy—has already had an impact on the country's foreign policies. It is exemplified by Iran's cooperation with regional states, despite Khomeini's will which explicitly warned against rapprochement with the 'government of the Hijaz' (i.e. Saudi Arabia); détente with the European Union, after the government of Khatami distanced itself from Khomeini's *fatwa* against Rushdie; and dialogue with the US government on Afghanistan and the situation in Iraq. It would be reductionist, however, to attribute these policies to power struggles between pragmatic 'reformers' organized around personalities such as Mohammad Khatami and his brother Mohammad-Reza Khatami, Ali Abtahi and Mostafa Moin, and pan-Islamic 'conservatives' supported by the office of the Leader Ayatollah Ali Khamenei. This dichotomous notion, too often presented in mono-causal terms (i.e. reformism equals pragmatism and pro-Western policies while conservatism equals pan-Islamicism and anti-Western agitation), is inadequate for examining why Iranian foreign policy elites have remained committed to certain core strategic principles of the state. Does the Islamic Republic not continue to represent itself as a 'moral superpower', as a force for change in international affairs? Does it not challenge US foreign policies repeatedly, in the Persian Gulf, in Iraq, in Central Asia? Does it not continue to support the Palestinian cause, with conferences, ideological propaganda, organized diplomatic initiatives? Is Iran's support for the Lebanese Hezbollah not equally consistent, whether under Khatami or Ahmadinejad? Doesn't the episode with the eight British servicemen in June 2004, when they were paraded in shackles in much the same way as Iraqi prisoners of war were paraded by the Americans and the British, indicate Iran's propensity for 'perception management' in international affairs? Wasn't a similar scenario replayed in March 2007, when Iranian Revolutionary Guards arrested 15 British Navy personnel in the Persian Gulf? Does the continued standoff with the International Atomic Energy Association (IAEA) over the country's nuclear programme not indicate Iran's obstinate adherence to the independence norm? Does the country not continue to advocate the case for the Islamic-republican model both at home and abroad? Like other states, it appears to me, the Iranian republic adheres to certain grand strategic preferences that transcend the faultlines of day-to-day politics.

Moreover, from the perspective of contemporary Iranian decision makers there appears to be no contradiction between the utopian-romantic *Leitmotif* of the revolution and multilateral engagement and détente—two elements that were central to the 'dialogue among civilizations' initiative put forward by the Khatami administration. Although the Islamic Republic has distanced itself from some of the confrontationist policies characteristic of the first decade of the revolution, *tabligh* and *dawat* continue to provide the strategic means to realize the preferences of the state:

> Fulfilling the utopian vision of the revolution's devotees inside and outside of Iran is a pressing necessity to ensure our survival. To assert our identity it is necessary to be present in all world forums and to defend Islam and Iran effectively in all international tribunals and conventions. But we cannot ultimately flourish and make our weight felt in the international scene—whose rules are set by our opponents—unless we maintain our unique idealism.[87]

Reiterating Iran's commitment to the ideal of an equitable world order, President Ahmadinejad exhibits a comparable political rationale when he calls for

> serious reform in the structure and working methods of the [UN] Security Council. ... Justice and Democracy dictate that the role of the General Assembly, as the highest organ of the United Nations, must be respected.

The General Assembly can then, through appropriate mechanisms, take on the task of reforming the Organisation and particularly rescue the Security Council from its current state. In the interim, the Non-Aligned-Movement, the Organisation of the Islamic Conference and the African continent should each have a representative as a permanent member of the Security Council, with veto privilege. The resulting balance would hopefully prevent further trampling of the rights of nations.[88]

To open a parenthesis here, I am not claiming that there is a consensus among the different factions of Iranian politics on every foreign policy decision. That would oversimplify the differences between the spectrum of political parties and institutions in Iran. After all, there are at least seven institutions involved in Iran's foreign policy process: the office of the Leader, the Foreign Ministry, the office of the President, the Head of the Expediency Council, the Supreme National Security Council, the Parliament (primarily through its National Security and Foreign Policy commissions) and the Strategic Council for Foreign Relations, which was established in June 2006 to oversee Ahmadinejad's performance. There is no doubt that these institutions follow different agendas. But there appears to be a culturally constituted consensus about the country's role in international affairs that is strong enough to transcend the factions of—and divisions in—Iranian politics. This foreign policy culture refers to a higher level of abstraction than the day-to-day affairs of the state. It functions as the guardian of identity, represents a web of shared ideals, images, norms and institutions, and provides for the foreign policy elites a coherent, if systematically abstract, overall orientation in the conduct of international affairs. Pro-Palestinian sentiments, anti-Zionism and anti-imperialism, Islamic communitarianism, 'third-worldism', and cultural and political independence functioned as the ideational points of fixation reconstituting the Iranian self during the revolutionary process of the 1960s and 1970s, and are not easy to discard. They have acquired the status of cognitively objectified and formally codified social institutions reabsorbed by Iran's contemporary elite, one that cannot escape the penetrative force of this cultural reality. Despite the domestic power struggles in Iran, then, the shared interests of reformers and conservatives meet where their competition ends: at the junction of Iran's foreign policy culture and—by implication—the grand strategic preferences of the state.

It is not at all obvious, then, that Iran's current strategic preferences represent a break from the ideals of the revolution. Nor is it clear that they result from 'socialization' in international structures. It is true that viewed from the perspective of leading Iranian foreign policy officials, the war against Saddam Hussein's Iraq played its part in confronting Iran with the brute realities of international life, with the immediate experience of 'war and destruction ... in the battlefields ... cities, neighbourhoods and homes' and the 'global indifference' regarding Saddam's war crimes.[89] But a utopia is always in the process of being realized because it is as much legitimization of what is as an aspiration towards what could be. This is the essential difference from ideology, which does not hold out the prospect for change, but legitimates the status quo. Iranian-Islamic utopianism is alive and well because it is still in the process of realizing its dual aim: democratization at home and positioning Iran as a central international player abroad. The reform movement has effected an eclectic reinterpretation of these goals and does not represent a revolt against the system.[90] Its vehicle is a reconstituted counter-utopia, a 'liberal-humanitarian' utopia that is directed against the 'chiliastic' moment of Iran's revolution. The crucial difference between the chiliastic and the liberal-humanitarian utopia, Karl Mannheim explains, manifests itself in the sense of time.[91] While the former makes an immediate promise—the transcendent moment is here and now, the immediateness of the transcendent overcomes the distance between the utopia and reality—the liberal-humanitarian utopia emphasizes evolutionary change. 'There is a sense of unilinear progress,' Ricoeur elaborates, 'and this philosophy of progress is directed exactly against the time sense of the chiliastic utopia. ... The idea is *post tenebras lux* (after darkness, light); in the end, light wins.'[92] The Iranian utopia of *imminent change* has therefore transmuted into the utopia of *generic growth*. This is the philosophical faultline of Iran's contemporary political culture: it manifests itself in the fight between an intellectual and scientific (enlightened?) world-view and a theocratic or clerical (orthodox?) one; it represents, in essence, a battle between progressive Islam and fundamentalist Islam, a struggle that goes beyond the Iranian context.[93] I found the influential ideas of the contemporary Iranian philosopher Abdolkarim Soroush emblematic of the former:

> If science develops, it would modernize and develop our politics, it would give meaning to justice and freedom ... and [it] would determine the rights of people. We should not forget that in the New World politics is scientific politics and management is scientific management. The new science modernizes even philosophy. Islamic philosophy is dear, but ... [w]e should not think that the answer to all questions could be found in this philosophy. Even on the scene of philosophy we should seek progress and renewal.[94]

The paradigmatic turn advocated by Soroush and others has engendered the critical deconstruction of Iran's pre-revolutionary identity discourse. According to the 'Kian school of Iranian philosophy', neither the 'return to the self' nor the idea of 'West-toxification' sufficiently addressed Iran's conflict with itself. Instead of essentializing Iran's Islamic heritage and castigating the 'West,' Soroush argues, Iranian thinkers need to evaluate critically the country's national (Persian), religious-Islamic (Shia) *and* Western heritage.[95] 'The difficulty arises,' Soroush asserts,

> when some people unreflectively assume a fixed and eternal cultural identity and distinguish friend and foe accordingly. Such people never realize that the self must be created, that it does not come prefabricated

and maintenance-free. ... The bid to 'return to oneself' will remain an empty slogan at best (and a slayer of culture and a source of stagnation at worst) if the boundaries of the self remain unspecified, if flexibility is denied. We cannot countenance a 'return to the self' that is counterposed to the reconstruction of the self.[96]

The contemporary foreign policy preferences of the Iranian state oscillate between the emerging, liberal-humanitarian utopia articulated by an increasingly vocal civil society and the chiliastic meta-structure woven into the institutional and intellectual fabric of the country during the revolutionary process. A critical, discursive, reconfiguring continuation rather than a break with the ideals of the revolution, this emergent culture has guided the Rafsanjani, Khatami and Ahmadinejad administrations towards advocating reform at home and abroad, while prioritizing an essentially conservative purpose: the preservation of the post-revolutionary, Islamic character of the Iranian system and the projection of Iranian power both regionally and globally. Iran's seemingly 'eclectic' pragmatism during times of crisis—arms deals with the United States and Israel during the Iran-Iraq war (the Iran-Contra affair), the diplomatic backing of the US invasion of Taliban Afghanistan in 2001, relative silence about Russian war crimes in Muslim Chechnya and Chinese suppression of Muslims primarily in the western provinces of the country, mute support for the war against Saddam Hussein in 2003, efforts to engage with the US diplomatically etc.— should be seen within that context.[97] They exemplify instances when diplomacy and the anarchic spaces of world politics are/were exploited in support of Iran's grand strategic preferences. They are not, as Tariq Ali and some others on the 'New Left' have argued, instances of the Islamic Republic's betrayal of the post-revolutionary foreign policy agenda.[98] Managing the intrinsic dichotomies of Iran's emerging 'utopian-romantic realism' will depend on the ability of the state, its willingness to accommodate the calls for internal reform, and its diplomatic resources to engage an international society struggling to accommodate the desires of a demanding Leviathan shaken by the events of 11 September 2001.[99] In the words of a senior member of Iran's foreign policy establishment:

> As regards the new international environment, the Iranian government must be cognizant of the fact that its powers derives from the degree of its popular support and legitimacy. Issues of security and identity must be taken more seriously. ... The identity that Iran projects on the regional and global level must be reconstructed in a way as to encourage a recasting of perspectives in the US towards both Iran and Islam. Thus a security shield can be provided.[100]

So Iran's foreign policy elites do not think of the international system in an ad-hoc fashion, they do not merely decide from crisis to crisis, their decisions are not singularly eclectic, they are not merely reactive as Soroush alleges erroneously.[101] Rather, they think of world politics in terms that have been bequeathed to them by preceding experience. As a result, a whole cultural ground exists upon which Iran's foreign policies figure as a surface effect. The nuclear issue is a case in point. Iran's refusal to compromise on mastering the full nuclear fuel cycle and the country's legitimate rights under the NPT can hardly be detached from cultural attitudes exemplified by the notion of 'mastering the machine' that was central to Al-e Ahmad's writings in the 1960s. A similar attitude towards technological innovation permeates Soroush's ideas when he ponders 'about the story of tradition and modernism or the relation of the so-called underdeveloped and developed countries', and when he invites us to

> [i]magine a long road where a train of cars is moving with a huge trailer driving slowly in front of them occupying the whole breadth of the road. Imagine that the engine of this trailer does not work properly and therefore, there is this suffocating smoke coming out of it bothering the people sitting in the cars trapped behind it. Although these people suffer from this thick smoke and have to linger behind, nevertheless they show

a lot of patience. But then finally they get tired of being patient and seek a solution. They sit down to talk and find out what they can do with that gory trailer. Some leisurely say, 'that's it. We have to give up and just follow the trailer and adjust our speed to it.' Others say 'we should go and fight with the driver, puncture the tire of his trailer and protest.' Some others believe that the trailer would soon be left without fuel and then we would be able to get rid of it. Still others try to find a way to get ahead of it and make a few attempts in this respect, but they soon find out that there is no way to pass that trailer as it occupies the whole width of the road. Finally some say quite despairingly that 'we should make a turn and go back. After all who says that we have to go through the same road and in the same direction, we can take the opposite direction,' but they also realize that it is now too late to turn back as they are already short of time. … We are sitting in the cars that by chance or the inescapable fate of history are located behind that smoke-producing trailer which is modernism or advanced technological development [and] we are seeking to find a way out of this trap.[102]

When analysts say that the nuclear issue has become a matter of national prestige for Iranians, they are right.[103] But they abstract from those cultural attitudes permeating Iranian society. 'Much technological innovation, in fact, is driven by a kind of utopianism: something new is introduced to the world that promises transformation,' argues the cultural critic Edward Rothstein pertinently.

Technology is disruptive, sometimes destructive, displacing older procedures, products, and ideas. And with each change comes the promise of further changes yet to come. Technology has also been connected with a form of gnosticism, an almost mystical attempt to purge illusion and reach true knowledge.[104]

This view of technology as a vehicle for change and, ultimately, prestige resonates with the utopian ideas of Iranian intellectuals from the 1960s until now. 'It's obvious that as long as we only use machines and don't make them,' warned Al-e Ahmad, 'we're Weststruck.'[105] Indeed, a critical analysis of Iran's nuclear strategy can be written only on the basis of what has been contemporaneous with it, that is in terms of the intellectual and theoretical *a prioris* established in the archives of Iran's contemporary history. It is in this sense that a cultural genealogy can give an account of the nuclear strategy, and thus opens up a complex, emotionally charged area in which the history of Iran's resistance to foreign dominance can be explained. It is through such an understanding that the national consensus in defence of Iran's nuclear energy programme can be linked to the 'Tobacco revolts' of 1891 against the concession of exclusive Tobacco rights in favour of Major G. Talbot (a British citizen), the nationalization of the Anglo-Iranian Oil Company in early 1951 initiated by Prime Minister Mohammad Mossadegh, and the Islamic revolution of 1979 in the name of the *mostazafan*. These central struggles against imperial interference constantly strike a chord with the 'Iranian psyche'. Today, the right of civilian nuclear self-determination has reached a comparable emotional status. Ultimately, it has engendered a political momentum uniting Iranians against what is perceived to be yet another chapter of imperial intrusion into the country's domestic affairs.

Foreign policy analysis, theory and 'Middle Eastern' Studies

We laid down at the outset that utopian-romantic ideals constituted the preference setting and goal orientation of the post-revolutionary Iranian state. What had emerged as a counter-hegemonic political culture during the 1960s and 1970s, it was argued, was codified as a revolutionary narrative and appeared as a transcendent, *de facto* reality, reacting on its agents. The introjection of the utopia of the just state, mantled in the romantic imagery of the millenarian Shia struggle for emancipation, constituted the pool of shared knowledge that informed the foreign policy culture of the Iranian state after the Islamic revolution in

1979. Once this aestheticized political reality was internalized cognitively and legitimated institutionally, the self-identification of the Iranian state as the vanguard of an international movement for emancipation guided the country towards challenging the international status quo that was perceived as intrinsically unjust and overbearingly hierarchical. Thus, for the sake of abstraction, we may assume that the changes in Iran's foreign policy may be attributed to a four-dimensional cultural genealogy: (1) The elite-driven invention of utopian-romantic Islamic theories in the 1960s and 1970s engendered a total redefinition of Iran's relationship with the world based on a new, Muslim-revolutionary identity for the Iranian state; (2) through the process of mass internalization of the revolutionary ideals and institutionalization in the post-revolutionary period, the utopias generated a powerful dynamism of their own (they attained systemic qualities); (3) socialized in this omnipresent, ideological system, Iranian foreign policy elites became used to accepting Iran's new role as legitimate and a reflection of the revolutionary ideals as formulated by Ayatollah Khomeini and others; (4) that process of institutionalisation and habitualisation constituted Iran's contemporary role identity *par excellence*—it introjected foreign policy elites with the idea that Iran's self-attributed moral high ground legitimated the country's special place in international affairs, which, by necessity, motivated (and motivates) them to challenge the prevalent status quo.

Let me conclude this part of the book with a necessary self-criticism that goes beyond the empirical focus on Iranian foreign policies. First, the way I framed my argument may suggest that the change from one dialectic to another occurs in a temporal sequence: elites externalize culture, culture is objectified, internalized etc. I may be open to the criticism that I am suggesting a causal transmission belt from one cultural dialectic to another. Such a conclusion would be erroneous. It is important to remember that this part of the book sketched a *continuous* dialectical process composed of four moments. Because they occur simultaneously, analysis of foreign policy culture needs to explore the full cycle of the four-dimensional dialectic. In other words, there is no real beginning or end to the dialectical process. Our search for analytical signposts and significance is essentially a modest (perhaps even 'primitive') one. It is limited to finding constitutive events that informed the grand strategic preferences of the country in question and establishing how they were formed, transformed and maintained to fit the central preferences of the state. Every political entity experienced such constitutive periods. How, for instance, can we divorce the idea of *la grande nation* from France's role in international affairs, the concept of *Handelsstaat* from Germany's international conduct, Wilsonian idealism from the international role of the United States, socialist anti-imperialism from the international outlook of Cuba, or pan-African empowerment from the conduct of the South African state? Few analysts would contend that these self-perceptions do not condition how successive governments in those countries perceive their mission in international affairs. Fewer still would doubt that formative periods such as the American Revolution, the French Revolution, the 'Third Reich', the ANC's anti-Apartheid struggle and the Cuban revolution influenced the way future generations of decision-makers in those countries interacted with other nations.

To give meaning to the outside world, the bearer of culture needs to revert to the pool of knowledge accumulated from previous experiences. Inventions of the past *have* an impact on the present. The practice of foreign policy depends on the existence (and introjection?) of intersubjective 'precedents and shared symbolic materials — in order to impose interpretations upon events, silence alternative interpretations, structure practices, and orchestrate the collective making of history.'[106] Appeals to the past explain why the US state typically is represented as an idealistic force committed to international justice, the German state as an anti-militaristic economic powerhouse, the French state as a European superpower, the South African state as a pan-African spokesman and the Cuban state as the vanguard for the emancipation of the Third World.[107] None of these abstract typologies would make sense without reference to culture and none would be effective if the states in question did not act out, reproduce and legitimate their self-depicted identities. I think it is a central purpose of critical analysis to identify those cultural reification processes and unravel them dialectically. That dialectical critique promises to make explicit the implicit contradictions of the stages of our four-dimensional genealogy.

Second, it may be alleged that my argument does not address sufficiently the degree of cultural pressures on foreign policy interests. How deterministic is culture in setting grand strategic preferences? The method explored here suggests that it is difficult to discern *a priori* if and when foreign policy culture has an impact on interests and preferences; this needs to be investigated in conjunction with empirical analysis. In other words, to explore the causal and constitutive effects of culture is a matter of the dialectical analysis, and is by no means predetermined by theoretical signposts. It is important to remember that cultural inventions, however monolithic and deterministic they may appear, are essentially human fabrications. Their objective status does not divorce them from human action. The relationship between the individual, the producer, and the cultural world, the product, is and remains a dialectical one. Both are in constant interaction with each other. These aspects receive their proper recognition once cultural systems are understood in terms of an ongoing dialectical process composed of the four moments of externalization, objectification, internalization, and introjection. I regret that the unsolved puzzles within these dialectic moments could not have been explored more fully; had we moved further down our path, we might have come to understand the inner dynamics and structure of our ideal-types.

Finally, as I have entered the well-maintained garden of 'Middle Eastern' and Iranian studies with the heavy boots of critical (cultural) theory, some empirically spirited readers may ask: Why bother with theory, why expose oneself to complex systems with all their inevitable consequences for language, elegance or parsimony?[108] My initial response to such valid criticism would be that theories are at the heart of what individuals and governments think and say about the determinants of world politics; they also become the method governments use to define their identity and their differences to others. The main issues in international relations are about war and peace, of course. But when it comes to who has the right to attack the other country, who has the right to dominate and exploit it, who is a legitimate resistance movement and who a terrorist, and who was 'our' enemy in the first place—these issues are debated, contested and sometimes decided within theory. Indeed, the seminal study of Eric Hobsbawm and Terence Ranger on the invention of tradition and Hobsbawm's ideas on the construction of nationalist ideologies provide enough incentive to think of nation-states themselves as theoretical constructs.[109] The power of theory, or the power to block alternative theories from emerging, is very important to the legitimation of culture and national and international policies. Indeed, our case might have demonstrated that the 'libidinous' energies of theory mobilized millions of people in Iran to rise up and oust the omnipresent Shah; a comparable force motivated the Russians, Chinese, Cubans and other movements with the principal aim of subverting established hierarchies of master and servant, top and bottom, have and have-nots. Is opposition to theory hence not too often 'really directed against the transformative activity associated with critical thinking'?[110] Does critical thought not emancipate and open up the room for intellectual exchange that partakes neither of orthodoxy nor of the partisan affirmation about the supremacy of one world-view?[111]

These questions refer to issues left embarrassingly incomplete in this part of the book. An important task for future research would be to synthesize the vast critical theory literature with the international politics of the 'Third World' in general and the politics of Iran in particular; to ask how one can study the political cultures of non-Western societies from a critical, or a non-deterministic and non-manipulative, perspective. Projects like these may engender rather more multicultural discourse among the growing international studies community, strengthening the case of those among us who advocate the benefits of inter-cultural dialogue. I hope that the following parts of the book can make a contribution to that beginning.

PART II
INVENTIONS OF THE IRAN-IRAQ WAR AND THE MYTH OF ENDEMIC 'PERSIAN-ARAB' ENMITY

'At the present moment agitation is intense in all Mohammedan countries … the report of agents and others confirm … the extreme vitality of the movement [Pan-Islamism]. … It is … essential that the country to whom Mohammedans look should not be Afghanistan. We should therefore create a State more convenient for ourselves, to whom the attention of Islam should be turned. We have an opportunity in Arabia.

Strategically:	Afghanistan is well placed for offensive action against India
Strategically:	Arabia is well placed, from our point of view, for defence
Tactically:	Afghanistan is difficult to attack.
Tactically:	Arabia is open to our attack from every quarter save the north.
Politically:	Afghanistan is difficult to control.
Politically:	Arabia can be controlled and influenced fully, if we only see that no other Power shapes her policy. This we have every right to insist upon.
Geographically:	Afghanistan is well placed to rally round her elements hostile to ourselves.

Geographically: Arabia is ideally placed to divide those elements, the more so if we are installed in Baghdad.'

Memorandum by Captain N. Bray, March 1917, 'A note on the Mohammedan question, its bearing on events in India and Arabia, the future of the Great Islamic revival now that Turkey ceases to be a power on which the hopes of the Moslem world were placed', from *Islam: Political Impact 1908–1972*, J. Priestland (ed.), British Documentary Sources, Slough, Archive Editions.

The legacies of the Iran-Iraq War (1980-1988)

The introduction to the book and the previous part elaborated on my critique of the way Iran is studied. I have argued that for many years now historians of West Asian affairs and analysts of Iranian politics have preferred to continue a positivistic reading of events affecting the Islamic Republic, as if they were trying to define law-like causalities, unchangeable continua or inevitable 'facts' amid the complex transformations and diversity intrinsic to post-revolutionary Iran.[1] The methods that enable these scholars to pursue this mode of analysis are partly engrained in the discipline of 'Middle Eastern' studies and partly borrowed from other social sciences with a strong positivistic and empiricist tradition, especially economics, political science and, albeit to a lesser extent and perhaps unconsciously, 'realist' international relations theories.[2] By virtue of this mainstream discourse, the great proliferation of writings about Iran has favoured total comparisons within artificial entities: Islamist vs. secular, Persian vs. Muslim, nation vs. *umma*, pragmatist vs. idealist, republicanism vs. Islamism etc. Thus the multiplicity of the country's realities is reduced to a system of variables all of whose values are defined, if not by a mathematical formula, at least by a facile and hermetically sealed description.

This part of the book develops my critique of positivist readings of Iranian affairs further. I focus on the causes and consequences of the Iran-Iraq war—primarily because I want to contrast the available mainstream analyses of the conflict with my own 'dissident' perspective, and secondarily because I share the view that Iran's relations with post-Saddam Iraq are of primary importance for both the future stability of the Persian Gulf area and the future of Iran's revolutionary project itself. Indeed, even a cursory look at current events in the region reveals that inventing the Iraqi quasi-state and reconstituting Iran's 'self' during this tumultuous period of the country's history has rekindled some of the insidious legacies of ultra-nationalistic thinking. Extreme nationalism was central to the legitimation of the Iran-Iraq war, and its excesses have impeded rather more symbiotic relations between the peoples of the region for a long time now. Alas, in accordance with this resurgent current, some commentators in West Asia have redefined their roles and ideological allegiances. They have turned their attention to 'Orientalist archaeology', that is to active excavation in the vast graveyards of failed ideologies in West Asia. In Iran, the Islamic-communitarian legacy left behind by Ayatollah Khomeini has thus far subdued ultra-nationalist experiments, but it is not at all clear that the Iranian state will not be forced to re-invoke radical nationalist norms in a period of crisis (as it did during the Iran-Iraq war). True, Iranian nationalism was at the nadir of its unpopularity during the days of revolutionary exaltation because it was immediately linked to the excesses of the Pahlavi dynasty. But the nationalist mummy has returned in a new disguise. For some acolytes of Iran's 'Persian ideal' it functions as a vehicle against the message and symbolism of Islamic communitarianism which is enshrined in Iran's constitution. For others, including President Ahmadinejad, it is an expedient short-cut to gain popularity with the resurgent bourgeois middle-class of Iranian society. The latent powers intrinsic to deeply internalized ideological constructs, it appears, do not disappear with the demise of states. The prevalent chauvinism against Arabs that continues to guide the thinking of some Iranian commentators (especially in the Diaspora) indicates that 'Persianism' nurtured by the Pahlavis has endured the internationalist momentum triggered by the Islamic revolution in 1979.

The reinvention of the Iraqi nation-state, in addition, might require reverting to the symbols and imagery of Arab ultra-nationalism and its anti-Iranian precepts at some stage of the lumbering state-building process. Indeed, there has been active encouragement to that end. Consider King Abdullah's view that he has a 'real problem with certain Iranian factions' political influence inside Iraq' and his statement that 'Iraq is the battleground, the West against Iran'.[3] Consider also Prince Saud al-Faisal's declaration that 'Iraq was effectively handed over to Iran', which provoked the Iraqi Interior minister Bayan Jabr to call him a 'Bedouin on a camel', depicting the al-Saud family as 'tyrants who think they are king and God'.[4] Similar views on Iran were expressed by Ehud Olmert, members of the Bush administration, Hosni Mubarak, Ayman al-Zawahiri, Osama bin Laden and others with political constituencies in the region and beyond.[5] Indeed, hasn't embedded suspicion about Iranian designs in West Asia motivated Saudi Arabia, Egypt and Jordan to accommodate efforts by the US and Israel to prolong cease-fire negotiations after the Israeli invasion of Lebanon during the summer of 2006? The answer is yes, I think.[6]

Long forgotten in the 'West', the ideological legacies of the Iran-Iraq war thus continue to have an impact on the international politics of West Asia.[7] In Iran itself, the war continues to be a central theme of the burgeoning film industry; central to the scripts of the *sinamay-e jang* (the war cinema) with its eulogistic treatment of the 'lost generation' who fought what continues to be referred to as *defa-ye moghadas* (the holy defence) or *jangeh tahmili* (the imposed war) in the official jargon of the Islamic Republic and by some Iranian analysts.[8] The war is also constantly re-invoked by the political elites, and increasingly by the buoyant right wing surrounding President Ahmadinejad who has pushed to monopolize the symbolism intrinsic to it. It is 're-evaluated' in the accounts of foundations such as the *Bonyad-e mostazafan va janbazan* (Foundation of the Oppressed and Self-Sacrificers), *Bonyad-e shahid* (Martyr's Foundation) and the *Bonyad-e omur-e mohajerun-e tahmili* (Foundation for the Affairs of the Imposed War Refugees); and, not least, it is 'relived' on a daily basis by those veterans who continue to die from the effects of the chemical weapons attacks by Saddam Hussein's forces.[9] In a narrative like this it is inevitable, I therefore think, to investigate the 'historical verdict' on the war.

A quick perusal of the mainstream literature on the conflict reveals three recurrent themes: first, that Saddam Hussein seized the favourable international moment that was conducive to a military attack against the newly established Islamic state in Iran (the realist, power politics argument);[10] second, that the Iran-Iraq war was inevitable because of the 'historic' enmity between the two peoples (the 'Orientalist' argument); and third, that the Ba'thist state felt threatened by the spill-over of the Islamic revolution and decided to pre-empt further Shii uprisings in Najaf, Karbala, Samarra, Kazimiyah, and Baghdad as a means to contain a Shii resurgence in the greater West Asian area (the balance of power argument).[11]

The challenges to those established arguments, which I would like to express in the following paragraphs, are aimed not so much at dismissing what has been discovered by students of West Asian affairs *in toto* but rather at dissecting some of the regular features that have been accepted too readily. The object, to be more precise, is to present the 'regime of thought' that precipitated and sustained the Iraqi invasion of Iran, by 'contextualizing' the empirical facts about the war with a narrative that appreciates the impact of norms, images, institutions and other invented cultural artefacts on international crisis situations.[12] To that end, I move in two directions. In the first section I suggest that the Ba'thist leadership in Iraq made its decision to launch a full-scale invasion of Iran within the inter-subjective context of Iraqi-Arab nationalism, its anti-Iranian precepts and the regime's internalized self-perception as the indispensable pan-Arab force in the region. What has been largely undervalued in the literature about the war, I suggest, is that the invasion was precipitated by a fundamental dialectic: on the one hand, the cultural manufacturing of the Ba'thist garrison state and its anti-Iranian precepts; on the other hand, the reification of this identity by regional states and the wider international community. I am conscious that some readers may argue that an *a posteriori* historical account of the events surrounding the Iran-Iraq war (and other major international events for that matter) always carries the risk of someone committing that most deplorable of intellectual sins, politically interested historical revisionism. However, those readers will find that I have rendered useful empirical material that was not available at the time when the 'official' history of the Iran-Iraq war was written. Moreover, I have embedded this material in a set of questions that allude to complementing factors about the way the war was produced, but not in order to reveal competing, all-encompassing causalities, or as a means to search for a new history of the conflict, or to proclaim a return to a more comprehensive 'science' of the Iran-Iraq war in particular and organized violence between political units in general. Rather, my ambition is much more modest: I am interested primarily in showing that collective, socially manufactured and continuously reified cultural inventions came into play when Saddam Hussein decided to invade Iran. It is this inter-subjective *Kriegskontext* that I will attempt to bring into focus. I will refrain from a positivistic reading of the Iran-Iraq war; instead I will start from a set of questions about the way perceptions, enemy images, and ideologies are created.

Imagining the Persian menace

A long-standing hypothesis put forward by cognitive and social psychologists claims that cultural constructs, such as norms, institutions, values or ideologies, are accessible to the extent that they have been activated and reified by previous knowledge.[13] 'Abundant evidence for this,' it is argued, 'comes from experiments in which researchers manipulate whether participants are exposed to a word or image related to a construct (a *prime*) and then measure the extent to which the participants' subsequent interpretations of a stimulus are influenced by the primed construct.'[14] I have attempted to differentiate the emergence and determining imprint of culture in the previous part, suggesting a four-dimensional dialectic: (1) it is through externalization that culture is a human product; (2) it is through objectification that culture becomes a reality *sui generis*; (3) it is through internalization that agents are products of culture; and (4) it is through introjection that culture constitutes the identities, interests and preferences of agents. Culture thus understood has a genealogy: it is both a producer of mindsets and world-views and a product of the same phenomena. It should become clear to the critically minded reader that the state has a pivotal interest in that socially constructed sphere, because it is the main locus where we tap into knowledge, where we find our place in society, where we draw the boundaries between ourselves and the enemy without and where, ultimately, militaristic ideologies habituate us to the expectation of war. '[T]he indispensable condition of war,' Gordon Allport argues,

> is that people must *expect* war and must prepare for war before, under war-minded leadership, they make war. It is in this sense that 'wars begin in the minds of men' ... personal aggressiveness does not itself render war inevitable. It is a contributing cause when people *expect* to vent their emotions in warfare. Similarly the alleged economic causes of war are effective causes only when people think war is a solution to problems of

poverty and economic rivalry. Otherwise they are not. What men expect determines their behaviour.[15]

Allport refers to a 'psychology' of war that affects our thinking about the enemy. Sociologists would add that written and spoken texts are the most important kind of cultural artefacts in the transmission of those salient images of the enemy. Exposure to texts activates implicit theories in the mind of the agent, by triggering relevant knowledge and affecting changes in the mindset in the direction of the internalized ideological content of a text. Hence the importance of studying the writings of intellectuals who as a group have the power to constitute 'truth conditions', as a legitimating system, as authoritative discourse, who can disqualify competing views from emerging and counter-narratives from questioning the status quo. Contemporary social psychologists agree:

> Both the informal texts of 'low culture' (e.g., folktales, television, commercials) and the more formal texts of 'high culture' (e.g., religious tracts, canonical works of literature) are capable of conveying and reinforcing conceptions of agency.[16]

I have argued elsewhere that the latter aspect of culture, that is the perpetuation of myths through cultural introjection, was rather more central to the production of the Iranian enemy image in Ba'thist Iraq.[17] Mythic narratives are particularly deterministic and functional in perpetuating and reproducing the boundaries between 'the' identity of the state and 'the' identity of the enemy. 'Myth is invention,' writes Gorki:

> To invent means to extract from the sum of a given reality its cardinal idea and embody it in imagery—that is how we get realism. But if to the idea extracted from the given reality we add—completing the idea by the logic of hypothesis—the desired, the possible, and thus supplement the image, we obtain that romanticism which is at the basis of myth, and is highly beneficial in that it tends to provoke a revolutionary attitude to reality, an attitude that changes the world in a practical way.[18]

'Inventing reality', in the Iraqi case, implied advancing the myth that there has been a perennial conflict between 'the' Persians and 'the' Arabs. The Ba'thist leadership soon realized that the fact that Arabs and Iranians have shared long periods of common history on both sides of the Shatt-al Arab required a systematic effort to invent strict boundaries between the 'Iranian other' and the 'Iraqi-Arab self'. Central to this strategy was (a) emphasizing the 'racial' composition of Iran, which was pursued by referring to the country as Persia; (b) historicizing the challenge of the Persians, which was pursued by projecting the conflict back to the reign of the Persian king Cyrus, who relieved the plight of the Jews deported to Babylonia and persecuted by king Nebuchadnezzar in the sixth century BC; (c) stressing the intrinsic hostility of Iranians, which was the central argument of state-sponsored poems, books, pamphlets etc.;[19] and (d) emphasizing the 'cultural' and 'racial' inferiority of the 'Persian race' by similar means.[20] At times, Ofra Bengio explains,

> the description of the Iranians as Mongols, Tatars, or barbarians was spelled out in greater detail. The "Persian Character" was described as aggressive, domineering, prone to war, and bloodthirsty. Persians, and in particular their rulers, were fanatics and likely to engage in the "collective killing" of thousands of people. ... Iraq must at all times keep one eye open to the east, "where the treacherous, the heretical, and the bloodthirsty are found." The Iranians would "cut off the breasts of Iraqi women unless their sons fought" to protect them.[21]

'Each period has its own Mongols', a poem by Rashid Majid reads much in the same vein,

They come, laden with hatred
Wearing different masks
and behind every mask
is the face of the new Hulagu
and other Mongol faces ...
The yellow pest coming

from the east
has passed but [its disappearance]
has not brought peace [22]

It is possible to deduce four central themes from the vast amount of anti-Iranian material available. First, Iranians are represented as *ajam*, an inferior people within the dominance of Islam, which was deemed to be first and foremost an Arab domain; second, they are described as being possessed by a destructive mentality (*aqliyya takhribiyya)*, which was deemed a racial attribute that had not changed since the days when Islam came into the Sassanian empire in the seventh century;[23] third, Ayatollah Khomeini himself is portrayed as an infidel (*kafir*) and heretic (*taghut*), unfit to preach Islam which was portrayed as an exclusive domain of the Arab peoples; and fourth, the Iran-Iraq war is officially referred to as Saddam's Qadisiyya or *Qadisiyyat Saddam*, projecting two central institutions of Ba'thist Arab nationalism: the romantic mystification of the leadership ideal on the one hand, and suspicion and antagonism towards Iranians on the other.[24]

Yet the effort to historicize the myth of seemingly endemic Persian-Arab enmity was not sudden or merely in response to the revolution in Iran, for it was not only power politics that propelled Saddam Hussein to demonize Persia. Arab nationalist activists have singled out Iranians as a main source of anti-Arab conspiracies at least since the writings of Michel Aflaq and Sati Khaldun al-Husri. Both were instrumental in the institutionalizing of the Arab nationalist ideal in Iraq: the former—who founded the Ba'th party in the 1940s—because of his decision to side with the Iraqi Ba'th of Saddam Hussein against the Syrian Ba'th of Hafiz al-Assad in the early 1970s, the latter because of his educational posts between 1921 and 1941.[25] Ultimately, the reification of this norm under Saddam Hussein's rule, central as it was to the nation-building process pursued by the state, was not entirely unrelated to the identity politics of the Pahlavi monarchs, the support given to Iraqi-Kurdish movements by the Shah in close collaboration with the US and Israel in the late 1960s until the Treaty of Algiers in 1975, and Ayatollah Khomeini's appeal to Iraqi-Shia movements. Consider in that context this excerpt from Saddam Hussein's speech marking the tenth anniversary of the end of the Iran-Iraq war in August 1998, that is during a period when Iraqi sovereignty was seriously constrained because of the international sanctions imposed since the end of the second Persian Gulf war in 1991:

The Arabs, including Iraq, with all hope, urge officials in Iran and the Iranian people not to be turned into a tool in the hands of the covetous foreigner to inflict harm on the Arabs, particularly Iraq. Muhammad Reza Pahlavi, the Shah of Iran, as well as his father and others, did so. Iraq and the Arabs were seriously harmed after 1979 ... The growing calls to use force, harm and aggression until the time war broke out on 4 September 1980, the continuation of the war with full intransigence, and the calls to do everything that contradicts and opposes peace cannot be explained except by saying that Iran had lost its senses ... Has Iran recovered, partially or fully from all that? ... Iraq, by virtue of geography, is the most able to monitor and check things. Many other historical, social and spiritual factors make Iraq the most able to understand Iran and realities there as they truly are, and not as they are presented on certain occasions. Arab brothers, Muslim brothers, for eight years we believed and worked on the basis that our objectives could be achieved through peace and, therefore, we called for it. Officials in Iran, on the other hand, believed, until the final days or final months before victory on the day of days, that their objectives could be achieved through war and aggression. The evidence on our part is all the traditions of the glorious Qadisiyah, including everything that was said and done day and night, and on the part of Iran everything in their tradition and everything they said and did day and night, including the last official speech by the most senior official accepting the ceasefire [i.e. Ayatollah Khomeini], which brought an end to the bloodletting. That official said: "I wish I had died before I ordered the cease-fire." He also said in the same speech that his acceptance of the UN Security Council resolution was more painful than drinking venom.[26]

From the perspective of Saddam Hussein, I am in no doubt, Iran *was* a threat to Ba'thist rule both before and after the revolution. Hence the perpetuation of the anti-Iranian norm, its internalization by the Ba'thist elites, and its impact on the perception and decision-making process before, during and after the war with Iran. The Persian enemy image thus functioned as legitimation for Iraq's invasion, suppression of the political ambitions of the Shia majority of the country and other measures to secure and prolong the rule of the Arab/Sunni/Tikriti minority commanding the Ba'thist leadership. But what has been ignored in the literature about the war is that the anti-Iranian norm also engendered its own 'reality', that norms belong to the domain of social objectification—that is, to what passes for 'reality' in a given social situation at a particular point of time. Norms thus have a status of objectivity quite independent from the minds of their agents. Norms do not only guide people towards what *ought to be*. They also tell them what *is*. In Ba'thist Iraq a whole cultural apparatus was put into operation in order to tell Iraqis that Iran *is* the eternal enemy of Arabs, that the Islamic revolution *is* directed against Iraq, that Persians *are* racists, that they *are* different etc. The anti-Iranian norm wilfully introjected its agents from above; from a political-cultural system that was invented more or less according to plan. In other words, the anti-Iranian norm was as much an ideological (utilitarian) tool to delineate the Iraqi-Arab self from the Iranian-Shiite other as it was firmly rooted in the belief system of the Ba'thist leadership: both power politics and Ba'thist political culture constituted Iran as *the* enemy. It is true, as Halliday points out, that the source of the Iran-Iraq war

> lies not in history, or disputed frontiers, or irreconcilable cultural differences. It lies in the way in which *modern* political regimes (Iran since 1921, Iraq since 1932) have sought through indoctrination and political rhetoric to demonise the other and have sought to promote their own interests by intervening in the affairs of the other. The Shah and Saddam Hus-

sein fought each other between 1969 and 1975 making use of Cold War rivalries. Saddam fought Khomeini from 1980 to 1988 because the latter's revolution threatened the stability of the Iraqi regime. The war gave Iraq a chance to supplant Iran as the dominant power in the Gulf.[27]

But our analysis shouldn't stop here. By attacking Iran, the Ba'thist regime not only wanted to make itself the pre-eminent force in West Asia, but also acted on the premise of a deeply embedded resentment against Iranian cultural and political outreach in the region and beyond. In my opinion this tactic was not only an act of political utilitarianism (or a matter of power politics) in the sense that it was suddenly invoked to rally the support of Arab states in reaction to the exogenous effects of the Islamic revolution; in addition, its system effects (i.e. the effects of the revolution in Iran) were interpreted and processed against the background of a pre-existing, deeply embedded 'paranoia' about Iranian expansionism. Halliday alludes to the centrality of cultural artefacts when he argues that Iraq's invasion of Kuwait cannot be adequately analyzed without understanding the 'nature of Ba'thism, with its dramatic idea of the Arab nation, its cult of war as the purgative fire, its glorification of *sharaf* or honour, its obsession with the strong man ... who will deliver the Arab nation'.[28] One has to agree. These cultural attitudes were of primary importance for the Ba'thist polity, especially during Saddam Hussein's leadership. Consequently, they must be considered central to understanding his decision to launch the invasions of his neighbours. These wars, in short, could only 'happen' because Ba'thist political culture *made* them happen.

Recently declassified US State Department documents and the 'Duelfer Report' presented by the US Chief Arms Inspector in Iraq, Charles Duelfer, provide further evidence for the Ba'thist obsession with Iran. Consider a meeting in 1988 between representatives of the US construction company Bechtel and Saddam Hussein's son-in-law Hussein Kamil (at that time minister of

Industry). During the meeting Kamil stated that the US Senate was controlled by Zionists who were responsible for undermining US-Iraqi relations 'since Iraq had defeated their Iranian ally and was now defeating their Kurdish surrogates in northern Iraq.'[29] Thus anti-Iranian (and anti-Israeli) rhetoric was not employed merely to rally support among Arab nationalists; Kamil was addressing representatives of an American conglomerate with close relations to the Israeli state, who were perhaps indifferent to Iran. In such a discursive context it did not make sense to accuse Iran and Israel of conspiring, except from a genuine belief that this was really the case.

The Duelfer report confirms the centrality of the 'Persian menace' to Ba'thist threat perceptions: 'From Saddam's viewpoint,' the author argues, 'the Persian menace loomed large and was a challenge to his place in history.' Moreover, the report suggests that Iran (not the United States) was the 'pre-eminent motivator' of Saddam's WMD (weapons of mass destruction) programme. 'All senior level Iraqi officials,' the interrogations revealed, 'considered Iran to be Iraq's principal enemy in the region.'[30] Indeed, this obsession with Iran can also be discerned from Saddam Hussein's comments during the war-crimes trial against him. He would take responsibility 'with honour' for any attacks on Iran using conventional or chemical weapons during the 1980-88 war, he proclaimed on 18 December 2006, a week before his lawyer's appeal against the death sentence was rejected by the Iraqi High Court. Hussein even blamed 'Iranian agents' (and the US) for the death sentence itself.[31]

Research into the social construction of reality by cultural theorists and social psychologists suggests that human beings construct their own realities.[32] This idea is not, of course, a new one; it used to be, for instance, the central philosophical tenet of the Mu'tazillah school of Islam (literally 'those who withdraw themselves')—the eighth-century Muslim 'social constructivists' who advocated contextual analysis of the Qur'an. It was also central to the writings of Nasir al-Din Tusi who provides a kind of early-day 'discourse analysis' in his *Sayr wa Suluk* (Contemplation and Action) published in the thirteenth century AD. Here, Tusi contemplates about the meaning of '"command (*amr*) or the "word" (*kalimah*), in accordance with the verse of the Qur'an: "Verily His command, when He desires a thing, is to say to it 'Be' and it is" (36:82)'. This verse, according to him, 'makes it clear that the issuing forth of existents from God depends on the expression "Be" (*kun*) and the word "verily" (*innama*) in Arabic serves the purpose of pinpointing [the scope of the expression], thereby making clear that the command is an expression for that word.'[33] Contemporary research supports the idea that ordering the environment and by extension inventing 'realities' is a natural function of human behaviour.[34] Steering towards political theory, we may add that invented realities that engender motivational drives towards war are especially pronounced within totalitarian political systems, where the institutionalizing of pluralistic discourse atrophies under the pressure of ideological introjection. 'There is both an objective and a subjective aspect to legitimation,' the sociologist Peter Berger explains:

> The legitimations exist as objectively valid and available definitions of reality. They are part of the 'objectivated' knowledge of society. If they are to be effective in supporting the social order, however, they will have to be internalised and serve to define subjective reality as well. In other words, effective legitimation implies the establishment of symmetry between objective and subjective definitions of reality. The reality of the word as socially defined must be maintained externally, in the conversation of men with each other, as well as internally, in the way by which the individual apprehends the world within his own consciousness. The essential purpose of all forms of legitimation may thus be described as reality-maintenance, both on the objective and the subjective levels.

In the case of Ba'thist Iraq, anti-Iranianism had been legitimated to the extent that it had acquired the quality of an immanent, autonomous reality, reacting back on its creator (this illustrates the introjective qualities of culture). Acting within this self-consciously chosen ideational habitat, Saddam Hussein was alienated from objective reality, failing to see that the reality guiding him had been produced by himself: the subject was assimilated into the object and followed the signals of external, objectified norms, institutions and structures. That Saddam Hussein tailored his actions according to this 'false consciousness' three times (against Iran, Kuwait and the United States) only reiterates the salience of the cultural belief system that framed the existence of the Ba'thist polity, and explains Saddam's gross misperceptions during the three Persian Gulf wars.

Manufacturing the Iraqi garrison state

Research by 'social constructivists' in the discipline of international relations suggests that perceptions, representations of reality and identities are not manufactured in isolation. States do not operate in encapsulated habitats, they are not 'cloistered', it is not possible to act decisively on a specific identity without perceiving a minimal degree of external recognition.[35] This means that 'the ideas held by individual states are given content or meaning by the ideas which they share with other states—that state *cognition* depends on states systemic *culture*.'[36] Neurophysiological research suggests a comparable pattern, hypothesizing that *visions* caught by the eyes are transformed into *perceptions* by the coordinated firing by millions of neurons all over the brain. This physiological process enables us to 'link' the invented category 'grandmother' to the mother of our mother and fill that category with meaning accumulated through previous interaction with that person.[37] In other words, we make sense of our environment through processes of physiological and social *interaction*. Applied to the inter-subjective context of Iraqi Ba'thism, this idea suggests that the Ba'thist leadership invented and legitimated its war role *in relation to* international society. The Iraqi state perceived itself as the main agent of pan-Arabism at least from the Ba'thist coup in 1968 onwards. That this subjective self-understanding was not confirmed during a period when the Iranian-Saudi dual pillar order was systematically legitimated (by the United States and the Gulf monarchies) prevented Iraq from playing a rather more prominent regional role in the 1970s. Revolution in Iran altered that constellation. In the reshuffling of regional relations, the way the Iraqi state viewed itself was approximated by the way it was addressed (Iraq's role was objectified). Indeed, it can be argued that Iraq became the agent for containment of the revolution for two reasons: it felt legitimated in its self-perception as the leader of the Arab world, and it was confirmed as the suitable vehicle to preserve the regional status quo.[38]

What may be termed the 'social manufacturing' of the Iraqi war role has not been made explicit in the literature about the causes and consequences of the Iran-Iraq war. Can Iraqi state identity, external confirmation and the decision to go to war not also be related causally? It appears to me that Saddam Hussein was convinced that military confrontation with Iran would be tolerated because the international community did not suggest otherwise; external signals were interpreted as a green light—if not *carte blanche*—by the government elites. Does not the fact that Saddam Hussein managed to organize a high degree of political, economic and media support both in the Arab worlds (apart from Lebanon, Libya and Syria) and in the Western hemisphere suggest that the Iraqi regime's expectation was at least partially accurate? Does this not suggest that the signals before the war must have been quite strong indeed? I think that the Iraqi war role was socially engineered in that it existed only *in relation to* the international system. To be more precise, the Ba'thist state could not have acted on its war role without its real and perceived objectification by international society. Having investigated the first process of this dialectic, that is the emergence of the Iraqi-Ba'thist self-perception, I now turn my attention to its confirmation by international actors, regional and global.[39]

The regional input: Saddam's financiers

The Gulf monarchies had already reacted positively to the tactical moderation of Iraqi behaviour in the period after the signing of the Algiers agreement in 1975 and the reshuffling of inter-Arab politics following the Camp David Accords in 1978. Diplomacy followed suit. In February 1979, Saudi Arabia and Iraq signed a security agreement that committed Iraq to defend the former in the case of war. The agreement was accompanied by high level diplomatic exchanges between the two countries and between Iraq and Ras al-Khaimah, Oman, and Kuwait.[40] From the perspective of Saddam Hussein, the recognition gained from the diplomatic exchanges was reason enough to believe that an invasion of Iran would be supported. Some commentators even speculate that the decision to take military action was approved beforehand.[41]

The least that can be argued is that regional states signalled that an invasion of Iran would be accommodated. Apart from Dubai and Sharjah, which continued to have cordial relations with the Islamic Republic, the other sheikhdoms were either directly or indirectly involved in the Iraqi war effort, especially after the failure of the Iraqi *Blitzkrieg* and the Iranian counteroffensive into Iraqi territory in 1982. Several measures were taken: Saudi Arabia and Kuwait agreed to forward the profits of oil production in the Khafji oil field, located in the neutral zone between Saudi Arabia and Kuwait, to the Iraqi government;[42] the two countries provided Iraq with loans ranging from an estimated US$ 35 billion to US$ 50 billion, most of them not necessarily meant to be repaid;[43] both countries opened up their ports for the shipment of products bound to the Iraqi market and the selling of oil on behalf of the Iraqi government; and the Saudi state arguably even offered to finance the rebuilding of the Iraqi nuclear reactor in Osirak, destroyed in a pre-emptive strike by Israeli warplanes in June 1981.[44]

Details of the support for the Iraqi war effort may be disputed, but the regional disposition to take sides was never at issue. The sketch of regional collusion with Iraq provided here should not mislead, however, for the support was not unequivocal. Concurrent with the quasi-alliance of Egypt, Jordan, Kuwait, and Saudi Arabia with Iraq, and Syria and Libya with Iran, the regional states were engaged continuously in containing the economic calamities and military spill-over of the war. Apart from sustained efforts to appease Iran, they also refrained from formalizing their relationship with Saddam Hussein. Indeed, the six states on the Arabian Peninsula littoral of the Persian Gulf established the Gulf Co-operation Council (GCC) in early 1981, soon after the war had started, and left out both Iran and Iraq.

Yet, viewed from the perspective of the Iraqi regime, the support for the country's war effort was seen as a boost to its claim to regional power and, more specifically, its self-bestowed role as the leader of the Arab world. The external approval and support from regional states were processed against the background of the Arab nationalist and anti-Iranian precepts of Iraqi Ba'thist state identity. From that viewpoint, supporting the war effort was considered only 'natural'— indeed the only logical response of Arab states against the threat to the eastern flank of the Arab nation. 'All Gulf countries are aware of Iran's ambitions in targeting them,' Saddam Hussein argued in a typical manner. 'They know that had it not been for Iraq, they would have been taken as prisoners to the lands of the Persians.'[45] A declassified memo of March 1985 indicates a similar attitude:

During a March 26 meeting with [NAMES RETRACTED] ... confirmed that the real importance of last week's visit of King Hussein and President Mubarak to Baghdad was that it occurred at all. He claimed that resumption of relations between Egypt and Iraq had not been discussed, but that Saddam Hussein had been moved by the gesture of support. He further indicated that Iraq, although initially unhappy about the silence of the Gulf states during the battle in the Marshes, was now very pleased with the "unprecedented" statement of support the GCC had given Iraq. The Iraqis, he said, felt that the Iranians could not help but note that their efforts to neutralise Gulf support for Iraq had failed abjectly. Whenever the Iranians launch a major offensive, he observed, the Gulf states quickly lose their complacency about the war and recall that the only thing that stands between them and disaster is Iraq.[46]

The international input: War crimes and Saddam's Western 'engineers'

Indeed, since the overthrow of the Iraqi monarchy in 1958, no Iraqi leader had enjoyed more international support than Saddam Hussein did during the war with Iran. There was even a strange fascination with the persona of Saddam Hussein himself within some diplomatic circles in Britain and the United States, especially in the late 1960s and early 1970s. In a telegram to the British Foreign and Commonwealth Office, for instance, the then British ambassador in Baghdad described Hussein as a 'serious character' with an 'engaging smile' which 'seemed part and parcel of his absorption with the subject in hand and not, as with so many of the others, a matter of superficial affability. I should judge him,' the ambassador went on, 'to be a formidable, single-minded and hard-headed member of the Ba'thist hierarchy, but one with whom, if only one could see more of him, it would be possible to do business.'[47] The US Assistant Secretary of State for

Near Eastern and South Asian Affairs, Alfred L. Atherton, Jr. appeared to have a comparable fascination with the character of Saddam Hussein in 1975. In a conversation with Henry Kissinger as part of a routine review of world events, Atherton described Hussein as a 'rather remarkable person' who is 'running the show' and is 'a very ruthless and pragmatic, intelligent power'.[48]

Thus Saddam Hussein already had been singled out as somebody who 'we can do business with' before he launched the invasion of Iran. During the war his international credentials were enhanced further by the then ruler of Jordan, King Hussein, who repeatedly acted as an intermediary between the Ba'thist regime and the United States, especially during periods of diplomatic crisis. A declassified cable from the US Embassy in Amman to the US State Department dated 19 March 1985, that is at a time when Iraqi chemical weapons attacks against Iranian soldiers and civilians already were well known, shows King Hussein's systematic efforts to enhance the international reputation of Iraq while fostering pan-Arab cooperation with Egypt. Symptomatically, King Hussein indicates to the then US ambassador in Amman that the Iraqis are 'very pleased' with American diplomatic support 'and with their overall cooperation with the U.S.'[49] In another cable dated 28 March 1985 and summarising a meeting between King Hussein, Hosni Mubarak and Saddam Hussein, it is stated that 'so long as Saddam was ruling the country, Iraq would continue on its present pragmatic course',' and this was expected to continue 'even after the war ended.'[50]

The reassuring international context before and after the invasion of Iran contributed to Saddam Hussein's ability to claim the right to go to war (*jus ad bellum*) and to avoid the right conduct of the war itself (*jus in bello*), even though international society condemns military aggression and the canons of international law provide some degree of protection against war crimes (at least formally).[51] In the case of Iran, the first international reaction to the conflict was emblematic for the pattern of behaviour that followed: after six days of hostilities, on 28 September 1980, the UN Security Council unanimously adopted Resolution 479, calling for an immediate cessation of hostilities without, however, naming Iraq as the invading force or calling for the country's withdrawal from Iranian territory (the call to return to internationally recognized boundaries came only after Iranian advances into Iraqi territory as a result of the counter-offensive in mid-1982).[52] In essence, Resolution 479 and the final Resolution 598 adopted after nearly eight years of fighting were similar with regard to the question of who started the war. Both failed to name Iraq as the invading party.

There was also calculated accommodation with regard to Iraqi chemical and biological warfare against Iran. Complaints from the Iranian side were made as early as November 1980. Yet it took the international community, including the most prominent non-governmental organizations (NGOs), at least three and one-half years to investigate the allegations systematically. The Stockholm International Peace and Research Institute (SIPRI) testified to that in May 1984:

> Three and a quarter years [after the first Iranian complaints in November 1980], by which time the outside world was listening more seriously to such charges, the Iranian Foreign Minister told the Conference on Disarmament in Geneva that there had been at least 49 instances of Iraqi chemical-warfare attack in 40 border regions, and that the documented dead totalled 109 people, with hundreds more wounded.[53]

The SIPRI report also indicated that after visiting several hospitals in Tehran, the International Committee of the Red Cross (ICRC) confirmed that 'substances prohibited by international law' were employed during hostilities (7 March 1984). This in turn was confirmed by the United Nations in the same month, with a report by the Secretary General, condemning the use of chemical weapons. Again, however, Iraq was not named as the perpetrating party.[54] During the period of the 'tanker war' and the 'war of the cities' the same pattern towards both Iraqi modes of warfare and the identification of the invading force could be observed.[55] Even the final UN Security Council Resolution 598, which ended the hostilities after being accepted by both Iran and Iraq, only deplored 'the use of chemical weapons' and merely determined 'that there exists a breach of the peace as regards the conflict between Iran and Iraq', and hence refrained from naming Iraq as the guilty party. Another SIPRI report dated 7 March 2001 even showed that there were concerted efforts to blame the gassing of Kurdish civilians and Iranian soldiers operating in Halabja on Iran. The Special Security Office of the US Defence Intelligence Agency issued a statement to that end on 23 March 1988:

> Most of the causalities in Halabja were reportedly caused by cyangen chloride. This agent has never been used by Iraq, but Iran has shown interest in it. Mustard gas casualties in the town were probably caused by Iraqi weapons because Iran has never been noted using that agent.[56]

The regional and global complacency towards Iraq's methods of warfare, including the employment of chemical and biological weapons, confirmed the impression of the Iraqi regime that it had been granted a 'free ride' role; this led to the paradox that by the use of Iraq to contain the Islamic revolution, the co-operative norms and institutions of international society itself were rendered useless, manipulated to function according to the overarching *Leitmotif* of preventing Iranian advances. In turn, this compromised the authority of the international community to act as a restraining force during the war, exemplified by this intercepted communication by Saddam Hussein's cousin Ali Hassan al-Majid, called 'Chemical Ali' after the *al-Anfal* (spoils of war) campaign against Iraqi Kurdish and Iranian forces operating in the Halabja area between February and March 1988:

> Jalal Talabani asked me to open a special channel of communication with him.[57] That evening I went to Suleimaniyeh and hit them with the special ammunition. That was my answer. We continued the deportations [of the Kurds]. I told the *mustashars*[58] that they might say that they like their villages and that they won't leave. I said I cannot let your village stay because I will attack it with chemical weapons. Then you and your family will die. You must leave right now. Because I cannot tell you the same day that I am going to attack with chemical weapons. I will kill them all with chemical weapons. Who is going to say anything? The international community? F… them! The international community and those who listen to them.[59]

It has been documented that from the outset of the war the US government provided Iraq with intelligence information about Iranian force deployments and movements collected by the US Airborne Warning and Control Aircraft (AWACS) that had been stationed in Saudi Arabia but were operated by the Pentagon.[60] There is compelling evidence suggesting that, after the end of the 'hostage crisis' and the change of US administrations from Jimmy Carter to Ronald Reagan (January 1981), as well as Iranian advances on the battlefield, intelligence sharing was supplemented by diplomatic, financial and military cooperation.[61] On the diplomatic front, the United States followed an active policy of reconciliation with Iraq, removing the country from the State Department's list of 'state sponsors of terrorism' in February 1982, and then officially resuming diplomatic ties in November 1984. Economic support ranged from authorization of supplies of dual use equipment, such as helicopters that could be converted to military use, and generous loans provided by the US Export-Import Bank (Eximbank) and other financial institutions. In a speech presented to the US House of Representatives, Henry Gonzalez (Democrat, Texas) outlined that '[b]etween 1983 and the invasion of Kuwait in 1990, Iraq received $5 billion in CCC [US Department of Agriculture's Commodity Credit Corporation] guarantees that allowed them to purchase United States agricultural products on credit.'[62]

In October of the same year, hearings before the Senate Committee on Banking, Housing and Urban Affairs revealed that the United States had not only exported agricultural products to Iraq, but also 'chemical, biological, nuclear, and missile-system equipment ... that was converted to military use in Iraq's chemical, biological, and nuclear weapons program,' and which in turn also were used against US soldiers in the Second Persian Gulf War.[63] The record of these hearings was compiled as the Riegle Report in May 1994. According to this report, the US government had approved sales of a wide-range of chemical and biological materials to Iraq,[64] including components for mustard gas, anthrax, Clostridium Botulinum, Histoplasma Capsulatum, Brucella Melitensis and Clostridium Perfringens.[65] The official 'tilt' toward Iraq actually was defined in a State Department Information Memorandum dated 7 October 1983; it concluded that the 'policy of strict neutrality has already been modified, except for arms sales, since Iran's forces crossed into Iraq in the summer of 1982', adding that the 'steps we have taken toward the conflict since then have progressively favoured Iraq.'[66] The range of US assistance to Saddam Hussein was confirmed by former National Security Staff Member Howard Teicher in an affidavit to a US district court in Florida:

> Pursuant to the secret NSDD,[67] the United States actively supported the Iraqi war effort by supplying the Iraqis with billions of dollars of credits, by providing U.S. military intelligence and advice to the Iraqis, and by clearly monitoring third country arms sales to Iraq to make sure that Iraq had the military weaponry required. The United States also provided strategic operational advice to the Iraqis to better use their forces in combat. For example, in 1986, President Reagan sent a secret message to Saddam Hussein telling him that Iraq should step up its air war and bombing of Iran. This message was delivered by Vice President Bush who communicated it to Egyptian President Mubarak, who in

turn passed the message to Saddam Hussein. Similar strategic operational military advice was passed to Saddam Hussein through various meetings with European and Middle Eastern heads of state where the strategic operational advice was communicated.[68]

From the perspective of Saddam Hussein, the US 'tilt' was a confirmation of his elevated regional role. During the various diplomatic encounters, Iraqi officials gave repeated attention to inter-Arab politics (the situation in Lebanon, Syrian expansionism, the reintegration of Egypt, the Israeli-PLO 'peace process' etc.), presenting Iraq as the pivotal power in the Arab world at the expense of Syria and Libya whose leaders were described as radical, revisionist and irrational. The Iraqi Ba'thist regime in turn was presented as moderate, pragmatic, modern, without ideological 'complexes', and acting 'within the context of five thousand years of Mesopotamian civilisation.'[69] Owing to the reawakened historic weight of Iraq under the leadership of the Ba'th party, it was argued, the country's role as a force for stabilization was indispensable: 'What ... would have happened to the states of the Gulf and Arabian peninsula,' Saddam Hussein asked during a meeting with Donald Rumsfeld in Baghdad in December 1983, 'if Iraq had not stood fast [against Iran]? No one would have been able to put out the fire. Zionism was in fact encouraging it to burn.'[70]

Nothing confirmed Saddam Hussein's war role more than the international silence about the use of chemical and biological weapons. In a State Department memo to then Secretary of State Shultz in November 1983, it was confirmed that the US knew 'that Iraq has acquired a CW production capability, primarily from Western firms, including possibly a U.S. foreign subsidiary' and that Iraq appeared to be using chemical weapons almost on a daily basis.[71] Further intelligence suggested that 'as long ago as July 1982, Iraq used tear gas and skin irritants against *invading* Iranian forces quite effectively,' and that 'in October 1982, unspecified foreign officers fired lethal chemical weapons at the orders of Saddam during battles in the Mandali area.'[72] US awareness of Iraq's chemical warfare is also confirmed by a former Defense Intelligence Agency officer, Lt. Col. Rick Francona, who served in the US embassy in Baghdad in 1987 and 1988. According to Francona, the US

> believed the Iraqis were using mustard gas all through the war, but that was not as sinister as nerve gas. ... They started using tabun [a nerve gas] as early as 1983 or 1984, but in a very limited way. They were probably figuring out how to use it. And in 1988, they developed sarin.[73]

Francona also revealed that the Reagan administration provided 'planning assistance' for the successful Iraqi offensive on the Faw peninsula in 1988. 'When I was walking around,' Francona told the *Guardian*, 'I saw atropine injectors lying around. We saw decontamination fluid in vehicles, [but] there were no insects. There was a very quick response from Washington saying, "Let's stop our cooperation," but it didn't last long—just weeks.'[74]

Moreover, in December 2002, Andreas Zumach, an investigative journalist working for the German *Tageszeitung* (TAZ), gathered and published classified information excerpted from a report presented to the United Nations by the Ba'thist regime in hopes of averting the ensuing invasion of Iraq in 2003.[75] According to the report, which was not circulated beyond the five permanent members of the UN Security Council, 14 American companies, including Hewlett-Packard, Unisys and Dupont, were directly involved in the buildup of Iraq's biological, chemical and atomic industries.[76] Ironically, if viewed in comparison with current US accusations about Iran's nuclear research programme, the report also listed the US Departments of Defense, Energy, Commerce and Agriculture and the nuclear research facilities Lawrence Livermore, Los Alamos and Sandia, as suppliers for Saddam Hussein's conventional and/or non-conventional weapons programmes.

Further evidence reveals that German and British companies were also implicated. The German involvement in Iraq's chemical weapons industry was initially concentrated on the chemical plant in Samarra, built by Iraq's State Establishment for Pesticides Production. The companies involved in this project were Preussag Heriger, Hammer, Rhein-Bayern, Karl Kolb/Pilot Plant and Water Engineering Trading, a company based in Hamburg. The German weekly magazine *Stern* reported on 10 December 1987 that Kolb/Pilot Plant exported to Baghdad a 'gas chamber' suitable for testing chemical weapons on dogs and cats. The same company was involved in the second-largest chemical weapons plant in Falluja. In 1990, a report submitted to the German parliament by the late German minister of Trade, Jürgen Möllemann, provided further insight into the involvement of Kolb/Pilot Plant in Iraq's chemical weapons industry. On page 22 it is stated that the German government believed as early as 1982 that German companies were involved in Saddam Hussein's chemical warfare industry and that these allegations were verified in 1984. The German government subsequently pursued 'informal' talks with the companies concerned, which did not yield any results.[77] In fact, Kolb/Pilot Plant constructed a new chemical plant in Falluja in 1988, a site which featured in former US Secretary of State Colin Powell's case for the invasion of Iraq, presented to the UN Security Council in February 2003. It also featured in a September 2002 report by Britain's Joint Intelligence Committee, to the great benefit of Prime Minister Tony Blair when he sought to justify the invasion.

In March 2003, *The Guardian* revealed that the British company Uhde was also involved in the Falluja chemical plant, which was central to Iraq's chemical warfare arsenal during a period when 'senior officials recorded in writing that Saddam Hussein was actively gassing his opponents.'[78] Uhde received the contract to supply a chlorine plant in December 1984, agreeing to pay its

German intermediary a commission of almost one million pounds. Uhde, which is based in Hounslow in the west of London, had only a handful of employees, and was run by German executives. It was wholly owned by a German firm of the same name, headquartered in Dortmund. This sister company, in turn, was at the time a subsidiary of the German chemical giant Hoechst.[79] The documents made available to *The Guardian* also showed that then UK Trade minister Paul Channon rejected a strong plea from the Foreign Office minister Richard Luce, who argued that the deal would ruin Britain's image in the world. 'I consider it essential everything possible be done to oppose the proposed sale,' Luce pleaded, 'and to deny the company concerned [Export Credit Guarantee Department] cover.' 'A ban,' Channon replied in line with the support for Saddam Hussein against Iran by the Thatcher government, 'would do our other trade prospects in Iraq no good.'[80]

True, before Donald Rumsfeld returned to Baghdad in late March 1984 for a second official visit, the United States, for the first time during the war, condemned the use of chemical weapons publicly.[81] Yet while acknowledging that the 'United States has concluded that the available evidence substantiates Iran's charges that Iraq has used chemical weapons,'[82] the press statement also condemned the Iranian insistence on the removal of the Ba'thist regime. This statement is historically interesting, even ironic, when viewed from the comparative perspective of events that have surrounded the US-led invasion of Iraq in March 2003. The US government in 1984 named Iran as the invading force, declaring that the 'United States finds the present Iranian regime's intransigent refusal to deviate from its avowed objective of eliminating the *legitimate* government of neighbouring Iraq to be inconsistent with the accepted norms of behaviour among nations and the moral and religious basis which it claims.'[83]

From Saddam Hussein's perspective, the calculated complacency of the Reagan administration and the continuous assistance to Iraq's chemical, biological and/or atomic weapons industries by companies from Belgium, Britain, China, France, Germany, Japan, the Netherlands, Spain, Sweden, and the United States confirmed his impression that Iraq's unconventional warfare was tolerated.[84] '[T]he [Iranian] invaders should know,' a public statement proclaimed in 1984, 'that for every harmful insect there is an insecticide capable of annihilating it whatever the number and Iraq possesses this annihilation insecticide'.[85] Asked whether Iraqi use of chemical weapons would affect relations between the White House and Saddam Hussein, a State Department spokesman replied at press briefing in March 1984: 'No. I am not aware of any change in our position. We're interested in being involved in a closer dialogue with Iraq.'[86]

The support for Saddam Hussein also extended to diplomatic cover at the United Nations. When the Iranian government submitted a draft resolution asking for UN condemnation of the chemical warfare by Iraq, the US delegate was instructed to lobby for a general motion of 'no decision' on the resolution. At a meeting between Iraqi interests section head Nizar Hamdoon and then Deputy Assistant Secretary of State James Placke on 29 March 1984, the former spelled out what the Iraqi government expected from the UN resolution. Hamdoon stressed that his country favoured a Security Council presidential statement rather than a resolution, together with reference to former resolutions on the war, progress toward termination of the conflict, and no mention of responsibility regarding the employment of chemical weapons. One day after the meeting, the Security Council issued the aforementioned presidential statement, condemning the use of chemical weapons without naming Iraq as the offending party. A State Department memorandum from 30 March 1984 acknowledged the successful diplomatic 'spin' in support of Iraq, noting that the 'statement ... contains all three elements Hamdoon wanted.'[87]

Actions during the latter half of the war, such as the US attacks on Iranian oil platforms during the 'tanker war' period and the shooting down by the USS *Vincennes* of an Iran Air passenger jet (an 'accident' in which 290 civilians were killed), only reconfirmed the Iraqi position.[88] The Iraqi regime even got away with an apology and the payment of US $27.3 million for hitting the USS *Stark* with a missile, an incident that killed 37 US Navy personnel and wounded 21.[89] The support for Saddam Hussein did not, however, preclude deals with the Iranian government. It was not knowledge about Iraqi war crimes that proved disastrous for the Reagan administration, but the much publicized Iran-Contra Affair. At the time congressional testimonies revealed that the Reagan administration, with Israeli complicity, was engaged in a massive arms deal with the Islamic Republic, the profits of which were intended to finance the guerrilla war of the 'Contras' in Nicaragua; this could be (and has been) interpreted as an effort to 'engage' with the Iranian state.[90] But recently declassified documents show that apart from the policy of balancing Iran and Iraq *against* each other, Israel also acted on the premise

> that moderate elements in Iran can come to power if these factions demonstrate their credibility in defending Iran against Iraq and in deterring Soviet intervention. To achieve the strategic goal of a more moderate Iranian government, the Israelis are prepared to unilaterally commence selling military material to Western-oriented Iranian factions. It is their belief that by so doing they can achieve a heretofore unobtainable penetration of the Iranian governing hierarchy. ... once the exchange relationship has commenced, a dependency would be established on those who are providing the requisite resources, thus allowing providers to coercively influence near-term events. Such an outcome is consistent with our policy objectives and would present significant advantages for US national interests.[91]

Replying to this memorandum authored by John M. Poindexter (and prepared by Oliver North), Ronald Reagan authorized assisting

> selected friendly foreign liaisons services, third countries and third parties which have established relationships with Iranian elements, groups, and individuals sympathetic to U.S. Government interests … for the purpose of: 1) establishing a more moderate government in Iran, 2) obtaining from them significant intelligence not otherwise obtainable, to determine the current Iranian Government's intentions with respect to its neighbours and with respect to terrorist acts and 3) furthering the release of the American hostages held in Beirut and preventing additional terrorist acts by these groups. Provide funds, intelligence, counter-intelligence, training, guidance and communications and other necessary assistance to those elements, groups, individuals, liaison services and third countries in support of these activities.[92]

Thus, in parallel with support for Iraq, the United States (and Israel) also attempted to weaken the leadership of Ayatollah Khomeini domestically in order to re-establish the pre-revolutionary strategic partnership between Iran, Israel and the United States. In the meantime, before a new Shah could be installed in Iran, the Reagan administration presented Saddam Hussein as the guarantor of the regional status quo in the Persian Gulf, lending him a prominent role in regional affairs. This in turn legitimated his self-perception as the bulwark against the revolutionary tide from Persia. '[Y]ou [were] not the ones who protected your friends during the war with Iran,' Saddam Hussein pointed out during a conversation with US Ambassador April Glaspie in the build-up to the second Persian Gulf War. 'I assure you, had the Iranians overrun the region, the American troops would not have stopped them, except by the use of nuclear weapons. I do not want to belittle you,' the Iraqi President went on, '[b]ut I hold this view by looking at the geography and nature of American society … Yours is a society which cannot accept 10,000 dead in one battle.'[93]

That the Reagan administration had balance of power calculations in mind does not contradict our argument. What is central is that by supporting Saddam Hussein, the US gave his regime the opportunity to act upon his plans to invade Iran. 'War roles' are never constituted merely in the encapsulated habitat of the nation-state. In order to enact effectively a certain role identity, social legitimation is crucial. During the Iran-Iraq war, international society granted that legitimation to Saddam Hussein. Without regional and global approval, the Ba'thist state would never have been able to act upon its role or follow the campaign of unrestrained warfare. At the end of the war (March 1988), this anarchic international context enabled Saddam Hussein to pursue the 'Anfal' campaign against Iraq's Kurdish population and Iranian army units operating in the area, culminating in the gassing of the eastern Iraqi town of Halabja and the killing of at least 4,000 to 5,000 people. The slaughter of Halabja, the 'use of poison gas and other war crimes against Iran and the Iranian people' and the claim that 'Iraq summarily executed thousands of Iranian prisoners of war as a matter of policy' were not on top of the international agenda when they happened.[94] They only became relevant as a means to legitimate regime change in Iraq in the late 1990s, and the invasion of the country in March 2003.

Orientalist myths and the ordering of West Asia

In the middle of the Second World War, Margaret Mead boldly asserted that war is neither a biological necessity nor a sociological inevitability, but an invented social institution that will be rendered obsolete once a better invention takes its place.[95] Contemporary theorists of war agree:

> [W]ar does not appear to be one of life's necessities—it is not an unpleasant fact of existence that is somehow required by human nature or by the grand scheme of things. ... War may be a social

affliction, but in important respects it is also a social affliction that can be shrugged off.[96]

What I have attempted to do in this part of the book, much in above spirit, is to discuss some of the inventions surrounding the Iran-Iraq war, in order to show that the conflict was not inevitable, that there was a cultural transmission belt that led to the conflict and sustained it. To that end, I have pursued a dual path: on the one hand, I outlined the cultural manufacturing of the Ba'thist garrison state and its anti-Iranian precepts. On the other hand, I investigated the accommodation of this identity by regional states and the wider international community. This 'cultural genealogy' of the conflict made explicit the connection between the political culture of Saddam Hussein's Iraq, the social manufacturing of international legitimacy, and the invasion of Iran. I am not saying that power politics or other 'realist' categories did not play a role in the war. Nor am I saying that culture is an explanatory concept that can account for most of what is happening in international society. Nor, certainly, do I believe that one should challenge historical teleology in order to present competing, all-encompassing 'truths', as if this narrative can be detached from my own academic socialization, personal history and intellectual interests. What I am saying is that without the invention of Ba'thist Arab nationalism and its anti-Iranian precepts; without its institutionalization and reification as Iraq's preferred state identity during Saddam Hussein's rule; without its internalization by the Ba'thist elites; and without the implicit objectification of this invented garrison state identity by the international community before and during the conflict, the Iran-Iraq war would not have 'happened'.

There was no historically ciphered enmity between Iraqis and Iranians, no automatism that triggered the invasion. Rather to the contrary, both peoples have shared long periods of common history within different Muslim and pre-Islamic empires, both are intermingled ethnically, religiously and culturally. Undoubtedly, there *are* subdued, yet indissoluble transnational ties between Iraqis and Iranians. Consider the network of institutions, charities, foundations and seminaries linking Qom and Mashhad to Karbala and Najaf, or the family, economic and cultural ties between Iraqi Kurds and Iranian Kurds, Iraqi Turkmens and Iranian Turkmens, Iraqi-Sunni businessmen and Iranian-Shia businessmen, and so forth. Indeed, once the Ba'thist polity was removed those ties evolved, exemplified by the range of Memoranda of Understanding signed between the Iraqi government and Iran in the fields of economy, security, and energy;[97] the al-Maliki government's vocal criticism of the detention of Iranian diplomats and governmental personnel by US forces in December 2006 and January 2007 respectively;[98] or the election of the critically acclaimed film *Half Moon*—directed by Iran's Bahman Qobadi and co-produced by Iraq, Iran, Austria and France—as Iraq's entry for the 2007 Academy Awards in Hollywood. Indeed, the only Iraqi forces opposing a peaceful relationship between the two countries are the remnants of the Ba'thist dictatorship and al-Qaeda activists such as Abu-Hamza al-Muhajir, who is viciously anti-Shia and anti-Iranian. Al-Qaeda in Iraq has in many ways inherited and further propagated the anti-Iranian norm invented by Saddam Hussein. Consider this statement of Muhajir released by al-Qaeda's al-Furquan Foundation, translated into English by the Al-Boraq Workshop and reproduced on the Jihad Unspun Website:

> He [President George W. Bush] turned to Sham [Syria and Lebanon] and terrorised its tyrant [Syrian President Basher Assad]. ... The blockade continued until he [Assad] had to open his country to hundreds and thousands of Persians to acquire citizenship in it, [to enable them to] support the charlatan agent of the anti-Christ, Nasr'allat [worshipper of idols] who is called Nasrallah [leader of the Lebanese Hesbollah]. ... Hence the old Persian empire has become complete, extending from the countries behind the river, Iran and Iraq ... to the Sham [Syria and Lebanon].[99]

Consider also the remarks of Adnan al-Dulaimi, the leader of the Iraqi Accordance Front, who warned in August 2007 that Baghdad was in danger of falling into the hands of the 'Persians' and 'Safawis'.[100] It is difficult not to see the parallels between these statements and the rhetoric of the Ba'thist state here. To al-Qaeda, Ba'thist loyalists, and some members of the governments of Saudi Arabia, Jordan and Egypt, who talk about Shia crescents, Persian hegemony etc., Iraq continues to be the battlefield between Arabs and Persians. But is it? Isn't the idea that conflict between Arabs and Iranians is inevitable an invention of Arab and Iranian ultra-nationalists?[101] Isn't this idea in many ways imported from the political culture of Iraqi-Ba'thism, and perpetuated within the anarchic spaces of international society; didn't the Iran-Iraq war 'happen' and wasn't it made to function in that international cultural episteme?[102]

One has to be critical of the monomaniac, 'neo-Orientalist' vogue whose arguments include notions about inevitable 'sectarian violence', the inherent split within the Islamic world between Shia and Sunni, the unbridgeable enmity between Saudi Arabia and Iran, the intrinsic weakness of nation-state structures vis-à-vis transnational loyalties, and so forth. I am wondering here if it is a coincidence that books like *The Shia Revival* by Vali Nasr and *The Foreigner's Gift: The Americans, the Arabs, and the Iraqis in Iraq* by Fouad Ajami have appeared during a period when US policymakers are in need of quick-fix manuals to help them understand the mayhem they have engendered in Iraq and elsewhere in the Muslim worlds.[103] How helpful is the framing of politics in the region along sectarian/religious lines? Aren't these kinds of grand categories too simplistic, too mono-causal, and are they not primarily geared towards the politics of the moment? I think the emphasis on allegedly historically codified Arab-Persian enmity or the seemingly unbridgeable Shia-Sunni divide leads to the exact opposite of a critical understanding of world politics in general and the international relations of West Asia in particular. Ultimately, once it is concurrent with government policies, such scholarship threatens to foster what Herbert Marcuse calls 'incestuous reasoning', that is 'the strengthening of the established power structure. Reasoning with it "from without" the power structure', Marcuse notes, 'is a naïve idea. They will listen only to the extent to which the voices can be translated into votes, which may perhaps bring into office another set of the same power structure with the same ultimate concern.'[104]

But then, how should we 'reason from without'? What does one tell an eager undergraduate struggling to find his way around the canonical schools of international relations and history that are part and parcel of 'systematic education', especially with regard to his or her focus on the Islamic worlds? Ibn Khaldun, Islam's fourteenth century historiographer and philosopher, had a useful piece of analogous advice to sceptical students dealing with matters of interpretation of the political world for the first time. In his *Muqadimah*, Ibn Khaldun argues that the science of history is special because, while related to rhetoric and civil politics, it is not synonymous with both. The historian's task, he says, is to find his place beyond the rhetoric of the day on the one hand and the politics of the moment on the other. A disinterested historical disposition hence engenders an open-ended process of exploration, into the subject matter, into one's own argument, into the transcendental. Only if society is driven by that momentum can it attain *'asabiyah*, the *Endziel* of a transformative process which carries it through different civilizational stages from barbarism and sociability to social solidarity. It is thus apparent how the critical task that we have set ourselves here is linked, in its profoundest possibilities (and perhaps limitations), to the destiny of 'anti-foundational' Islamic philosophy as it was established from the eighth century AD onwards. It is trying, in effect, to move my own focus away from the rationality of that which *is* and that which *can be* within the dominant reality I am writing in. It is an effort, in short, to find 'Reason as the critical power of negation'.[105]

Thus critical practice, quite obviously, cannot support a particular 'science' or political philosophy, realist, liberal, constructivist, post-modern or other. It is limited to looking at the cultural inventions permeating particular societies at particular points in time, to grasp better the dynamics of a particular social situation. On the basis of what historical narratives are ideas and ideologies propagated and reified? How do societies constitute themselves in opposition or in relation to others? And how, then, does this socially engineered self-perception affect the grand strategic preferences of the state? It would be salutary for future research on conflict in West Asia to focus on the political-cultural processes that permeate the dialectic between states and societies in the region, be they Muslim, secular, Jewish or other. There is no 'Da Vinci code' and no 'holy blood' or 'holy grail' that condemns West Asia to recurrent periods of conflict. A critical approach toward the politics of the region, in my opinion, may give impetus, as far and as wide as possible, to the undefined work of regional peace. To that end, several questions remain to be answered: has ultra-nationalism in West Asia become an obsolescent shibboleth? Do deeply embedded political cultures fade away with the demise of states? Have we finally re-entered a new era of intellectual engagement that is liberated from retroactive, exclusionary ideologies? I think that at this stage—despite the current engagement between Iraq and Iran—we are perhaps more hopeful than reassured that regional elites have learned the lessons of the bad old days of nationalist exaltation. Remember Ibn Khaldun's cautionary note: the development of a contiguously defined nation-state contains the element of its own destruction. Only a higher form of transnationally defined *'asabiyah* can ensure long-term, structural cohesiveness; only at that stage can we designate the necessary 'inter-subjective condition for the creation of a higher form of collective existence'.[106]

Let me end on a topical note. That Saddam Hussein's war crimes have not been comprehensively covered—legally, intellectually and normatively—indicates that his trial and his perversely chaotic execution did not occur in a vacuum. National and international law is embedded in 'international political culture', a ferociously contested space where ideas, norms and institutions compete and where legitimacy is socially engineered rather than legally constituted.[107] International behaviour during the war reveals in what way this international culture made manifest the existence of unrestrained anarchy, and how the Iran-Iraq war owed its ferocity to the non-existence of a restraining order, regional or global. Here lies the normative claim of the critical disposition I have set out in this book: a critical reading of conflict in West Asia in general, and the Iran-Iraq war in particular, opens up a process whose aim is to rediscover on what basis Halabja became possible; within what international context chemical warfare was legitimated; on the basis of what historical narrative, and in the service of what power, Saddam Hussein could appear as somebody with whom 'it would be possible to do business' for over a decade, only to be branded the new Adolf Hitler after his invasion of Kuwait. Remember that the monster in Mary Shelley's *Frankenstein* became evil only when he was rejected by his creator. The real monster and source of evil in *Frankenstein* is, naturally, the creator of the monster, Dr Frankenstein himself.

A critical disposition that dispassionately dissects the ordering of West Asia in accordance with hegemonic interests would start a process of self-reflection whereby Arabs, Jews, Christians, Iranians, Kurds, Turkmens, Assyrians etc. comprehend that they share a common fate, that crisis in Iraq affects Iranians, that war in Palestine has repercussions for Turks in Istanbul, that imperial power is a process which is decisively dependent on the collaboration of native agents. Such a process, moreover, would bring to light the international context in which Halabjas, Abu Ghraibs, Sabra and Shatilas and Jenins can happen. It would reveal how states have grounded their militaristic policies and thereby have fostered an international order that is not moving towards perfection, but rather towards recurrent crisis, especially in the Muslim worlds. In holding states responsible, in short, what should appear are those political configurations that have given rise to anarchy in West Asia. Such an enterprise perhaps is not so much a legal effort as an intellectual endeavour aimed at finding empathetic antidotes for the existing calamities of international life.

PART III
IRANIAN-AMERICAN ENCOUNTERS: THE ISLAMIC REPUBLIC IN THE NEOCONSERVATIVE MIND

Now, certainty consists in believing that the existence of what has been recognized as true can never be other than what we believe, and to believe, in addition, with respect to that belief that it cannot be otherwise, so that if it is taken as belief with respect to the first belief, then it cannot be otherwise, and so on ad infinitum.

—Abu Nasr Farabi, *'Kitab al-burhan* (Paraphrase of Aristotle's *Analytica Posteriora*)

Dialectic consists not in trying to discover the weakness of what is said, but in bringing out its real strength. It is not the art of arguing (which can make a strong case out of a week one) but the art of thinking (which can strengthen objections by referring to the subject matter).

— Hans-Georg Gadamer, *Truth and Method*

US neoconservatism and the ideology of political reality

Nearly eleven centuries and seemingly unbridgeable intellectual cultures separate the Muslim philosopher Abu Nasr Farabi, who died in 950 AD at the age of eighty, and Hans-Georg Gadamer, the German philosopher and pupil of Martin Heidegger who died in 2002 at the age of 102. Yet despite their disparate locations in time and culture, both men formulated surprisingly comparable ideas on method and 'construction' of reality. Gadamer's most famous book *History and Truth*, which was published in 1960, presents a theory of hermeneutics that attacks the objectivity of positivistic theories and argues that prejudice is present in all interpretation. In Gadamer's view any act of understanding is both bound by context and determined by language. 'The anticipation of meaning that governs our understanding of a text,' Gadamer states, 'is not an act of subjectivity, but proceeds from the commonality that binds us to the tradition.' That tradition, he argues, 'is not simply a permanent precondition; rather we produce it ourselves inasmuch as we understand, participate in the evolution of tradition, and hence further determine it ourselves.'[1]

Abu Nasr Farabi expressed a comparably sceptical view of scientific determinism when he argued that 'every demonstration is … the cause of the scientific knowledge acquired thereby, but not all demonstration conveys the knowledge of the cause of the thing's existence.'[2] Although I am oversimplifying, it is probably correct to say that both men's ultimate argument is that one must not presume the existence of a sphere of human relations somehow detached from a manufactured context, historical, economic, philosophical, traditional, ideational, political or other. *All* human facts, Gadamer and Farabi agree, are invented, objectified, internalized and ultimately introjected.[3]

Although that brief sketch may make the ideas of both thinkers appear commonsensical enough to accept, we too often continue to assume that facts are somehow detached from a manufactured context, that they exist on their own without a historical background and ontological present signifying them.[4] It has been a central methodical argument of this book that notions of unchangeable laws constrain our capacity for understanding that facts are socially engineered, that they are elastic, relative, differentiated.[5] To some post-modern and critical theorists, this may seem unchallengeable, but if we switch our focus away from these approaches to the reality of contemporary international relations studies in general and analyses of West Asia in particular, we see that the majority of scholars tend to take 'facts' for granted, that they fail to focus on the social engineering of world politics.[6] One serious consequence of the absence of a 'critical school' in our empirical field of study, I have argued, is that the image of Iran as a country in the grip of enigmatic, hostile revolutionaries led by intransigent, retroactive Mullahs is surprisingly salient. Part of the problem, I claim in the following paragraphs, is that the Islamic Republic has occupied a prominent place in the imagination of influential neoconservative strategists with direct links to the decision-making process in Washington and immense resources to influence the public discourse in the United States.[7] Together with their allies in the Likud party in Israel (some of them are now members of Kadima), that neoconservative coterie has manufactured an image of Iran, which has made the country's 'aggressive nature' an established fact amongst influential strata of international society.[8]

The missing link in that cause-effect relationship is the role of a specific context (in our case neoconservatism) in the production of reality (in our case the image of Iran as an 'international pariah' governed by irrational religious zealots), a dialectic which both Farabi and Gadamer well understood. It would be a mistake to underestimate that dialectic, especially with regard to the nuclear question. For is the ideological representation of Iran not governed by the strategy to expel from competing realities the notion of a Third World country trying to exercise its right to national development, to contain the view that Iranians are as rational as the Japanese, Germans or other nations who have developed a nuclear energy programme? The answer is yes, in my opinion, which explains my focus in the following paragraphs on the neoconservative habit of producing the image of Iran as an 'international pariah'. I am not so much interested in quantifying the proliferation of anti-Iranian discourses in neoconservative circles. It is rather more central, I think, to account for the way Iran is spoken about, to analyze who does the speaking, to explore the institutions which codify people to speak about the country, and to understand the political culture that signifies and legitimates the things that are said. What is at issue in this part of the book, in short, is the overall discursive representation of Iran by neoconservative ideology, the way in which Iran is 'translated' to us by an exalted, cumbersome, coterie of activists with an overtly and self-consciously anti-Iranian agenda.[9]

After Babylon, Persepolis? Narrating the war script

No manufacturing of consent, no engineering of facts, no ideological effort to 'produce' reality, no campaign to transform a specific political consciousness could function if it did not constitute an overall strategy, through a pattern of institutions, functionaries, and media outlets. And, inversely, no such strategy could achieve lasting effects if it was not based on a consensus serving, not as a headquarters, conspiracy or predetermined, static outcome, but as the smallest common denominator among its adherents. With regard to Iran that consensus is built by influential, idea-producing conglomerates established by neoconservative functionaries and activists with close links to influential lobbying organizations and like-minded parties in Israel. These all adhere to a common interest: to subvert the Iranian state and, by extension, to recode Iranian behaviour in accordance with American and Israeli interests in West Asia and beyond.[10] Let me start exploring some of the strategies pursued to that end from a comparative perspective, by investigating the involvement of neoconservative functionaries in the build-up to the invasion of Iraq in 2003.[11]

'Anyone can go to Baghdad'[12]

It is no secret that there are strong ideological and institutional links between the neoconservative coterie surrounding the White House and various parties in Israel.[13] 'No lobby has managed to divert US foreign policy as far from what the American national interest would otherwise suggest,' write John J. Mearsheimer, Professor at the University of Chicago and Stephen Walt, dean of Harvard's Kennedy School of Government, 'while simultaneously convincing Americans that US and Israeli interests are essentially the same'.[14] One oft-cited example of this nexus is a paper by Douglas Feith (among others), who was US Undersecretary of Defense for Policy from July 2001 until August 2005. The paper bears the curious title, 'A Clean Break: A New Strategy for Securing the Realm.' Produced in July 1996 by the Institute for Advanced Strategic and Political Studies, a think tank based in Washington and Jerusalem, the paper urges Israel to reconsider its strategic posture. The report advocates the 'principle of preemption, rather than retaliation alone'. It suggests that Israel work with 'moderate' regimes such as Jordan and Turkey in order to 'contain, destabilise, and roll back some of its most dangerous threats'. In addition, it recommends that Israel 'focus on removing Saddam Hussein from power in Iraq—an important Israeli strategic objective in its own right—as a means of foiling Syria's regional ambitions.' Historically valuable, if viewed within the context of the current situation in Iraq, the paper also suggests that Israel support Jordan in advocating restoration of the Hashemite monarchy in Iraq.[15]

The list of functionaries involved in the production of the paper reads like a Who's Who of the neoconservative cabal (it will become clear later that the same people are involved in the campaign against Iran). Apart from Douglas Feith, the list includes Richard Perle, one of the central advocates of the Iraq war and until recently chairman of the Pentagon's Defence Policy Board; Charles Fairbanks Jr., a personal friend of Paul Wolfowitz; David Wurmser, formerly of the American Enterprise Institute (AEI) and former special assistant to John Bolton at the State Department, and his wife Meyrav Wurmser, who runs the Hudson Institute and directed the Washington office of the Middle East Media Research Institute (Memri, an invention of Col. Yigal Carmon, who spent 22 years in Israeli intelligence and later served as counter-terrorism adviser to the Israeli Prime Ministers Yitzhak Shamir and Yitzhak Rabin).[16]

In July 1996, the then Prime Minister of Israel Binyamin Netanyahu presented the central strategic tenets of the 'Clean Break' paper to the US Congress. The case for an invasion of Iraq was followed up by the Jewish Institute for National Security Affairs (JINSA) and the Project for a New American Century. JINSA's board of advisers included Vice President Dick Cheney, US Ambassador to the United Nations John Bolton, and Douglas Feith before they entered the Bush administration. Leading neoconservatives such as Richard Perle, Michael Ledeen, Stephen Bryen, Joshua Muravchik, and former CIA director James Woolsey continue to be members of the board at the time of writing. The Project for a New American Century's declared goal is 'to promote American global leadership'.[17] It is chaired by William Kristol, editor of the right-wing *Weekly Standard.* Already in January 1998, the Project sent a letter to then US President Bill Clinton advocating a 'strategy for removing Saddam's regime from power' and demanding a 'full complement of diplomatic, political and military efforts' to that end. This appeal was followed by a letter to Congressional leaders Newt Gingrich and Trent Lott in May 1998, urging, 'US policy should have as its explicit goal removing

Saddam Hussein's regime from power and establishing a peaceful and democratic Iraq in its place.' Out of the seventeen signatories to the two letters, eleven have held posts in the Bush administration since the invasion of Iraq was launched in March 2003. Elliot Abrams, who had orchestrated the Iran-Contra operation when the Reagan administration used the proceeds of arms sales to Iran (despite its own embargo) to circumvent a congressional prohibition on funding Nicaraguan rebels, was recruited as Senior Director for Near East, Southwest Asian and North African Affairs on the National Security Council (promoted to Deputy National Security Adviser, responsible for advancing Bush's strategy of advancing democracy abroad);[18] Richard Armitage was named Deputy Secretary of State; John Bolton, Under Secretary, Arms Control and International Security (promoted to US Ambassador to the United Nations); Paula Dobriansky, Under Secretary of State for Global Affairs; Zalmay Khalilzad, Special Presidential envoy to Afghanistan and 'Ambassador-at-large for Free Iraqis' (promoted to US Ambassador to Iraq); Richard Perle, chairman of the Pentagon's Defence Policy Board; Peter W. Rodman, Assistant Secretary of Defense for International Security Affairs; Donald Rumsfeld, Secretary of Defense; William Schneider, Jr., chairman of the Pentagon's Defense Science Board; Paul Wolfowitz, Deputy Secretary of Defense (promoted to Director of the World Bank); and Robert B. Zoellick, the US Trade Representative (promoted to US Deputy Secretary of State).[19]

It would be naïve to assume that the institutionalizing of the neoconservative nexus in a myriad of think tanks and lobbying organizations did not create the structural platform to advocate the case for war against Iraq. Let me put forward a general hypothesis here. Neoconservatism does not reject aggression. On the contrary, it habituates us to accept war as rational, it puts into operation an entire machinery for producing 'true' facts in order to legitimate militaristic foreign policies. Not only do neoconservatives speak of aggression and urge everyone to do so; they also present an 'aestheticized' version of war. Via neoconservatism justice, patriotism, morality, even chivalry find an opportunity to deploy themselves in the discourse of war. Not, however, by reason of some naturally positive property immanent to war itself, but by virtue of the properties neoconservatism and other militaristic ideologies ascribe to it. Let me turn to explaining how a comparable *Kriegskontext* with the same 'eponymous heroes' is manufactured with regard to Iran.[20]

'Real men go to Tehran'[21]

One newly established link in the chain of neoconservative think tanks tied to lobbying organizations advocating confrontation with Iran is the Coalition for Democracy in Iran (CDI). Founded in 2002 by Michael Ledeen and Morris Amitay, who used to be executive director of the American Israel Public Affairs Committee (AIPAC), the organization aims to foster political support for regime change in the Islamic Republic. Members include Raymond Tanter of the Washington Institute for Near East Policy, itself an invention of the AIPAC; Frank Gaffney, president of the Center for Security Policy (CSP); and Rob Sobhani, who has close personal and political links to the son of the deposed Shah of Iran, Reza Pahlavi. Ledeen, Amitay and Sobhani joined forces at the American Enterprise Institute (AEI) in May 2003 in a seminar entitled 'The Future of Iran: Mullahcracy, Democracy, and the War on Terror', co-sponsored by the Hudson Institute and the Foundation for the Defense of Democracies. All three have connections with the media agency Benador Associates which manages both their op-ed placements and television appearances. Eleana Benador represents Richard Perle, James Woolsey, Charles Krauthammer, Martin Kramer and other neoconservatives tied to the Bush administration. The Foundation for the Defense of

Democracies also supports the Alliance for Democracy in Iran (ADI), which is backed by prominent political strategists such as Jerome Corsi. Whereas the CDI and ADI support the restoration of monarchy in Iran, the Iran Policy Committee (IPC) acts as a lobbying organization for the Mojahedin-e Khalq (MEK), which is listed as a terrorist organization by the US State Department and the European Union.[22]

Through institutionalization, an ideology is transmuted into another sphere of synthesis, a coherent policy. In other words, through creation of more and more interlinked foundations, think tanks, and lobbying organizations, goals, causes, norms and ideas are brought together with an artificial unity of a whole and complete political action. It is this synthesis that brings neoconservative ideology close to the foreign policy process in the United States. Hence, in the US Congress, the Iranian government has been targeted by several bills, including the Iran Freedom and Support Act sponsored by Senators Rick Santorum (Republican, Pennsylvania) and John Cornyn (Republican, Texas), and a comparable bill proposed by Representative Ileana Ros-Lehtinen, a Florida Republican and strident anti-Castro campaigner. Funding of US$ 3 million for Iranian opposition activities had already been inserted by Congress in the 2005 budget on the initiative of Senator Sam Brownback, a Kansas Republican and a member of the Institute on Religion and Public Policy which has recently launched its in-house 'Iran Project'. This is aimed at enhancing 'the understanding of Iran's policy-making process and politico-Islamist system'.[23] Santorum advocated regime change in an address to the National Press Club on 'Islamic fascism' in July 2006, stating that 'every major Islamic leader has openly identified the US as its enemy.'[24]

Influence on the levers of power in Washington is not only secured through lobbying efforts. There is also persuasive evidence of covert activity. In August 2004 it was revealed that classified documents including a draft National Security Presidential Directive devised in the office of then Undersecretary of Defense for Policy, Douglas Feith, were shared with AIPAC and Israeli officials. The document set out a rather more aggressive US policy toward Iran and was leaked by Lawrence Franklin, an 'expert' on Iran who was recruited to Feith's office from the Defence Intelligence Agency.[25] An FBI counterintelligence operation revealed that the same Franklin repeatedly met Naor Gilon, the head of the political department at the Israeli embassy in Washington, and other officials and activists tied to the Israeli state and pro-Israeli lobbying organizations. Franklin was sentenced to 12 years and seven months in jail in January 2006 for disclosing classified information to Steven Rosen and Keith Weissman. Both were members of the AIPAC.[26]

Douglas Feith, whose office invented the idea that the regime of Saddam Hussein had ties to al-Qaeda—which in turn was used to legitimate the invasion of Iraq[27]— has longstanding ties to Zionist pressure groups. The Zionist Organization for America (ZOA), for instance, honoured him and his father for their service to Israel and the Jewish people in 1997. He is also cofounder of 'One Jerusalem', a Jerusalem-based organization whose ultimate goal is securing 'a united Jerusalem as the undivided capital of Israel.'[28] A second cofounder of this organization is David Steinmann who is chairman of JINSA (see above). He is also a board member of the Center for Security Policy (CSP) and chairman of the executive committee of the Middle East Forum. Two other cofounders of 'One Jerusalem' are directly tied to the Likud Party: Dore Gold was a top adviser to former Prime Minister Ariel Sharon and Natan Sharansky was Israel's Minister of Diaspora Affairs from March 2003 until May 2005 (he resigned from the cabinet in April 2005 to protest against plans to withdraw Israeli settlers from the Gaza Strip).

Let me sketch now how the neoconservative machinery works within a specific political context, namely Iran's ninth presidential elections in June 2005. Here, the strategy to inject the public discourse with false facts and predictions was evident before, during, and after the election of Mahmoud Ahmadinejad. 'Any normal person familiar with the Islamic republic knows that these are not elections at all,' wrote Michael Ledeen of the American Enterprise Institute (AEI) in an article entitled 'When Is an Election Not an Election'. He said they were 'a *mise en scene*, an entertainment, a comic opera staged for our benefit. The purpose of the charade is to deter us from supporting the forces of democratic revolution in Iran.'[29] Kenneth Timmerman reiterated the neoconservative message in an article for the *National Review Online* (NRO) entitled 'Fake Election, Real Threats', which was reprinted by the *Washington Times*. Citing Abolhassan Banisadr, the first president of the Islamic Republic, who fled to exile and has not been in Iran for nearly 30 years, Timmerman predicted that no more than 27 per cent of eligible voters in Iran would participate in the elections (his estimate missed the real turnout by over 34 per cent).[30] Danielle Pletka, vice president for foreign and defence policy studies at the AEI, made a similarly misleading prophecy. In 'Not Our Man in Iran', she argued that Ali Akbar Hashemi-Rafsanjani was handpicked by the 'machinations of the mullahs' to win the election (Rafsanjani lost, of course, having received seven million votes less than Ahmadinejad).[31]

The campaign to trivialise the emergent democratic process in Iran before and during the elections served a dual, interdependent purpose: rendering the ninth Presidency of the Islamic Republic illegitimate *a priori* and by extension, representing Iran as an irrational actor, as a country where there is no regulative context in which decision-makers and others operate.[32] Such manipulation helps produce the image of Iran as a 'rogue' country, and this in turn serves the important function of legitimating diplomatic and, potentially, military aggression. The strategy has appeared to be at least partially successful. After the election leading journalists, including John Simpson of the BBC, alleged that Ahmadinejad had been one of the students responsible for holding US diplomatic staff captive between 1979 and 1980.[33] This rather apocryphal claim was rejected by the CIA only after it had its impact on global public opinion. Crucially, the strategy adopted minimized the diplomatic power of the Ahmadinejad administration before its first serious engagement with the international community at the United Nations in September 2005. (All that happened before Ahmadinejad's excessive tirades against Zionism in general and the Israeli state in particular.)

Let me add in parenthesis that tracing the impact of neoconservatism on the way Iran is portrayed is not, of course, to defend the political process in Iran. The Islamic Republic has not established a representative democracy at this stage of its development[34] and I don't think that Mahmoud Ahmadinejad's raucous and bellicose posture in general and his abominably limited understanding of the history of the Holocaust are representative of the political culture of the country.[35] Ahmadinejad and his institutional supporters represent that strata of Iranian society which resort to reactionary policies whenever it comes to issues such as freedom of speech, gender equality and societal empowerment vis-à-vis the state, because they do not have much to contribute intellectually on these matters. Yet it should also be added emphatically here that neoconservative activists favour this type of politician. '[T]here are benefits to having an enemy that openly bares its teeth,' suggests Daniel Pipes in that regard, '[f]or Westerners, it clarifies the hostility of the regime much more than if it subtly spun webs of deceit.'[36] 'Let us state the obvious,' writes Reuel Marc Gerecht of the AEI in a similarly congratulatory mood. 'The new president of the Islamic Republic of Iran, Mahmoud Ahmadinejad, is a godsend.'[37] Ilan Berman, the author of *Tehran*

Rising: Iran's Challenge to the United States, agrees: 'Thank goodness for Mahmoud Ahmadinejad.'[38] The Muslim democrat, I am in no doubt, is anathema to the neoconservative *Weltanschauung*.

Neoconservative 'science fiction' and Iran's nuclear file

Mahmoud Ahmadinejad unconsciously serves neoconservative interests because he has made it that much easier to portray Iran as a monolithically irrational, even fascist country. In another parallel to the way Iraq was portrayed before the invasion,[39] likening Iran with absolute evil, in contemporary world politics always epitomized by Nazi Germany, has become a central pillar of the neoconservative campaign to demonize the country. Ahmadinejad 'has cast himself as Adolf Hitler reincarnated,' writes George Melloan in a column for the *Wall Street Journal*, representatively.[40] The same message, i.e. 2007 equals 1938 and Iran equals Nazi Germany, has been put forward by Binyamin Netanyahu.

Moreover, one tends to agree with Ahmadinejad's many critics in Iran that by adopting a retroactive political discourse permeated by a static notion of Shia-millenial imagery as a means to appeal to the (neo)conservative factions of Iranian society and especially the orthodox clergy, Ahmadinejad further inhibited Iran's bargaining power with regard to the nuclear issue. It should not come as a surprise that the neoconservative apparatus feeds on his dismally anachronistic rhetoric, knitting his abominations closely together in one thoroughly anti-Iranian episteme: 'So a Holocaust-denying, virulently anti-Semitic, aspiring genocidist, on the verge of acquiring weapons of the apocalypse,' writes Charles Krauthammer, 'believes that the end is not only near but nearer than the next American presidential election. ... This kind of man,' Krauthammer continues, 'would have, to put it gently, less inhibition about starting Armageddon *than a normal person*.'[41] 'There is a radical difference between the Islamic Republic of

Iran and other governments with nuclear weapons [*sic*]', Bernard Lewis agrees. 'This difference is expressed in what can only be described as the apocalyptic worldview of Iran's present rulers. ... Mr. Ahmadinejad and his followers clearly believe that the terminal struggle has already begun ... It may even have a date, indicated by several references by the Iranian president to giving his final answer to the US about nuclear development by Aug. 22 [2006]. ... This year, Aug. 22 corresponds, in the Islamic calendar, to the 27th day of the month of Rajab of the year 1427. This, by tradition is the night when many Muslims commemorate the night flight of the prophet Muhammad on the winged horse Buraq, first to the "farthest mosque," usually identified with Jerusalem, and then to heaven and back (cf, Koran XVII.1).' Lewis delves even deeper into the realms of ideological mythology when he tells us that 'it would be wise to bear the possibility in mind' that 22 August 'might well be deemed an appropriate date for the apocalyptic ending of Israel and if necessary of the world.'[42] The same theme was picked up by Kenneth Timmerman: 'As the world prepares to confront an Iranian regime that continues to defy the International Atomic Energy Agency over its nuclear programs,' he warns, 'we must listen to what Iran's leaders say as we watch what they do. A religious zealot with nuclear weapons is a dangerous combination the world cannot afford to tolerate.'[43] Timmerman heads the Foundation for Democracy in Iran (FDI) and is a member of the Committee on the Present Danger.[44] The latter organisation issued a policy paper in January 2006 calling for more sanctions against Iran and lobbys the Bush administration to 'energetically assist dissidents to bring about the downfall of the Iranian state.'[45]

Occasionally, the neoconservative campaign to present Iran as an irrational polity receives setbacks.[46] In May 2006, bloggers and investigative journalists exposed as wholly invented a story by Amir Taheri whose opinion pieces are managed by Benador

Associates (see above).[47] In an article for the *National Post* of Canada, Taheri had claimed that a new law would require Iranian Jews to 'be marked out with a yellow strip of cloth sewn in front of their clothes while Christians will be assigned the colour red. Zoroastrians end up with Persian blue as the colour of their zonnar.'[48] According to Taheri 'the new codes would enable Muslims to easily recognise non-Muslims so that they can avoid shaking hands with them by mistake and thus becoming *najis* (unclean).'[49] To reiterate the message, the article ran alongside a 1935 photograph of a Jewish businessman in Berlin with a yellow, six-pointed star sewn on his overcoat. The *National Post* was forced to retract the bogus piece and apologise publicly. But by then the *New York Post*, part of the media empire controlled by Rupert Murdoch, the *Jerusalem Post*, which also featured a photo of a yellow star from the Nazi era over a photo of Mahmoud Ahmadinejad, and the *New York Sun* had picked up the story.[50]

Moreover, in another *New York Post* column in 2005, Taheri claimed that Iran's ambassador to the UN, Javad Zarif, was one of the students involved in the capture of US diplomats in Tehran between 1979 and 1981. The story was retracted after Dwight Simpson, a professor at San Francisco State University, wrote to the newspaper explaining that the allegation was 'false'. On the day of the seizure of the US embassy in Tehran, Zarif was a 'graduate student in the Department of International Relations of San Francisco State University. He was my student,' Simpson told the editors, 'and he served also as my teaching assistant.'[51] Despite this track record, Amir Taheri was amongst a group of 'experts' on Iran and the region invited to the White House in a meeting with Tony Blair and George W. Bush in May 2006.[52]

As I have mentioned earlier, Taheri and others would not have been able to publicize their stories so effectively without the excessive rhetoric of the Iranian government, and here especially Ahmadinejad's infamous speech questioning the factual circumstances of the Holocaust. Let me take this argument one step further now. What the dialectic between the rhetoric of the Ahmadinejad administration and its reinvention by sympathisers of the neoconservative agenda shows is that a whole range of individuals is trading in the business of 'reality production' when it comes to Iran, that we are constantly alerted to accept their ideas, that a whole armada of politicians, activists, journalists etc. dilute facts in order to further their agenda, and that this process affects the way we are able to 'see' Iran. What they intend to do, ultimately, is to concoct a 'reality' that can be superimposed on the 'facts on the ground'. As a result, in this case, knowing the history of Iranian Jews becomes almost impossible. Rather immediately, the neutral observer is artificially divorced from the fact that the Old Testament describes the Persian king 'Cyrus the Great', as God's 'anointed' and 'chosen' ruler, because it was he who relieved the plight of the Jews deported to Babylonia by king Nebuchadnezzar in the sixth century BC. Quite suddenly it is rendered irrelevant that Cyrus is mentioned in the Torah as a saint and saviour of the Jewish people; that one of his successors on the Persian throne, Xerxes I, married a Jewish woman, Esther, the daughter of one of his ministers, that the tomb of Esther in the north-Western Iranian city of Hamadan (ancient Ecbatana) draws Jewish pilgrims from all over Iran, especially during the holiday of Purim (the walls of the building explain the origins of Esther in Hebrew).

As a result of Ahmadinejad's tirades and the myths invented by Taheri, one is compelled to forget that at a time when Nazi Germany was busy implementing the *Endlösung*, Iranian diplomats offered hundreds of Iranian passports to European Jews in order to facilitate their exodus, especially from Poland (this is the theme of a popular Iranian TV series titled 'Zero Degree Turn', there is still a sizeable Polish-Jewish minority in Iran to this date); that the Islamic Republic itself guarantees the rights of Iran's Jewish minority, which is the largest in West Asia outside Israel and Palestine; that the 25,000 to 60,000 Jews of Tehran, Shiraz, Isfahan, Boroujerd and Yazd have their own cemeteries,[53] which, in contrast to Europe and Russia, are not desecrated by skinhead mobs; that they attend packed synagogues, send their children to Jewish schools, buy their meat in kosher butchers, are exempt from prohibitions on alcohol; that their political representation in the Iranian parliament (*majlis*) is secured in the Iranian Constitution; that many Iranian Jews fought Saddam Hussein during the Iran-Iraq war (1980-88); and that in August 2006, the 'Association of the Iranian Jewish Community' and the management of the Sepir Jewish hospital in Tehran facilitated medical aid for Palestinians wounded by Israeli armed forces during the latest *Intifada* against the occupation.[54] All these 'facts on the ground' quite suddenly do not matter, because the plots engendered by Taheri and Ahmadinejad opened up a whole new reality into which another, rather nasty image of Iran could be pasted rather more conveniently.[55]

It should not come as a surprise, in this context, that the AIPAC has made fears about Iran's nuclear energy programme a central pillar of its congressional agenda. At its largest ever policy conference in May 2005, the AIPAC presented a Disney-inspired multimedia tour aimed at fostering the argument that Iran is developing nuclear weapons. Similarly, the American Jewish Committee (AJC) has taken out full-page advertisements in influential US newspapers since April 2006, entitled 'A Nuclear Iran Threatens All', depicting radiating circles on an Iran-centred map to show the potential reach of the missiles. 'Suppose Iran one day gives nuclear devices to terrorists,' the ad reads. 'Could anyone anywhere feel safe?'[56] The same message is reiterated by Manuchehr Ghorbanifar, who was a central player in the Iran-Contra affair and who met envoys from the Pentagon in Rome in July 2006.[57] In a declassified document dated 25 July 1984, entitled 'Fabricator Notice Manuchehr

(Gorbanifar)', it is indicated that prior to the Islamic revolution Ghorbanifar had been 'an informant for Iranian Intel' and that he 'claimed to have access to many senior ranking officers in [the Iranian] military as well as access to Iran[ian] underworld characters of various illicit hues.' In the same document it is also stated that he was implicated in the

> abortive coup of 3 July 1980 which resulted in curtailment of his trips to Iran. ... He had a history of predicting events after they happened and was seen as a rumourmongerer of occasional usefulness. In addition, the information collected by him consistently lacked sourcing and detail notwithstanding his exclusive interest in acquiring money.[58]

Amir Abbas Fakhravar, who presents himself as an 'Iranian student leader' and who advocated the policy of 'regime change' in his testimony to a Senate Homeland Security Committee in July 2006, appears to follow a similar career.[59] In an interview with the *Sunday Telegraph* in July 2006, Fakhravar reverted to the neoconservative themes explored above, stating that the 'world has to do something—whatever it takes—so that Mahmoud Ahmadinejad does not become another Hitler'.[60] Sitting comfortably in his office at the Foundation for the Defense of Democracies, Fakhravar even promotes military action against Iran: 'Whatever the world does against the Iranian regime,' he assures us much in the same way Iraqi exiles did in the build-up to the Iraq war, 'the Iranian people will be supportive.'[61]

The theme of equating Iran with Nazi Germany, which is one of the many neoconservative themes that strengthen the agenda against the Islamic Republic, has already entered the political consciousness of decision-makers in western Europe and the United States. Jim Lobe, the prolific investigative journalist of the *Inter Press Service*, states that Senator John McCain has likened the nuclear stand-off with Iran with the situation in Europe in the 1930s.[62] Angela Merkel, leader of the 'Grosse Koalition' between the conservative Christian Democratic Union (CDU) and the centre-left

Social Democratic Party (SPD) in Germany, appears to adhere to a similar view: 'Looking back to German history in the early 1930s when National Socialism was on the rise, there were many outside Germany who said "It's only rhetoric—don't get excited",' Merkel told policy makers at the 2006 Munich security conference.[63] 'There were times when people could have reacted differently and, in my view, Germany is obliged to do something at the early stages. ... We want to, we must prevent Iran from developing its nuclear programme.'[64] George W. Bush himself alleged repeatedly that the government of Iran 'has proclaimed its desire to build a nuclear weapon', in total disregard of the repeated proclamations by Iran's Supreme Leader Ayatollah Ali Khamenei that 'developing, producing or stockpiling nuclear weapons is forbidden under Islam'.[65] Another prominent policy maker to adhere to that threat scenario is Newt Gingrich who argued that Iran could be planning for a preemptive nuclear electromagnetic pulse attack on the United States that would turn one third of the country 'back to a 19th century level of development.'[66] Gingrich, it should be added, is a member of the Senior Advisory Board of the United States Commission on National Security/21 Century. The Commission has produced a series of policy recommendations that discuss US national security challenges until 2025.

Iran in the 'war on terror'

At the theoretical level, neoconservatism is not ordered according to a unifying headquarters or conspiracy.[67] Contemporary neoconservatism should be represented rather as an ideological space open in three dimensions. In one of these we have already situated the neoconservative functionary, for whom writing the script, the speech, the terminology of a specific political discourse is central (e.g. the 'axis of evil' invented by David Frum). In a second dimension we may situate the decision-maker, neoconservatism's public face, who proceeds by relating diversified but consensual discourses in such a way that they are then able to claim causal validity and strategic value (e.g. Richard Perle, Dick Cheney, Donald Rumsfeld, Paul Wolfowitz). These two dimensions are largely empirical in that they are part of the day-to-day affairs of politics in Washington (and the 'think-tank belt' scattered around Dupont Circle, for that matter). The third dimension, in my opinion, is that of strategic value, which develops as a long-term state interest out of the second; it forms a salient grand strategy and hence is not easily discarded or altered. It is here that we meet the legitimation of war, and its translation from the empirical realms of day-to-day politics into theorized reality; it is this realm that is least transparent, causal, ontological. What evidence is available to us today if we seek to explore Iran's position in that third dimension? Let me frame this question with two political realities that define Iran's place in the strategic imagination of contemporary US neoconservatives.

First, the 'global war on terror' and the doctrine of pre-emption proclaimed by President Bush have emerged as the primary elements of US foreign policy. Both prescribe military intervention against potential adversaries even if they are not considered an *immediate* threat to US national security.[68] According to Norman Podhoretz, who was editor-in-chief of the influential neoconservative magazine *Commentary* between 1960 and 1995, the 'global war on terror' is instrumental in producing a 'new species of imperial mission for America, whose purpose would be to oversee the emergence of successor governments in the [West Asian] region more amenable to reform and modernisation than the despotisms now in place.[69] After taking Baghdad,' Podhoretz prophesied, 'we may willy-nilly find ourselves forced by the same political and military logic to topple five or six or seven more tyrannies in the Islamic world.'[70]

The preemptive strategic doctrine, which was announced in June 2002 by President Bush at the military academy at West Point, provides the political legitimacy for such an agenda. Setting out an interventionist framework for US foreign policy, President Bush declared that the country would confront 'evil and lawless regimes', if necessary by military force.[71] The US National Security Strategy published three months later institutionalized the 'Bush doctrine'. According to its authors, the US 'has long maintained the option of preemptive actions to counter a sufficient threat. … The greater the threat', it states, 'the greater is the risk of inaction and the more compelling the case for taking anticipatory action to defend ourselves, *even if uncertainty remains as to the time and place of the enemy's attack*.'[72] There is enough evidence to conclude that Iran is on that target list. First, there is the circumstantial evidence, such as the repeated warnings by Seymour Hersh, Scott Ritter, Dan Plesch, Paul Rogers and others that the war against Iran is already on its way,[73] and the reports leaked to the *Sunday Times* indicating that 'under the American plans Britain would be expected to play a supporting role, perhaps by sending surveillance aircraft or ships and submarines to the Gulf or by allowing the Americans to fly from Diego Garcia'.[74] Second, there is the factual evidence exemplified by the classified version of the National Security Presidential Directive (NSPD) 17 and Homeland Security Presidential Directive 4,[75] leaked to *The Washington Post*. This broke with 50 years of US counter-proliferation efforts by authorizing preemptive strikes on states and terrorist groups that are close to acquiring weapons of mass destruction or the long-range missile capable of delivering them. In a leaked, top-secret appendix, the directive named Iran, Syria, North Korea and Libya among the countries that are the central focus of the policy.[76]

Moreover, NSPD 17 also sets out to respond to a WMD threat with nuclear weapons. This nuclear 'first strike' policy is reiterated in presidential directive NSPD 35 (Nuclear Weapons Deployment Authorisation), issued in May 2004, the Nuclear Posture Review in January 2002 and the Doctrine for Joint Nuclear Operations published in March 2005. In addition, US Senate Joint Resolution 23 ('Authorisation for Use of Military Force') empowers the president 'to take action to deter and prevent acts of terrorism against the United States' without consulting Congress.[77] There are even calls to change international law to legitimate the policy of pre-emption. In another similarity to the Iraq war, when scholars such as Fouad Ajami covered the invasion with an 'academic canopy', Harvard Law professor Alan Dershowitz argues that '[b]y deliberately placing nuclear facilities in the midst of civilian population centres, the Iranian government has made the decision to expose its civilians to attacks ... if all else fails', he demands, 'Israel, or the United States, must be allowed under international law to take out the Iranian nuclear threat before it is capable of the genocide for which it is being built.'[78]

Second, Iran was mentioned sixteen times in the latest National Security Strategy of the United States, a 'wartime document' that uses such emotionally charged phrases as 'tyrannical regime', 'ally of terror' which 'harbor[s] terrorists' and is an 'enemy of freedom, justice, and peace' to describe the Islamic Republic.[79] Moreover, the NSS also spells out a policy of subversion against the Iranian state, as a means to 'protect our national and economic security against the adverse effects of their bad conduct.'[80] To that end, the US State Department has established an in-house 'Iran Desk, 'Iran watch units' in Dubai as well as US embassies in the vicinity of Iran, and a US$75 million programme aimed at 'expanding broadcasting into the country, funding nongovernmental organizations and promoting cultural exchanges.'[81] In another parallel to the build-up to the Iraq war, US officials have also set up an Iran Syria Policy and Operations Group (ISOG) whose actions include

increasing the military capabilities of Arab allies such as Saudi Arabia, the United Arab Emirates, and Bahrain ... providing covert assistance to Iranian dissidents and building international outrage toward Iran by publicizing its alleged role in a 1994 terrorist attack in Argentina.[82]

Students of recent Iranian history agree that the policy of subverting the Iranian state violates the Algiers Accords of 19 January 1981 which laid down that the United States 'pledges that it is and from now on will be the policy of the United States not to intervene, directly or indirectly, politically or militarily, in Iran's internal affairs'. Yet despite these legal restrictions, it is further diversified by a parallel process probing tensions between Iran's ethnic minorities and the central government in Tehran. A research project to that end was implemented by the Marine Corps Intelligence which focuses on 'crises and pre-deployment support to expeditionary warfare'.[83] This strand of current US policies vis-à-vis Iran, unsurprisingly, is overwhelmingly endorsed by neoconservative functionaries, as exemplified by an AEI conference in October 2005 entitled 'Another case for Federalism'. 'The "Iranian" people have no connection to a glorious past,' we are told much in that same spirit, 'and thus no foundation for a flourishing future.'[84] Michael Rubin agrees: 'Iran is more an empire than a nation. ... When the Islamic Republic collapses, a strong unified Iran will be a force for stability and a regional bulwark against the Islamism under which the Iranian people now chafe.'[85] 'To the extent that the different nationalities each have their own identities and oppose the essentially Persian regime,' Edward Luttwak joins the chorus, 'they are likely to applaud external attacks on the nuclear installations rather than rally to the defense of their rulers.'[86] Luttwak ignores, of course, the fact that both President Ahmadinejad and Supreme Leader Ayatollah Ali Khamenei are members of the Turkish speaking community, which is the second second largest in contemporary Persia.

The logic of US foreign policies in West Asia

Realist insiders of the foreign policy establishment in Washington such as Joseph Nye are aware that the contraction of diplomatic power is always precipitated by the demise of international legitimacy.[87] By waging what was perceived (at least by the majority of states and peoples) to be an illegal war against Iraq, and by continuing to inscribe the narrative of endemic conflict in world politics, US neoconservatives have reified the notion of international anarchy, the dangerous kill-or-be-killed rationale of a Hobbesian world. 'There are ideas, and ways of thinking, with the seeds of life in them,' writes Raymond Williams, 'and there are others, perhaps deep in our minds, with the seeds of a general death.'[88] It appears to me that neoconservatism nurtures the latter kind of thinking, the desire to manufacture war, to dominate imperially, a desire that transcends the faultlines of domestic politics in the United States.[89] I have argued that to that end, the neoconservative apparatus mediates between three dimensions of the political cycle within the US and, by extension, within the transnational spheres of international society: (international) public discourse, (international) politics and (international) grand strategy.

Ultimately, neoconservatism functions as a mediation between individual events and the target enemy. To be more precise, by establishing a presence in public discourse through the media and institutions, in politics and in the foreign policy process of the United States, neoconservatives transform disparate crisis situations into a clear and immediate threat to the national security of the country. As a consequence, an event in West Asia is presented as more than just a singular occurrence. It is metamorphosed into a giant conspiracy against the United States (and Israel). Typically, it is alleged that a single, prime mover can be detected, *the* enemy par excellence, exemplified by Saddam Hussein after his invasion of Kuwait and now increasingly by Iran. Consider the statements during the Israeli invasion of Lebanon in the summer of 2006 in that regard.[90] 'No one should have any lingering doubts about what's going on in the Middle East,' Michael Ledeen stated. 'It's war [and] there is a common prime mover, and that is the Iranian mullahcracy, the revolutionary Islamic fascist state that declared war on us 27 years ago and has yet to be held accountable.'[91] Ledeen groups the Israeli invasion of Lebanon and the complex politics surrounding it into one whole encapsulated in the term 'Middle East'. He then moves on to link the conflict to Iran, the 'fascist state' that is considered to be the 'prime mover'. A similar logic motivates Larry Kudlow when he writes that '[a]ll of us in the free world owe Israel an enormous thank-you for defending freedom, democracy and security against the Iranian cat's-paw wholly-owned terrorist subsidiaries Hezbollah and Hamas.'[92] According to him they are not only 'defending their own homeland and very existence, but they are also defending America's homeland as our frontline democratic ally in the Middle East.'[93] So a conflict that emerged from the capture of Israeli soldiers by the Lebanese Hezbollah, and has a complex historical dynamic, is turned into a conflict between Iran, Hamas and Hezbollah on one side and the forces of freedom, Israel and the United States on the other. By means of this constellation, a whole new agenda opens up. Quite suddenly Iran is represented as a clear and immediate threat, not only to the United States but to Western civilization as a whole:

> What's happening in the Middle East, isn't just another chapter in the Arab-Israeli conflict. What's happening is an Islamist-Israeli war. … Better to say that what's under attack is liberal democratic civilization, whose leading representative right now happens to be the United States. … Communism became really dangerous when it seized control of Russia. National socialism became really dangerous when it seized control of Germany. Islamism became really dangerous when it seized control of Iran … The right response is renewed strength - in supporting the governments of Iraq and Afghanistan, in standing with Israel, and in pursuing regime change in Syria and Iran. For that matter, we might

consider countering this act of Iranian aggression with a military strike against Iranian nuclear facilities. Why wait? Does anyone think a nuclear Iran can be contained? That the current regime will negotiate in good faith? It would be easier to act sooner rather than later. Yes, there would be repercussions - and they would be healthy ones, showing a strong America that has rejected further appeasement.[94]

I hope that the reader will excuse the wide-ranging, perhaps excessive quotation from neoconservative writings in this part of the book. I have chosen to make them primarily as a means to show how neoconservatives invent political plots that often have had a 'causal' impact on policy. As we have seen, by means of these plots facts, myths, ideology, international crisis situations and US domestic politics are brought together within an artificial unity. It is this synthesis of the heterogeneous, the expression of complexity in a language that is approachable, which make these plots so appealing and which bring them so close to politics. By bringing together and integrating into one whole and complete unity complex and scattered issues, neoconservatives schematize and structure the direction of US foreign policies. This is especially pronounced and effective vis-à-vis an adversary that has an under-represented presence in the mainstream of American political culture because (a) many analysts and journalists in the United States have not moved beyond a largely perverted image of Iran and (b) the Iranian state continues to reify its anti-American posture on an almost daily basis (especially under the current Ahmadinejad administration).[95] A critical reading of these representations of Iran, which of course includes a critical view of what is being proposed in the present study, requires that you, the reader, grasp the mechanism and operations that unify disparate issues for political ends. You may thus deem it useful to delve into the 'prehistory' of political ideologies such as neoconservatism. The plots that I have tried to cover in this part of the book in relation to Iran emerge from that background. With this emergence also comes to the fore the implied target, in our case the Islamic Republic. In my opinion, understanding how this *target* is constituted as the prototypical *enemy* is central to understanding the manufacturing of war. Ideally, it would empower us to recognize 'an ideology as such, hence to pick it out from the properly argumentative modes, hence also to place it within the scope of a critique of ideology'.[96] It would equip me and you, in short, with a critical consciousness vis-à-vis world politics.

The density of neoconservative ideology engendered by the prolific writers mentioned above, and carried into the public domain by a myriad of think tanks and lobbying organizations does not of course mean that there are no competing narratives in the United States. Let there be no misunderstanding in this regard: I do not claim that neoconservatism has a total grip on the political culture in the country. This is quite impossible in a pluralistic democracy. But there is no escaping the fact that neoconservatives have a strong influence on the levers of power in Washington. This has been repeatedly lamented by former high-ranking officials. For example Graham Fuller, a former Vice-Chairman of the National Intelligence Council for long-range forecasting at the CIA, concedes that 'efforts to portray Iran with some analytical balance have grown more difficult, crowded out by inflamed rhetoric and intense pro-Israeli lobbying against Tehran in Congress'.[97] Stephen Walt and John J. Mearsheimer are equally critical. In an emphatic article published by the *London Review of Books* they argue that 'the thrust of US policy in the region derives almost entirely from domestic politics, and especially the activities of the "Israel Lobby".' Walt and Mearsheimer define that lobby as 'the loose coalition of individuals and organisations who actively work to steer US foreign policy in a pro-Israel direction.'[98] Zbigniew Brzezinski, another critic of the neoconservative agenda, goes one step further, relating these policies to cultural attitudes towards Muslims:

Government at every level has stimulated the paranoia. Consider, for example, the electronic billboards over interstate highways urging motorists to "Report Suspicious Activity" (drivers in turbans?). Some mass media have made their own contribution. The cable channels and some print media have found that horror scenarios attract audiences, while terror "experts" as "consultants" provide authenticity for the apocalyptic visions fed to the American public. Hence the proliferation of programs with bearded "terrorists" as the central villains. ... Hence the TV serials and films in which the evil characters have recognizable Arab features, sometimes highlighted by religious gestures, that exploit public anxiety and stimulate Islamophobia. Arab facial stereotypes, particularly in newspaper cartoons, have at times been rendered in a manner sadly reminiscent of the Nazi anti-Semitic campaigns. Lately, even some college student organizations have become involved in such propagation, apparently oblivious to the menacing connection between the stimulation of racial and religious hatreds and the unleashing of the unprecedented crimes of the Holocaust.[99]

One must agree with Walt and Mearsheimer that there is no such thing as a neoconservative headquarters, manifesto, conspiracy or even party. There are Republican and Democrat activists, Jewish and non-Jewish functionaries, Christian fundamentalist and Muslim sympathizers, entertainers such as Glenn Beck and 'historians' such as Andrew Roberts. Indeed, the empirical evidence suggests that the pervasive concentration of think tanks and activists—the neoconservative apparatus—transcends the faultlines of domestic politics in the United States. Ultimately, the term neoconservatism denotes the latest manifestation of America's contemporary imperial strategy. Because this strategy is lodged within an overarching imperial attitude, it permeates the overall political culture of the country to its core, which explains why it is not easily discarded. So when Democrat leaders such as Barack Obama announce that in dealing with Iran 'we must never take the military option off the table,'[100] or when Hillary Clinton states that 'to those who believe we should become involved only if it is easy to do, I think we have to say that America has never and should not ever shy away from the hard task if it is the right one,'[101] they reveal a comparable, if less raucously stated belief in the special status of the United States. It is this general consensus about America's 'indispensable' global leadership role, the firm belief in unipolarity, in the US-centric configuration of world politics, that has engendered and sustained the image of Iran as an 'international pariah' which is shared by both neoconservatives and 'missionary' liberals. Along with this image goes a 'macro-culture'. This is the overarching habitat I have explored at the beginning of this part of the book in relation to the ideas of Gadamer and Farabi, the place where the image of Iran as an international threat is implanted. For what gives the country its negative image in the 'West' is not its own ontological content, not even the confrontational rhetoric of the Islamic Republic, but the act of institution, an installation, a consecration that gives significance to what has, in itself, a neutral content.[102] It is within a comparable, very tight-knit, very ubiquitous cultural habitat that the invasion of Iraq was made possible, and it is within a similarly pervasive *Kriegskontext* that the idea of military intervention against Iran is cultivated.[103] I hope that I have made it clear that neoconseravtive ideology is central to this process, because it groups disparate issues together and integrates them into one whole, because it cuts down alternatives, because it reduces complexity, because it continuously works to give quasi-legitimacy to its ultimate aim, which is war:

> Make no mistake, President Bush will need to bomb Iran's nuclear facilities before leaving office. It is all but inconceivable that Iran will accept any peaceful inducements to abandon its drive for the bomb. Its rulers are religio-ideological fanatics who will not trade what they believe is their birthright to great power status for a mess of pottage. Even if things in Iraq get better, a nuclear-armed Iran will negate any progress there. Nothing will embolden terrorists and jihadists more than a nuclear-armed Iran.

The global thunder against Bush when he pulls the trigger will be deafening, and it will have many echoes at home. … We need to pave the way intellectually now and be prepared to defend the action when it comes. In particular, we need to help people envision what the world would look like with a nuclear-armed Iran. Apart from the dangers of a direct attack on Israel or a suitcase bomb in Washington, it would mean the end of the global nonproliferation regime and the beginning of Iranian dominance in the Middle East.

This defense should be global in scope. There is a crying need in today's ideological wars for something akin to the Congress for Cultural Freedom of the Cold War, a global circle of intellectuals and public figures who share a devotion to democracy. The leaders of this movement might include Tony Blair, Vaclav Havel, and Anwar Ibrahim.[104]

The purpose of revealing transnational neoconservative propaganda is not to deny differences in US foreign policies. I am not suggesting a monocausal link between neoconservatism and hostiltity towards Iran, not any automatism or inevitable political outcome. Neither do I claim that Iranians are naïve bystanders in all this. The Campaign Against Sanctions and Military Intervention in Iran (CASMII), for instance, has spearheaded a public relations strategy in order to counter media distortions about Iran's nuclear file in particular and the foreign affairs of the country in general.[105] The Iranian state itself on the other side, has tried to counter US moves to isolate the country by strengthening its commercial transactions with South Africa, India, China and Russia; by 'bandwagoning' with leftist leaders in Latin America, particularly Hugo Chavez in Venezuela, Fidel Castro in Cuba, Evo Morales in Bolivia and Daniel Ortega in Nicaragua; and by 'reassuring' other leaders in the Third World and the wider Muslim worlds about its nuclear intentions.

Yet the transnational neoconservative media, many leading US politicians, the Israeli state, a whole range of activists and journalists, and some academic experts continue to reify the general consensus that Iran is a threat to world order, if not to 'Western' civilization. Now this is not the same as saying that only deliberately subjective things are said about Iran. Neither does it mean, as Sadeq Zibakalam and Mashallah Shamsolvaezin stated after the first direct Iranian-American inter-governmental negotations since the Islamic revolution—talks focused on Iraq and held in Baghdad on 28 May 2007—that Iran and the US could not overcome their differences. It does mean, however, that neoconservatives and their allies will continously and rather relentlessly exert pressure to derail any type of diplomatic engagement between the two states. What I have hoped to explore in this part of the book, then, is the nihilistic international agenda that neoconservatism promotes, the social engineering of a militaristic ideology which has secured a place in that ferociously contested space I have called 'international political culture'.[106] How else can we interpret the comments of Patrick Clawson at a symposium organized by the militant *FrontPageMag.com* in July 2005? Clawson bluntly advocated covert operations in order to sabotage nuclear facilities in Iran: 'Accidents are known to happen (remember Three Mile Island or Chernobyl). If there were to be a series of crippling accidents at Iranian nuclear facilities, that would set back the Iranian program.'[107]

Ultimately, then, neoconservative functionaries inscribe the narrative of war in international relations; they inscribe it in stituions (e.g. the Committee on the Present Danger), language (e.g. the 'axis of evil'), mindsets (e.g. 'Why do they hate us?'), and policies (e.g. the doctrine of preemption). This strategy transforms other countries into replaceable variables. To be more precise, preemption and the 'war on terror' are made into versatile ideological agents that can be employed to legitimate war *globally*—not only in the Iraqi, Somali, Iranian, Venezuelan or Syrian context, but also with regard to other conflict scenarios (China-Taiwan, Russia-Chechnya, etc.). From this perspective Lebanon, Palestine, Afghanistan, Iraq, Iran are just episodes in the same imperial project, namely the 'Fourth World War' invented by Eliot Cohen and popularized by James Woolsey. This political strategy is reassuringly mimetic: once a specific war project has bedded in, its supposed chivalry is loudly trumpeted, bundled up in a morally righteous and infallible narrative—in essence the legitimation of US imperialism—and stitched into the political fabric of contemporary America. It is in this sense that neoconservatism reveals itself as war—a war continued by other means. The perverse irony of this ideology is that it makes some of us think that it serves the liberation of mankind.

PART IV
IRAN'S PLURALISTIC MOMENTUM AND THE FUTURE OF IRANIAN DEMOCRACY

The City, then, in which people aim through association at co-operating for the things by which felicity in its real and true sense can be attained, is the excellent city, and the society in which there is a co-operation to acquire felicity is the excellent society; and the nation in which all of its cities co-operate for those things through which felicity is attained is the excellent nation. In the same way, the excellent universal state will arise only when all the nations in it co-operate for the purpose of reaching felicity.

—Abu Nasr Farabi, *'Mabadi ara ahl al-madinat al-fadilah'* (The Perfect State)

The nature of the Prophet's religious experience, as disclosed in the Qur'an … is individual experience creative of a social order. Its immediate outcome is the fundamentals of a polity with implicit legal concepts whose civic significance cannot be belittled merely because their origin is revelational. The religious ideal of Islam, therefore, is organically related to the social order which it has created. The rejection of the one will eventually involve the rejection of the other. Therefore, the construction of a polity on national lines, if it means a displacement of the Islamic principle of solidarity, is simply unthinkable to a Muslim.

—Muhammad Iqbal *(Struggle for Independence)*

The failures of the reformists and the making of the Ahmadinejad Presidency

At the end of its fifth national congress in November 2003, the Islamic Iran Participation Front (IIPF), one of the main reform parties in Iran, issued a strategic communiqué referring to the seventh parliament (*majlis*) election as 'a turning point in the reforms movement of the country', emphasizing that the survival of the movement depended on the presence of those who favour 'the mentality of reforms at the polls'.[1] A turning point it was: their candidates barred, major legislation delayed, the trust of Iran's younger generation lost, the reform movement had to accept that for the time being institutionalized power proved to be stronger than the calls for change articulated by Iran's burgeoning civil society. Consequently, on 1 February 2004, a date symbolically chosen as the anniversary of the return of Ayatollah Khomeini to Tehran 25 years earlier, 120 Iranian members of parliament resigned in protest at the mass barring of candidates from the 'Seventh Islamic Consultative Assembly' election.[2] In their declaration to then *majlis* speaker Mehdi Karroubi they said they were unwilling 'to be present in a parliament that is not capable of defending the rights of the people and which is unable to prevent elections in which the people cannot chose their representatives.'[3] In a speech entitled 'Advocating the Republic' at Tehran's Amir Kabir University, Mohsen Armin defended the election boycott:

> The Islamic Revolution took place with the Islam propagated by Ali Shariati, late Ayatollah Morteza Motahari and the late Imam Khomeini. If we replace it with the Islam of the dignitaries, we will face the situation we are facing right now … Islam in the Islamic Republic comes from the hearts of the people which is separate from the Fiqh-oriented Islam.[4]

But the election boycott turned out to be self-defeating. Without a parliamentary mandate, the reformers failed to solicit piecemeal compromises from the ruling clergy, which was the initial aim of the strategy advocated by Said Hajjarian.[5] As a result the Guardian Council, which functions as a 'Supreme Court' in charge of vetting the candidates for the parliamentary elections, won out, the chaperones of Iranian (neo)conservatism took over and the *majlis* lost its popular mandate for political and socio-economic change.[6]

The ninth presidential election, in June 2005, caused another blow to the IIPF. Despite its alliance with the semi-official Iran Freedom Movement, a group founded in the 1960s by the late Mehdi Bazargan and currently headed by Ibrahim Yazdi (the first foreign minister of the Islamic Republic after the revolution in 1979),[7] the party failed to mobilize support beyond the intelligentsia and the student population. In retrospect, it did not come as a surprise that the chief candidate of the IIPF, Mostafa Moin, received a disappointing share of the vote.[8] With the defeat in the ninth presidential election, the reformers lost their last bastion of institutional power; this indicated a steady demise of the movement since the parliamentary elections in June 2000. In that year, reformers controlled the executive and legislative branches of the government, as well as the municipal councils.[9] Yet despite the popular mandate, they failed to meet the demands of the electorate. The economy of the country remained stagnant, the socio-economic gaps within Iranian society widened and cultural freedoms remained stymied. The mixed results of the reformers were conceded by Mohammad Khatami in his 47-page philosophical 'letter for the future' addressed to Iran's youth amidst growing disappointment with the pace of reforms: 'We do not pretend that our attempt to defend the rights of the people have succeeded in every domain,' he proclaimed, maintaining, nonetheless, that there 'have been changes of such an extent in social, cultural and political relations that it is impossible to return to the period of before the reforms'.[10]

The previously unknown Islamic Iran Developers Council (*Etelaf-e Abadgaran-e Eslami*) capitalized on the widespread discontent with Khatami in the municipal elections in 2003, winning the majority of seats in Tehran. The members of the Council promptly elected Mahmoud Ahmadinejad as Mayor in April 2003. A year later the *Abadgaran*, in tandem with the second major neoconservative party, the Society of Devotees of the Islamic Revolution (*Jame-e Isargaran-e Enqelab-e Eslami*), won the largest number of parliamentary votes including most of the seats in Tehran. Using the term 'neoconservative' to describe these factions needs some qualification here. The first thing I would like to mention is that domestically, Iranian neoconservatism is not monolithically 'capitalistic', and in terms of foreign relations, it does not have expansionary aims. The Right elsewhere, as in the United States or the United Kingdom for instance, usually has a strong tendency towards deregulated capitalism which manifests itself in tax-cuts for the upper classes and less emphasis on social welfare. There is also typically a propensity for aggresssive foreign policies (e.g. Reaganism and Thatcherism). Mahmoud Ahmadinejad and his institutional backers, on the contrary, have advocated social welfare for the poor, capital redistribution and anti-corruption measures, and have thus far pursued a rather 'pragmatic', if rhetorically confrontational, foreign policy agenda. So what makes Iran's right-wing 'neoconservative'?

A quick perusal of the 'sociology' of Iranian neoconservatism shows that the movement has emerged out of the cultural attitude of patriarchal traditionalism among those orthodox strata of Iranian society whose ultimate aim is to preserve (rather than reform) the political structure of the Islamic Republic and reify (rather than reinterpret) the political tenets of 'Khomeinism'. Ultimately, Iran's right wing has inherited the chauvinism of Persian nationalism heralded by the Pahlavi monarchs, and the populism of the early revolutionary years. Thus they are representative of

Iran's political culture both before and after the Islamic revolution in 1979. On the one hand, not unlike the Shah, Ahmadinejad and his followers feel quite comfortable advocating equality, emancipation, justice and virtue abroad, while closing down reformist newspapers, intimidating intellectuals, banning internationally acclaimed films and classical literature, and harassing nongovernmental organizations within Iran. And on the other hand, they portray themselves as the guardians of the 'Imam's line' (*khatt-e imam*, Ayatollah Khomeini's legacy), ignoring the fact that Khomeini led a movement for revolutionary change, not reification of the status quo. Thus far this new breed of Iranian conservatives has successfully merged shrewd political brinkmanship vis-à-vis the country's clerical elite with an agenda of 'Islamic socialism' aimed at the majority, lower-income strata of the Iranian population.[11] It was not least through successful implementation of this dual strategy—mobilizing the right wing of Iranian politics on the one side and appealing to the lower middle class of Iranian society on the other—that Mahmoud Ahmadinejad was able to take the ninth Presidency of the Islamic Republic in June 2005.[12]

Women's rights activists, civil society and Iran's pluralistic momentum

If we would measure the success of Iran's reformers by their own standards, we need to accept the dismal prospect that the reform movement is dead. There have been many signs pointing in that direction: the announcement by the minister for Culture and Islamic Guidance, Mohammad Hossein Saffar-Harandi, that the ministry will block the activities of non-governmental associations as well as newspapers that 'attack' religious values; the closure of a range of reformist newspapers; the campaign to tighten the censorship regime of the internet by contracting the Iranian company Delta Global;[13] the arrest of writers and activists and the prolonged detention of human rights lawyers, as documented in the quarterly human rights report from the 'Defenders of Human Rights Centre' in Tehran which is directed by the Nobel Prize winner Shirin Ebadi.[14] Yet, for every report of anti-democratic measures by the Iranian government, one may cite consequential changes within the seemingly undifferentiated Islamic polity itself.

In my opinion, emphasis on what is going wrong in Iran needs to be complemented with the achievements of Iranian society vis-à-vis the state. Consider the increasingly bold women's rights movement in Iran, which receives scant coverage in the 'liberal', 'pro-emancipatory' 'Western' press, and here especially the success of women candidates in the municipal elections of 2007. Out of 264 seats available on councils in provincial capitals, 44 went to women; there were majority votes for female candidates in Shiraz, Hamadan, Qazvin, Ardebil and Arak. In the former two cities, female candidates who are still in their twenties polled the most votes.[15] Consider also the 'One Million Signatures' campaign, 'which is designed to help reform discriminatory laws … and is a continuation of the women's peaceful gatherings on 12 June 2005 and 2006, that ended by violent attacks of the police and security forces. From both tactical and strategic points of view', Nayereh Tohidi explains,

> this latest campaign is in line with an envisioned future where powers, opportunities and social goods are not divided based on gender differences or sexual orientation. Primarily initiated by the younger generation of women's rights activists, this campaign seems to be turning into a point of convergence among many groups and individual activists in different parts of Iran. … By employing a door-to-door and face-to-face educational strategy, the One Million Signatures Campaign will teach our activists a lot about social realities on the ground. In light of these teachings, instead of throwing themselves in the harms way and carrying the brunt of reform costs, separate from people, the women's movement's activists will be able to have a wider and more practical impact in unison with people, one that is accompanied by pressure

from people and their full participation. … As evident from the writings of the activists in this campaign, unlike political parties, the women's movement has neither the intention of over-throwing the government, nor of seizing the state power. They reach beyond governments and aim at transforming the dominant cultural, social, economical, and political relations to achieve greater equality. Women's struggle in today's Iran is primarily a cultural and legal one, which is fought in a historical context rather than a battlefield.[16]

The indicators cited in the World Bank's 2007 report on Economic Development and Prospects in the Middle East and North Africa region show the upward social mobility of Iranian women. According to the report, women's participation in economic affairs increased from 33 per cent in 2001 to 41 per cent in 2006. In addition, the number of female graduates starting a career has risen by 10 per cent every year between 2000 to 2005.

The Iranian reform movement, then, has more depth than its contemporary institutional infrastructure reveals. If we were to reduce the movement to the party manifestos of the IIPF, the Organization of the Islamic Republic's Mojahedin (*Sazeman-e mujahedin-e enqelab-e eslami*) or the third largest reformist organization, the Solidarity Party (*Hezb-e hambastegi*), we would neglect the history and intellectual breadth of Iran's democracy project. Those with some insight into the domestic politics of Iran would agree that the reform movement is rooted in—and nurtured by—an increasingly pluralistic civil society.[17] To put it in more rigorous terms: contemporary Iranian reformism manifests itself as a trajectory, yet original and indigenous, political culture that feeds into the political process in a bottom-up process—from society to the state—not the other way around.

A quick look at some of former President Mohammad Khatami's speeches and the manifestos of the main reform parties reveals that they are heavily influenced by the thoughts of key contemporary Iranian intellectuals such as Javad Tabatabai, Mohsen Kadivar, Mohammad Mojtahed Shabestari, Abdol-Karim Soroush and others.[18] These thinkers are the vanguard of what Reza Shakeri, Hamidreza Jalaeipour and others call the 'neo-Islamic' heirs of Ali Shariati's critical theory.[19] They have embarked on a perilous theoretical journey to redefine the ideational tenets of the Islamic Republic and here especially what Soroush calls the 'fascist' disposition of some segments of Iranian society. Iranian women activists and gender theoreticians make a comparable impact: 'As non-Western women,' Nushin Ahmadi Khorasani pointed out on Iran's International Women's Day in March 2000, 'we have over a century of experience in the women's movement … Regardless of any "ism" or school of thought, the quest for justice is what we women have nourished in our children's minds.'[20] 'The women's movement in Iran is comprised of diverse groups, various activities and tactics,' Nayereh Tohidi elaborates:

> Some are engaged in organizing anti-violence workshops and anti-war activities as *Zanan-e Solh* (Women of Peace); some focus on feminist consciousness raising and egalitarian cultural production through print journals such as *Zanan* (Women) and *Hoquq-e Zanan* (Women's Rights), some are doing this through internet journals such as *Zanestan* (http://www.herlandmag.org), *Hastia Andish*, *Kannon-e Zanan-e Iran* (http://www.irwomen), *Meydan* and [through student organizations] such as 'The Women's Committee of the Office to Foster Unity' and the 'Alumni Organization of Iran' (*Advare Tahkime Vahdat, Sazemane Daneshamookhtegane Iran*).

The development of Iran's women's rights movement—to the extent that within one generation many Iranian women have ceased to think as they had been thinking up till then and have reinterpreted their social role—has been initiated by opposition women activists seeking to overthrow what is perceived to be Iran's overbearing patriarchic social order from within. As a result, the entire gender equation propagated by the Islamic Republic, the idea of the ultimate model of the Muslim woman (*olgu-ye zan-e mosalman*), finds its fundamental ideological content modified.

The relative success of this emergent counter-culture is due to the fact that its agents are spread around Iranian society. They include filmmakers like Rakhshan Banie'temad, Samira Makhmalbaf, Niki Karimi and Tahmineh Milani, prominent human rights lawyers such as Shirin Ebadi and Mehranguiz Kar, publishers and editors such as Shahla Lahiji and Shahla Sherkat, and other activists such as Jamileh Kadivar, Azam Ala'i Taleghani, Shahla Habibi, Zahra Rahnavard and Fakhrosadat Mohtashamipour.

It is beyond the scope of this part of the book to outline the political theory of the activists and intellectuals on both sides of the gender divide in more detail.[21] Suffice it to say, at this stage, that many segments of Iran's post-revolutionary generation are attracted to the critical reading of the Islamic Republic advocated by them.[22] What is important for our line of argument is that these thinkers' ideas are part of a pervasive culture of reformist thought that transcends the confines of the state. They attempt to reconcile such seemingly incompatible concepts such as faith and freedom (Shabestari), reason and revelation (Kadivar), *sharia* and democracy (Soroush), philosophy and religious ordinances (Tabatabai), and feminism and Islam (Tusi). In the first decade of the Islamic revolution the fundamental political and socio-economic order was that of total systems and each particular faction of society was lodged within this overall configuration (those who opposed it were 'dislodged').[23] In present-day Iran, every issue is subjected to proof by interpretation, that is, nothing will be accepted until society is persuaded to 'lodge' into the political and socio-economic process. This is the fundamental difference between revolutionary Iran and post-revolutionary Iran: whereas during the former period consensus was established without reference to an exterior agent (i.e. society), the latter establishes consensus and order through mediation *with* society. One may thus say, more specifically, that the intellectual tradition carried forward by critical Iranian intellectuals on the one side, and the burgeoning infrastructure of Non Governmental-Organizations (NGOs), professional unions, and grassroots advocacy groups on the other, have fostered a de-monopolization of the political process and, *ipso facto*, have led to a 'pluralistic momentum.'[24] It is this pluralistic momentum, I think, that engenders the imperceptive driving force of the post-revolutionary democratic movement in Iran.[25] One has to be careful with historical comparisons, but in that specific sense, Iran's current transformation process is not entirely different from changes in other post-revolutionary societies. Consider Leon Trotsky's diagnosis of post-revolutionary Russia in the late 1920s:

> The process of economic and cultural development in the Soviet Union has already passed through several stages, but has by no means arrived at an inner equilibrium. If you remember that the task of socialism is to create a classless society based upon solidarity and the harmonious satisfaction of all needs, there is not yet, in this fundamental sense, a hint of socialism in the Soviet Union. To be sure, the contradictions of Soviet society are deeply different from the contradictions of capitalism. But they are nevertheless very tense. They find their expression in material and cultural inequalities, governmental repressions, political groupings, and the struggle of factions. Police repression hushes up and distorts a political struggle, but does not eliminate it. The thoughts which are forbidden exercise an influence on the governmental policy at every step, fertilising or blocking it. In these circumstances, an analysis of the development of the Soviet Union cannot for a minute neglect to consider those ideas and slogans under which a stifled but passionate political struggle is being waged throughout the country. History here merges directly with living politics.[26]

Towards a reformation of the Islamic Republic?

The central characteristic of the pluralistic momentum in Iran is that the clerical establishment can no longer take for granted the allegiance of their client social strata. Pluralism engenders competition, state policies have to be 'sold' to an audience that is no longer obliged to 'buy' from one source. In this 'market situation' the monopoly on political power is dissected. As a result, institutions and elites operating within the domain of the state have to organize themselves in such a way as to mobilize their respective constituencies. They enter into a competitive situation with other groups who follow the same political rationale. Comparing electoral campaigns in Tehran, Shiraz, Ahwaz, Tabriz, Isfahan, Boroujerd and other cities during the summer of 2005, I considered it as one of the rather more remarkable aspects that the presidential candidates, including Mahmoud Ahmadinejad, scarcely employed Islamic imagery or reference to the political will of Ayatollah Khomeini to further their agenda. Political allegiance in contemporary Iran, it appears, is no longer directed primarily at the institution of the Leader. It is not the approval of the *Rahbar* that political parties struggle for. It is *public* opinion that matters.

Secondly, all institutions attached to the state are under pressure to produce 'results', especially in the economic sphere. In turn, this pressure in a competitive situation engenders the 'rationalization' of policies. This explains why both reformers and conservatives advocate economic growth and public participation in the political and cultural process. In a pluralistic situation where political parties become marketing agencies of the state, reform ceases to be a monopoly of the self-declared reformist parties. In other words, the reform agenda is of necessity intrinsic to the political process comprising all state institutions; it transcends the monocausal conservative-reformist divide, because the functioning of the whole state apparatus depends on the participation of the public. Public relations with the client social strata, lobbying, fund-raising, involvement with the secular economy—in all these aspects of the humdrum affairs of the state, the Islamic Republic is dependent on the civil society of the country. In such an interactive situation is it not impossible (for conservatives and reformists alike) to sell policies to a population of consumers without taking their wishes concerning the content of those policies into account? I think it is impossible. I am not claiming that the institutions within the domain of the state have conceded their formal powers—they have retained them, of course. But the pluralistic momentum has 'functionally differentiated' the *Machtkonsens* (power consensus) amongst the political elites in Iran. During the first decade of the Islamic Republic, it was Ayatollah Khomeini who authoritatively expressed that consensus. His legitimacy, albeit not total, was sufficiently massive and durable to maintain the political elites within the revolutionary framework (the Islamic Republican Party was the most influential manifestation of the power consensus dictating Iranian domestic politics in the first decade of the revolution). That framework expanded after his death in 1989. Not that Iran emerged as a 'republican democracy' in the Habermasian sense.[27] But the differentiation of the revolutionary polity into competing factions has reduced the ability of the state to conduct politics in the consensual mode.[28]

The anatomy of change in Iran

A comprehensive account of Iran's painful post-revolutionary transformation process has to move beyond an analysis of the state. It is Iran's active civil society that constitutes the momentum of the country's pluralistic situation, not the government. The pluralistic momentum, emerging from below, negates the binary and total opposition between political 'masters' and 'slaves' at the root of state-society relations. Where there is pluralism there is critique, defiance and opposition exercised from innumerable points within society. The pluralistic momentum is therefore not something that can be channelled, redirected or hermetically contained by a political faction or strata of society. There is no single locus, no unitarian institution, no ideational agent, no sacrosanct HQ to be conquered. The pluralistic momentum in Iran is by definition an omnipresent yet polymorphous phenomenon.

True, the demands articulated by women's rights activists, students, and intellectuals do not, by themselves, determine the substantive contents or direction of political and socio-economic reforms. They simply generate the dynamic making change possible. However, there are some other factors in Iran's contemporary societal situation that have substantive influence on the character of this change. Insofar as the highly educated Iranian population has access to the instruments of modern mass communication, their preference settings will reflect this. This is an important prerequisite for the emergence of a pluralistic society. The ability to choose and to evaluate alternative world-views requires freedom to go beyond state-manufactured 'facts'. Such freedom depends on socio-economic conditions which provide access to alternative world-views, not least through education and modern mass communication.[29]

There is a common theme to the foregoing: Iranian civil society on the one side and the technological opportunities that are available to the highly educated population of the country on the other have set off the de-monopolization of Iranian politics. The mass distribution of ideas through the internet and satellite television, for instance, have de-emphasized the importance of the state-controlled media and have, quite literally, penetrated the Iranian living room with a whole new set of ideas, values, norms and world-views.[30] In this struggle, does the state not yield its function as the monopolist of political ideas? Does its ability to impose renunciations and restrictions upon society not atrophy under the pressures of a 'cumbersome' population which is no longer bound to accept a single ideology?

I think the Iranian state has lost its monopoly over the political culture of the country to other sources of political thinking, to a whole assemblage of intellectuals, filmmakers, women's rights activists, student leaders, and so on, who all represent the realities of Iranian society far better and—crucially—far more effectively than the state does.[31] In fact, the contemporary Iranian state cannot fulfil the central goal expressed in article 3 of the Constitution, that is, 'raising the level of public awareness in all areas, through the proper use of the press, mass media, and other means', because the pluralistic situation has created new outlets for the dissemination of news and information. 'One should not be misled by the continuity in the regime's ideological language and some features—such as the handful of intellectuals of the pre-revolutionary years who continue to be revered: Ahmad Shamlu, Mehdi Akhavan Sales, Nima Yoshij, Forough Farrokhzad, Ali Shariati,' Fariba Adelkhah remarks. 'Society has become differentiated and more complex, and none of the actors can hope any more for a monopoly over it.'[32] In other words, the Iranian state is no longer the only authoritative representative of the country's political reality. Somehow the entire balance of power is changing. And it seems to me that it is the new, post-revolutionary generation that slowly imposes the political realities on the establishment, and not the other way around.[33]

Moreover, in a situation where the state cannot sustain order and its own legitimacy except by force, society will celebrate those who are condemned, those who dare to challenge the all-encompassing claim of an authoritarian state. This is what happened to Ali Shariati and Ayatollah Khomeini in the 1960s and 1970s. They continue to be revered by Iranians because they dared to speak out against the dictatorship of the Shah and because this 'crime' was widely advertised by the Pahlavi state. A comparable 'crime' and a comparable process elevated the condemned of the Islamic Republic to national stardom. The killings of the Foruhars in 1998, the prison sentences on Akbar Ganji and Eshkevari, the trials of Hashem Aghajari, Abdollah Nouri and Mohsen Kadivar, transformed the protagonists into 'folk heroes' both by the sheer extent of their widely advertised 'crimes' and by their protests against the oligarchs, against the rich, against the powerful, against a system that criminalizes freedom of speech thus blurring the boundaries between the murderer and the intellectual. Consequently, the silent residue of the powers of authoritarianism in Iran is a whole cadre of 'criminal intellectuals' who are not only pardoned by society but revered for their crimes. Indeed, criminalizing freedom of speech has transferred the ability to make legitimate judgement from the state to society itself, because common sense dictates that there is a normative difference between speaking one's mind and theft, because every condemnation brings into play the dissymmetry between the subject who has dared to make a public statement and the sovereign who displays his all-encompassing powers. Every show of force of this kind reminds Iranians that there continues to be a huge discrepancy between the libertarian demands articulated during the Islamic revolution and the reality on the ground, thus engendering political activism to close that gap. This is what an Islamic revolution in the name of the oppressed legitimated; it granted Iranians the absolute right to rise up and criticize those who exercise worldly power and claim transcendental authority at the same time.

The dialectics of Iran's emerging political economy

Some sceptics will point to the fact that the state continues to have a central presence in Iranian society, especially in the economic spheres. But is society always at the receiving end of political-economic dynamics? Is there a hierarchical relationship between the market and the state on the one hand and society and the individual on the other? Let me elaborate on those questions for a moment. The most prominent approaches to the political economy of West Asia—post-colonial approaches, but also to a certain extent the rentier state model and Marxist theory—tend to presume a causal transmission belt between economic macro-structures and events 'on the ground', i.e. changes within society. I am aware that I am simplifying, but it is perhaps true to say that all three approaches agree on a basic methodological premise: they tend to analyze 'political-economics' in a top-down fashion, from the core to the periphery, from the macro-structure of the world economy to society, from the capitalist system to the individual, and they tend to consider the state as the primary locus for political-economic activity and the main focus of socio-economic change. These common points may be called 'macro-structural economism' in the analysis of state-society relations: the view that material dynamics are the primary factor determining the inter-relationship between state and society, and that the parameters of this interdependence are primarily defined by political and/or economic macro-structures which affect society from 'above'. That emphasis on material factors is most prominently pronounced in Karl Marx's Preface to *Critique of Political Economy* which was published in 1859:

In the social production which men carry on they enter into definite relations that are indispensable and independent of their will; these relations of production correspond to a definite stage of development of their material powers of production. The sum total of these relations of production constitutes the economic structure of society—the real foundation, on which rise legal and political superstructures and to which correspond definite forms of social consciousness. The mode of production in material life determines the general character of the social, political and spiritual process of life. It is not the consciousness of men that determines their existence, but, on the contrary their social existence determines their consciousness. ... With the change of the economic foundation the entire immense superstructure is more or less rapidly transformed. In considering such transformations the distinction should always be made between the material transformation of the economic conditions of production which can be determined with the precision of natural science, and the legal, political, religious, aesthetic, or philosophic—in short, ideological forms in which men become conscious of this conflict and fight it out.[34]

The primacy of material factors is re-emphasized by Friedrich Engels:

According to the materialist conception of history, the determining element in history is *ultimately* the production and reproduction in real life. More than this neither Marx nor I have ever asserted. If therefore somebody twists this into the statement that the economic element is the *only* determining one, he transforms it into a meaningless, abstract and absurd phrase. The economic situation is the basis, but the various elements of the superstructure ... also exercise their influence upon the course of historical struggles and in many cases preponderate in determining their form. There is an interaction of all these elements, in which, amid all the endless host of accidents (i.e. things and events whose inner connection is so remote or so impossible to prove that we regard it as absent and can neglect it) the economic element finally asserts itself as necessary.[35]

For Marx and Engels the mode of production in material life determines and constitutes the general character of the social, political and spiritual process of society. The superstructure in which ideological factors reveal themselves is a matter of human consciousness which is dependent on—even a product of—the economic structure and the consequent social relations There are interactions, but in the final analysis a Marxist would deny that the laws of human consciousness and the ensuing norms, ideas and cultures are the prime movers of society; the primary factor is the economic process. What alternatives are there if we would want to reverse this interrelationship analytically, in order to further our understanding of the way the pluralistic momentum functions within Iranian society? How can we develop a perspective that explores action on the societal level and not the seemingly pervasive economic structures penetrating it from 'above'?

If, for genealogical purposes, we want to 'locate' the source of political-economic action in contemporary Iran, it seems logical to ask about its 'agents' or 'engineers' in the first place. From the perspective of some mainstream political scientists, the answer is quite obvious: it must be the 'self-interested' state that constitutes the primary unit of analysis, with regard to both national and international politics: 'Throughout modern history,' writes Robert Gilpin symptomatically,

> states have pursued policies promoting the development of industry, advanced technology, and those economic activities with the highest profitability and generation of employment within their own borders. As far as they can, states try to create an international division of labour favourable to their political and economic interests. Indeed, economic nationalism is likely to be a significant influence in international relations as long as the state system exists.[36]

Indeed, in our case, a quick look at the economic transformations immediately after the Islamic revolution in 1979 appears to show that the state is at the centre of the economic process in Iran. Applying the state-centred economic theory advocated by the 'liberal-left' factions of the Iranian revolution organized around the first President of the Islamic Republic, Abol-Hassan Banisadr, and the first Prime Minister, Mehdi Bazargan (differences notwithstanding), the revolution in 1979 initiated a massive programme of nationalization of major sectors of the economy, including all private banks, insurance companies, all heavy industries (automobile, mining and metals etc.) and all factories and organizations that had accumulated unrecoverable debts. The Iranian state hence assumed direct and indirect authority over the national economy primarily through the National Iranian Industries Organization, the Industrial Development and Renovation Organization and a range of charitable and semi-public foundations such as the *Bonyad-e Mostazafan va Janbazan* (Foundation of the Oppressed and Self-Sacrificers), *Bonyad-e Shahid* (Martyr's Foundation), *Bonyad-e Panzdah-e Khordad* or the *Bonyad-e Astan-e Qods-e Razavi*. But does this economic structure automatically mean that society is always in a subordinate position relative to the state and its economic macro-system? Is society always the 'recipient' of 'macro-pressures'?

In the first place, the appropriation of state power over the national economy is not concomitant with the expansion of state authority over society. It is not only that expanding the size of the state in fact raises popular expectations; that the state is likely to be held accountable for real and perceived socio-economic injustices, corruption in the public sector and social deprivation, especially if the state presents itself as a moral and ethical guide as it does in the Iranian case.[37] There is also a major methodological issue at stake here. In my opinion, the 'formal' power over economic regulations, administrations and institutions exercised by the state should not be confused with the 'informal' power of society to criticize, refuse to submit, and change these formal structures. The political economy of Iran, in other words, cannot be explained in terms of the difference between that unit of analysis which is thought to formally hold near-total economic power (i.e. the state) and the agent that submits to it (i.e. society). This is not only because the recent government-sponsored privatization of major sectors of the economy including the banking sector, and the provision of free trade areas, have contracted the presence of the state in the national economy, a trend that has been re-emphasized by Ayatollah Ali Khamenei's 'Action Plan' aimed at ceding 80 per cent of the shares of large companies to the Iranian public—which according to him will lead to a shift in the government's role 'from direct involvement in ownership and running the large companies to supervisory and guidance of different sectors of the economy to meet the regulations of the World Trade Organization (WTO) gradually'.[38] It is not only this trend towards 'deregulation' which has empowered society vis-à-vis the state that challenges the premise that economic macro-structures primarily operate in a top-down fashion.[39] There is also the fact that the political economy always circulates, that it cannot be monopolized by one single unit, the state, the multinational company or other agents.

Rational-choice theory has accustomed us to study political-economic phenomena in terms of cost-benefit calculations and/or the utility-maximizing drive of *homo oeconomicus*. This type of analysis presumes that rationality is unitarian, that it is solely based on material self-satisfaction and that the modern state, its complementary institutions and individuals themselves embody and exercise this rationality on a daily basis. But insofar as rationality is relative and not merely reducible to material concerns, rational choice theory does not tell us much about the way preference settings emerge. Consider the opposition of the bazaar network to the policies of the Shah, which was central to the success of the Islamic revolution in 1979. A simple cost-benefit analysis would deem that opposition 'irrational'—there was no immediate material gain involved. But in my opinion, it is problematic to analyze economic and political processes merely in terms of 'rational choice theory', as if self-interest is equal to material profit, as if it can be detached from what the constitution of the 'self' is in the first place. Political-economic phenomena are both cyclical (rather than strictly hierarchical) and structural (they are overlaid by other factors, e.g. norms, values, and other cultural artefacts). They are engineered by a range of self-conscious agents which may be positioned on a multidimensional 'analytical cycle' encompassing the state, society, the bazaar, and the fruit merchant at the end of the street, who all have different preferences that are not merely material. These 'agents', then, are not external to the political economy. They are its effects, they are effected by the political-economic system but are also the social engineers of that very system. As a structural phenomenon then, the political economy is nothing other than the amalgamation of a certain number of interdependent agents (state, society, merchant, company etc.) which find themselves intrinsic to a pluralistic system that affects their identities all the way down to their respective preferences and (material and non-material) interests.

A second issue is implicit in the aforementioned: insofar as the political economy is a social construction, a structural phenomenon inhabited by a range of agents, it embodies not only a material rationale, but a spectrum of normative incentives that are not necessarily 'rational' in a strict cost-benefit sense. In other words, at the heart of the political economy there exists something that defines it as a project, and this is not the 'treasury' (which functions as a means to achieve those aims) but values, norms and other cultural factors. In the Iranian context, this normative rationale has been quite explicitly stated in the writings of Ayatollah Taleghani:

> Islamic economics are founded on the principles of right and justice, and are not based on any special group or class. In fact, from the point of view of Islam, the appearance of the features of classes is not a necessary inevitable thing or a irremediable social necessity. The appearance of classes is the result of the defect of individuals and society [due to their] not following right and just principles. It is the byproduct of transgression, oppression and colonialism. The form of society is only the reflection of individual relationships and individual relationships externalise the thoughts, minds and morals of persons. Let the thoughts and spirits of individuals change into any other form and the communal relations and social form must also change. *Indeed God does not change the condition of a people, until they have changed it for themselves* (Qur'an 13:11). Thus in history and in different areas in both large and small manifestations we can observe the appearance of societies bound together without class.[40]

A comparable emphasis on normative factors, albeit with a transnational connotation, can be found in Ayatollah Muhammad Baqi al-Sadr's *Iqtisaduna*:

> If we look on this morality which man in the Islamic world lives as a truth represented in the being of the umma, we can put it to use in the economic program within the Islamic world by placing that program in

a framework which marches with that morality so that it may become a force of impulsion and movement just like the morality of modern European economic programs was a great factor in the success of those programs because of the harmony between the two.[41]

For both Taleghani and Sadr normative ordinances informed by Islam have priority over the cost-benefit rationale prescribed by capitalism. Moreover, according to them, the individual is not to be conceived as the lowest part of a hierarchical chain, an agent on which the state exercises unrestrained power, in the process moulding the individual without being moulded itself. The state is penetrated from 'above' by the *umma* and the normative structure of Islamic economics, and from below by society and individuals themselves. This corresponds to the primary thrust of the pluralistic momentum. The state is but one actor within this momentum, and a comprehensive analysis of it has to appreciate the impact of other agents and systemic configurations as well (the capitalist world economy, globalization etc.).

There is a third issue that follows from this: when I say that the political economy is cyclical, it does not mean that political or economic power is distributed democratically or anarchically. This would be an idealist distortion of the empirical reality facing us on a daily basis. But it is unhelpful analytically to start with the international market system, globalization, the state or governmental institutions and evaluate their impact on socio-economic factors assuming a causal transmission belt along the way. A typical example for such 'descending' analysis is the rentier-state model. The oil boom in the late 1960s and 1970s, it is typically argued, expanded the vulnerability of oil economies to the world market and fluctuations in the oil price, and increased consumption demand beyond the supply capabilities of these economies led to inflation and increasing dependency on imports, especially of luxury goods.[42] One can always make these seemingly causal statements and one can always back them up with empirical 'facts'. Indeed, it is a simple matter to argue that the dependency of oil economies on the world market as measured by the foreign trade/Gross Domestic Product (GDP) ratio rose from 50 to 84 per cent in the period between 1970 and 1982. But to conclude that this trend increased the vulnerability of oil economies to fluctuations in world markets (i.e. their insecurity) is only one possible interpretation.[43] One can always argue the opposite case, that increased interaction with the world economy enhanced the bargaining power of the 'oil economies', that the Saudi Arabian state would not be a trusted ally of the United States without its oil exports to that country, that Dubai would not have expanded into an international enterprise with economic stakes all over the world without its massively expanded links to the global economy, and that Iran would not have been able to sustain a functioning economy in the face of the harsh sanctions regime imposed by the United States without its multifarious presence in the world economy—and so on.

In my opinion, many factors can be deduced from macro-economics, the state, the international economy or other systems. But the central question remains: are these effects hierarchical, do they occur on a causal transmission belt starting with the most abstract entity and going down to society and the individual? I think that in order to better understand the functioning of Iran's emerging political economy, it is useful to reverse analytically our units of analysis, establishing an ascending (as opposed to descending) order of political and economic action. For that one needs to explore historically, commencing from the lowest unit of analysis, how the political economy functions within society, within the family and with regard to those strata of society that are largely marginalized from the political and economic process such as children, the elderly, or even the mentally ill. We need to identify the mechanisms that led to stratification of society, and the material dispossession or betterment of a specific social group, rather than lumping disparate objects of analysis together under abstract categories such as 'demand' or 'supply', 'market' and 'state', or 'institutions' and 'society'. Such a view is especially pertinent to the impact of the '20 year vision' economic development programme initiated by the State Expediency Council in 1999 and aimed at turning Iran into the strongest West Asian economy by 2025.[44] In order to capture the ensuing socio-economic changes analytically, it is helpful to direct our research at the nature of Iran's political economy in its entirety, not merely at the micro- and macro-economic indicators, growth rates, utility-maximization, or other 'factual' abstractions. Sustainable development in Iran demands critical analyses, research that is geared towards ascending micro-structures, towards the pluralistic momentum driving Iranian society and affecting government from below, towards the devastating effects of environmental destruction, towards localized systems—in short, towards 'strategic planning' that appreciates how political-economic dynamics at a given moment, in a precise socio-economic context, function with regard to the smallest carriers of Iranian society. In my opinion, it is only if we explore the micro-mechanisms, investigate their economic utility and political rationale in a given cultural context, that we can comprehend how they constitute themselves within the emerging political economy of Iran and, by extension, the country's pluralistic momentum.

Resistance and democratic evolution in the Islamic Republic

The pluralistic momentum, then, refers to more than 'organisational pluralism' —that is, to more than 'the existence of a plurality of relatively autonomous (independent) organisations (subsystems) within the domain of a state.'[45] The pluralistic momentum in post-revolutionary Iran transcends the domain of the state; it exists in a decentralized, diffuse fashion and is located in innumerable discourses permeating Iranian society. Let us not, therefore, try to find out who generates the pluralistic momentum in Iran. Let us ask, instead, how it affects state-society relations, how it translates opposition into political practice, and how it differentiates the power consensus among the ruling elites. In other words, rather than ask ourselves what the state has done to foster reforms (e.g. the 'Khatami effect'), we should try to investigate the manifold empirical manifestations of opposition and criticism within Iranian society. What, for instance, is the common theme between the resignation letters of the Friday prayer leader of Isfahan, Ayatollah Jallaleddin Taheri, who resigned in 2002, of the members of the Iranian parliament who protested to Ayatollah Ali Khamenei in 2003, and of Mohammad Ali Abtahi, who resigned as Khatami's vice president and chief of staff in 2004? Which factors led to the judiciary's decision to ban torture and solitary confinement in 2004, the unprecedented acknowledgement by the same ministry that Iranian prisoners continue to face physical, psychological and sexual ill-treatment thereafter, and the introduction of jury trials for press offences?[46] How does the critique of the internationally acclaimed Iranian *cinéma nouveau* translate into cultural preferences? What is the impact of conservationist groups and other environmental lobbying organizations on Iran's relationship to 'modernity'? And how are cultural artefacts such as norms of proper behaviour, moral obligations and ideological inhibitions reified in the first place? Capturing these instances of political, cultural and socio-economic change in Iran amounts to nothing less than a critical approach to Iranian politics.

Such an understanding alerts us to a second methodological precaution. The pluralistic momentum in Iran is not a commodity that can be possessed by this or that group; there is no engine that can be localized here or there. It must be analyzed as a 'gliding' phenomenon that is in constant motion. A trajectory of its infinitesimal movements requires analysis of the multifarious discourses, ideas, political cultures that constitute the Iranian polity. Therefore, I study the pluralistic momentum in Iran in the way that Michel Foucault studied the dialectics between power and domination by the state:[47]

> [W]e should direct our researches on the nature of power not towards the juridical edifice of sovereignty, the State apparatuses and the ideologies which accompany them, but towards domination and the material operators of power, towards forms of subjection and the inflections and utilisations of their localised systems, and towards strategic apparatuses. We must eschew the model of Leviathan in the study of power. We must escape from the limited field of juridical sovereignty and State institutions, and instead base our analysis of power on the study of the techniques and tactics of domination.[48]

Such an approach avoids identifying some single locus of the pluralistic momentum, such as 'the state' or 'the ruling elites'. It does not analyze it in terms of the interests and motives of political parties and institutions in a top-down fashion—from the 'ruling classes' to the 'proletariat' as Marxists suggest. Instead, it focuses as much as possible on the vehicles of the pluralistic momentum in Iran: students, non-governmental organizations, women's rights activists, writers, poets, intellectuals, film-makers etc. It pays attention to processes of differentiation, reification, deconstruction, theorization and other ideational sources of reform emanating from Iranian civil society. It establishes, in short, a genealogy of reform emancipating 'the local', i.e. Iranian society vis-à-vis 'the whole', i.e. the state.

With this understanding of the pluralistic momentum as a background, one may assert that a dynamic element is introduced into Iran's state-society relations that is intrinsically opposed to the very idea of conservatism and traditionalism. I have argued in Part One that this competition manifests itself in the fight between an intellectual and scientific (enlightened?) world-view and a theocratic or clerical (orthodox?) one. The late Edward Said understood this dynamic years ago, when he observed that Iran 'is in the throes of a stunningly energetic debate about law, freedom, personal responsibility, and tradition that is simply not covered by Western reporters.' Charismatic lecturers and intellectuals, clerical and non-clerical alike, he elaborated, 'carry on the tradition of Shariati, challenging centres of power and orthodoxy with impunity and, it would seem, great popular success.'[49] Ervand Abrahamian agrees, elaborating that the key words employed by Iranian intellectuals have changed from revolution, imperialism, martyrdom, dispossessed, solidarity, roots, and 'Westtoxifcation' to democracy, liberty, equality, pluralism, human rights, civil society, modernity, dialogue, political participation and 'a new term coined in the late 1990s shahrvandi (citizenship).'[50]

The existence of an active counterculture does not necessarily mean that there will be drastic changes, or that the principle of 'unchangeable laws of the Islamic revolution' will be surrendered ideologically, but the possibility of change is there and is there to stay. What we are currently observing in Iran, I would therefore assert, is not the demise of reformism. It is a dispute about how to exploit that possibility of change for political gains. There may be a 'communication lag' between the demands for reforms by Iran's civil society on the one hand and the acceptance of these demands by the state on the other, but the dynamics of societal preferences continuously exert pressures on the policy-making process of the government. Does this political culture not make it increasingly difficult to maintain the revolutionary ideals as unchanging verities? Even the most outspoken critics of the clerical establishment in Iran, such as Akbar Ganji, Hashem Aghajari, Said Hajjarian, Alireza Alavitabar and Abdollah Nouri, have answered this question with a tentative yes.[51] They might differ on the strategy to reinterpret the Islamic Republic, but they agree on the basic premise that the Iranian system can be reformed from within. 'The transition to democracy,' argues Akbar Ganji in that regard, 'is like a game of chess where dictators are sitting on one side and democrats on the other. We must enter the game and use all the pieces in order to check and mate the opponent.'[52] There is, moreover, an emerging consensus amongst the Iranian intelligentsia that reforming the Islamic Republic is a gradual process, that it is dependent on the country's civil society, that pluralism emerges from below. '[A]mong the general public, and in particular among the intellectual, political and cultural elite', argues Eshkevari,

> there has never been such a strong and deep awareness, such democratic and reformist demands, such a public will and the necessary consensus for [having] freedom and democracy and [attaining them by] peaceful and rational means. Of course it is the case that many conditions must be met before entering on the stage of democracy and realising a democratic system of government. … the necessary public understanding of modern conceptions of society, humanity, free will, freedom, democracy, the rights of individuals, the state, the nation and so on. … In the course of a hundred years of struggle against despotism and cultural, social and political backwardness, and after many setbacks, today freedom, democracy and citizens' rights have become more important for us than ever before. In the past, neither the people nor even the intellectuals and the political elite gave much priority to democracy — at least they did not place the necessary value on the means for attaining the goal of democracy. But both [the end and the means] have now become important for all.[53]

The Iranian revolution did not emerge out of an armed insurgency, but rather out of an 'unarmed insurrection whereby ordinary citizens engaged in methods of non-violent action, such as protests, demonstrations, strikes, boycotts, and civil obedience', a political strategy that was explicitly emphasized by Khomeini and his followers.[54] Such 'non-violent action' against the state has a long history in modern Iran. Thus, by emphasizing that the current reform movement is one stage in the 'hundred year long struggle' for democracy in the country, Eshkevari and others place it within the genealogy of resistance to the state in Iran, exemplified most prominently by the tobacco revolts of 1891, the Constitutional Revolution of 1906/07, the popular campaign for the nationalization of the oil sector between 1951 and 1953, and the Islamic revolution in 1978/79. In all these instances, collective non-violent action encouraged non-institutional protest emerging from innumerable loci of Iranian society. The momentum thus engendered provoked acts of omission, 'whereby people refuse to perform acts expected by norms, custom, law, or decree'; indeterminate actions, where the outcome of a protest is not defined in advance; and acts of commission, 'whereby people perform acts that they do not usually perform, are not expected by norms or customs to perform, or are forbidden by law, regulation, or decree to perform'.[55] The reform movement thus qualifies as a case study par excellence or the endurance of 'people's power' in the dialectic between the state and society in democratizing countries in general and contemporary Iran in particular.

Anyone who has travelled to Iran regularly and with an 'open eye' would concur that the reforms implemented during the eighteen years since the death of Ayatollah Khomeini provide enough evidence to conclude that the Iranian polity is capable of changing, and that it is quite innovative in its efforts to legitimate these changes on the level of ideological theorizing.[56] Ultimately, these changes have been forced upon the political elites by the people of Iran who have repeatedly and successfully lifted the sacred canopy laid out by their conservative opponents. Yet the many forms of resistance to an all encompassing, sacrosanct meta-narrative are not provoked by a single institution, a political party, or even a set of ideological currents. The pluralistic momentum engendered change in an irregular fashion and the instances of resistance appeared in varying strengths: confined and definitive (the sit-in by Iranian parliamentarians in the *majlis* in February 2004); symbolic and defiant (the repeated strikes by the Iranian Teachers Union and the Union of Bus Company Workers);[57] satirical and humoristic (the Mowj satire describing a young man's fictional encounter with the Imam Mahdi); tentative and hermetic (the protests of hundreds of former agents of Iran's dreaded pre-revolutionary secret service SAVAK to demand back wages in 1999); legal and righteous (the human rights campaign led by Shirin Ebadi); artistic and imaginative (the films of '*auteur*' filmmakers such as Abbas Kiarostami, Dariush Mehrjui, Jafar Panahi and the Makhmalbafs);[58] transnational and symbiotic (the increasing engagement between diaspora Iranians with their homeland, especially in terms of economic, artistic and academic exchanges); powerful and emotive (the popular music of Reza Sadeghi, Mohammad Esfahani and Ali-Reza Assar); and overwhelming and violent (the student demonstrations in the summer of 1999). These are but a few empirical instances of the pluralistic momentum in Iran that have led to a differentiation of Iranian politics.[59] As long as the country's civil society is driven by this momentum, it seems to me, Iranian reformism will elicit political results and—to highly dissimilar degrees—continue to provoke the silent subservience of central institutions of the state.

PART V
IN PLACE OF A CONCLUSION: TOWARDS CRITICAL IRANIAN STUDIES

Hafiz is a mystery. Who, indeed, is this *qalandar* [dervish], ascetic blasphemer who— during the darkest periods of the hypocritical rulership, at the table of the wily ones and in an era where even the proud, cannibalistic executioners like Amir Mubariz al-Din and his son Shah Shuja'a based their government on giving lashes, breaking wine jars, *nah-yi az munkar* and religious wars— solely denies the promise of resurrection, considers God as love and Satan as reason while passing, jumping around and dancing, he is chanting:

This cloak of mine better given in pawn for wine, And this register of nonsense better drowned in pure wine.
I, who can already gain Paradise today
why should I believe the zahid's promise of tomorrow?

—Ahmad Shamlu, *Hafiz-e Shiraz be revayat-e Ahmad Shamlu*

Some are going to object that by employing terms such as utopia, romantic, pluralism and democracy to explore what is happening in Iran, I have dealt in a methodology that is more loose than critical; that these ideal-types abstract from the fact that the Islamic revolution has failed, that what we should really focus on is the failure of 'political Islam', as Olivier Roy demands.[1] But isn't this only one possible interpretation of such a vastly discriminatory term such as 'failure'? I mean, couldn't we point to the *nobility* of failure which is so central to Shi'i Islam and its foundational legends? Isn't the task of dissolving the boundaries between the subject, the Islamic *umma*, and the object, 'Islamutopia' embodied in the idea of *madinat-al nubi*, the ideal community under the leadership of the Prophet Mohammad, by implication unattainable? Is it a cultural coincidence that Iranians revere those members of the Prophet's household who have 'failed' in their political mission: Imam Ali who 'failed' to assume the leadership of the *umma* immediately after the Prophet's demise, and Imam Hussein whose failure in the face of overwhelming force is celebrated on the day of Ashura during the month of Moharram and re-enacted in the Iranian drama of *ta'zieh*? I think that the Shia-Islamic imagery which was so pronounced during the Iranian revolution did not capture only a motivation to struggle for a better world, but also the heroic impossibility of this task which periodically produces exultation and despair, only to be reinvigorated through ideological means. Like Odysseus who did not try to defy the power of the sirens, who did not take another route that would have enabled him to escape sailing past them, and who still failed to pass over to them, Hussein derives his heroic status entirely from his failure to fulfil his mission to 'rescue the world from corruption'. Tragic 'failure' could equally be portrayed as *Erlebnis*, 'something unforgettable and irreplaceable, something whose meaning cannot be exhausted by conceptual determination'[2]—even after the naïve self-esteem of the moment has waned.

There is, then, always more than one 'truth' to a specific issue. One man's failure may well be another man's *Erlebnis*, just as for one class, as Marx said, the Eighteenth Brumaire of Louis-Napoleon Bonaparte could be a tragedy, while for another class it was a farce. Likewise, there will always be more than one 'Iran' that we can refer to. Ideally, a critical approach would shield us from favouring one Iran over the other, it would alert us to avoid judging on the basis of national, racial, cultural, educational or professional affinities or methodical or theoretical preferences. Ultimately, it would tell us that any object of analysis in the social world, when it is explored to its traces and when an attempt is made to extract its positivistic content, always reveals the epistemology that gave it meaning. This is not to say that facts do not exist. No one disputes the fact that Reza Khan, the first monarch of the Pahlavi dynasty, actually lived. But there is a great deal of interpretative controversy as to whether his rule was beneficial for the country, or disastrous. Such interpretation is the purpose of history which is constantly *in the making*. It is also the stuff from which we derive our knowledge of the social world and through which we establish our proper place in society. Hence the importance of knowing who writes the history, who does the interpretation, for what purpose, for whom, and within what kind of cultural, political and socio-economic episteme. According to Hayden White:

> There does, in fact, appear to be an irreducible ideological component in every historical account of reality. That is to say, simply because history is *not* a science, or is at best a protoscience with specifically determinable non-scientific elements in its constitution, the very claim to have discerned some kind of formal coherence in the historical record brings with it theories of the nature of the historical world and of historical knowledge itself which have ideological implications for attempts to understand "the present," however this "present" is defined. To put it another way, the very claim to have distinguished a past from a present world of social thought and praxis, and to have determined the formal coherence of that past world, *implies* a conception of the form that knowledge of the present world also must take insofar as it is *continuous* with that past world. Commitment to a particular *form* of knowledge predetermines the *kinds* of generalisations one can make about the present world, the kinds of knowledge one can have of it, and hence the kinds of projects one can legitimately conceive for changing that present or for maintaining it in its present form indefinitely.[3]

Therefore, the first thing to be aware of when interpreting history is that we have not inherited archives that are disinterested, scientific, or causally 'pure'. This is true especially when it comes to such ferociously contested places such as Iran. Indeed, if the reader has not considered this argument by now, I must have failed in my ambition to show how the politics surrounding the interpretation of Iran affect the way we perceive the country. I would have lost an opportunity to show how the Persian presence in international society has engendered myth making, quasi-factual inventions and pseudo-scientific theories; how US neoconservatives, Iraqi Ba'thists and not least Iranians themselves are busy creating a whole set of interpretations regarding the Islamic Republic, which are designed to have constitutive effects on their addressees; that they are designed to persuade us that Iran *is* monolithically violent, that the Iranian government *is* unchangeably hostile, that Iranian society *is* a place of minimal saturation, or the exact 'opposite'—that the Islamic Republic is thoroughly revolutionary, that Iran has a single, eternally valid meaning, that Persian history is synonymous with Iranian history.

If the reader rejects this out of hand, I have failed to show that these discourses enveloping Iran tend to reduce rather than extend the meanings of the country, singularize rather than pluralize Iran's identities. If not, the previous essays may claim a partial success in that they have captured ephemerally some of the dynamics which falsify (in a non-Popperian sense) such unadulterated positivism about Iran, whilst strengthening my thesis that the question of the Islamic Republic can only be posed and answered in the plural, that Iran in fact cannot be captured because Iranians number over seventy million, because life and culture in Lorestan are not the same as in Sistan-Baluchestan, because I don't know of any effective methodology that could capture Iranians in their entirety, from the Iranian-Jew in Boroujerd to the Iranian-Baha'i in exile. In short, if it convinces readers this book will have been successful in arguing that any reduction of Iran along a set of easily digestible propositions has a political purpose, typically carried by the myth making apparatus outlined in the previous parts of my argument.

To this end, I have tried to explore, even to theorize cautiously, instances of Iran's contemporary politics. This may appear contradictory, even paradoxical. How can one theorize (i.e. abstract) whilst claiming simultaneously that one is opposed to reducing contemporary Iran to a set of arguments or a single, all encompassing dynamic? My initial response to such criticism is that it would be irrational to argue that the social world can be approached without theoretical abstraction. Indeed, neuroscientists have long established that the human brain is biologically coded for abstraction, that it is instrumental in mapping our world, that it corrects the 'errors' of our other senses in order to 'interpret' our surrounding habitat. This is why you can read the following sentence: *In raeedinng a wrord, the olny naccassrey tihng is taht the frist and lasat ltteer be at the rghiet pclae. yuor mnind sppuliies the wrods form tohse cuees alnoe. It filtires out all tohse worngly palced lteters. Gmaes lkie bnrain tsear and yrou wrod sepll cehk oprate on a slimilar lgoic.*[4] Moreover, while you are reading this book, a whole 'perception-making' apparatus is involved: the lens of the eye which contracts and expands under muscular control, and which is itself part of an optical system that directs external impulses on the rods and cones of the retina, passes on these effects to the back of the brain where they are processed to create 'meaning'. Psychologists and physiologists explain that the initial information we thus receive is subjected to elaborate changes and transformations; much information is perverted or lost altogether and a good deal is added, probably through the interaction between genetically innate and learned or adopted information. According to Adorno and Horkheimer: 'Between the true object and the undisputed data of the senses, between within and without, there is a gulf which the subject must bridge at his own risk. In order to reflect the thing as it is', they explain, 'the subject must return to it more than he receives from it. The subject creates the world outside himself from the traces which it leaves in his senses. … The real ego', in short, 'is the most recent constant product of projection.'[5] We may add a sociological 'corollary' to this process:

> Man must make a world for himself. The world-building activity of man, therefore, is not a biologically extraneous phenomenon, but the direct consequence of man's biological constitution. … In the process of world-building, man, by his own activity, specialises his drives and provides stability for himself. Biologically deprived of a man-world, he constructs a human world. This world, of course, is culture. Its fundamental purpose is to provide the firm structures for human life that are lacking biologically. It follows that these humanly produced structures can never have the stability that marks the structures of the animal world. Culture, although it becomes for man a "second nature," remains something quite different from nature precisely because it is the product of man's own activity. Culture must be continuously produced and reproduced by man. Its structures are, therefore, inherently precarious and predestined to change. The cultural imperative of stability and the inherent character of culture as *un*stable together posit the fundamental problem of man's world-building activity. … [W]hile it is necessary that worlds be built, it is quite difficult to keep them going.[6]

Critical theory is interested exactly in those mechanisms 'necessary to keep the world going'. Far from revealing generalizations, critical theory attempts to disentangle particular cultural configurations, not in order to enclose them hermetically but to open them up for further investigation. Theory interrogated by a critical consciousness, I agree with Said,

> is awareness of the differences between situations, awareness too of the fact that no system or theory exhausts the situation out of which it emerges or to which it is transported. … Theoretical closure like social convention or cultural dogma, is anathema to critical consciousness, which loses its profession when it loses its active sense of an open world in which its faculties must be exercised.[7]

Much of what I have been saying may be consolidated finally by a few central methodological questions for future research on Iran. First, one has to find out who is speaking—who, among the totality of people speaking about Iran, is privileged by the media? Who claims the contested space in the public domain? Who legitimates his/her special position, and from whom does (s)he get the assurance that what (s)he says is true? What is the status of the author, intellectual, Mullah, decision-maker, analyst, and how does society sanction, by law or tradition, his or her privileged status? The status of *Mojtahed* (Islamic legal scholar) in Iran involves formally defined criteria of education, competence and knowledge; formal and informal institutions, norms and other cultural parameters that give the *Mojtahed* the right to be a privileged member of the religious and political establishment. The same applies in much less formalized ways to the societal position of '*Seyyeds*' (descendants of the Prophets household, or *ahl-e bayt*). What is their competition and neutral interaction with other individuals or groups that also possess their own status, from the businessman to the village preacher? And how are these self-attributed roles negated or accepted by society in the first place? The status of the *Marja'e taghlid* (source of emulation, the highest Shia religious rank) functions in society because there is (more or less) a cultural understanding of what this role implies and represents. This status is generally a rather special one in Iranian society and in Shia societies as a whole: religious ordinances cannot be expressed and interpreted by just anybody, their power, value, efficiency, cannot be divorced from the institutionally legitimated person who has the right to express them and to claim for them transnational and transcendental relevance (in form of *fatwa*s, for instance). But we also know that this status in Shia societies in general and in Iran in particular is in the process of being profoundly modified and differentiated. Tracing these movements is central to understanding the power of authority in contemporary Iran.

In the second place we must also explore the institution through which the Mullah, author, intellectual, etc. makes his or her discourse, and which legitimates the powers of their authorship. In Iran these are for example the mosque, a place where social activity, politics and spirituality merge; the *howzieh*, autonomous places of education, long distinct from the modern University, where religion, society, politics etc. are debated and where Islam is interpreted and re-engineered; the University, the place of 'secular' education, systematic observation, method, and the institution that has been at the heart of political protests in modern Iran; the think-tank, which has occupied the semi-autonomous space between the state and the scholarly community organized in the universities and the *howzieh*; the non-governmental-organization (NGO) which positions itself within civil society; the party, which faces the NGO from the opposite side because it operates within the domain of the state; the trade union, an artefact of Iran's 'Leftist' political culture engendered by the activism of the Tudeh party from 1941 onwards;[8] the professional association, which empowers its members to articulate a particular position on a particular issue whilst disqualifying others from doing so; the *Zurkhaneh* ('house of strength'), the place where Persia's knights prepared themselves for battle and where, since ancient times, Iranians have merged physical exercise with spiritual enchantment—and so on.[9]

And ultimately we have to find out how these agents, norms and institutions are positioned within the overall culture of Iran: within the domain of Iran's political culture, which currently has a transnational connotation that in turn demands analysis going beyond Iran and considering the impact of the wider Muslim political culture in West Asia, the contribution of Iranians living outside the country, and the impact of international factors extending beyond the confines of political-cultural dynamics within the Iranian/Islamic/Shia polity. It also demands exploring how those agents are treated and positioned within Iran's 'high culture', the arts, poetry, critical films etc. and the media of the country, which include the internet, radio, television, newspapers and other outlets. These cultural expressions define in complex ways individuals' distance from or closeness to their surrounding world, and hence are of central importance. Of the way in which immediate experience is emasculated by this 'culture industry', Adorno and Horkheimer say:

> In the culture industry the individual is an illusion not merely because of the standardisation of the means of production. He is tolerated only so long as his complete identification with the generality is unquestioned. Pseudo individuality is rife: from the standardized jazz improvisation to the exceptional film star whose hair curls over her eye to demonstrate her originality. What is individual is no more than the generality's power to stamp the accidental detail so firmly that it is accepted as such. The defiant reserve or elegant appearance of the individual on show is mass-produced like Yale locks, whose only difference can be measured in fractions of millimetres. The peculiarity of the self is a monopoly commodity determined by society; it is falsely represented as natural. It is no more than the moustache, the French accent, the deep voice of the woman of the world, the Lubitsch touch: finger prints on identity cards which are otherwise exactly the same, and into which the lives and faces of every single person are transformed by the power of the generality.[10]

It would be naïve to ignore the introjective effects of the 'culture industry' on individual perceptions. Media representations are instrumental intermediaries enabling us to appropriate our surrounding world. They are also a primary locus where ideas are externalised and objectified. If, in political discourse in Iran, either the office of the Leader of the Revolution or the Presidency is represented as the office of the true 'sovereign' or head of state, the 'truth' of this statement is not only established by 'measuring' institutionalized power: a whole set of cultural agents are involved in reproducing and interpreting that formal authority (and indeed, if these cultural agents are linked by a system of relations, institutional, normative. ideological etc., they may even oppose the cultural status quo altogether).

It follows, in conclusion, that when one explores Iran's state-society relations, foreign policies, relations with the United States, Persian art, literature and poetry, it is not in order to link them together on the basis of a single methodology or a set of a-historical truths; it is not to reify the processes that encapsulate the Islamic Republic as a whole.[11] The horizon of critical Iranian studies is not science *per se*. Rather, its purpose is to engender dialectical analysis that divides up the diversity of contemporary Iran, and to invalidate movement towards positivistic unification. So it defines limited spaces where we can engage Iran theoretically, ontologically and empirically. To that end, the previous parts of this book were designed to capture some of the discourses exercised over contemporary Iran. They were designed to ask 'how' rather than 'what', to present alternatives rather than imperatives, to diversify rather than unify, to explore the making of politics, culture, norms, institutions rather than getting engaged in the grand project of reifying them. Indeed, what is the aim of scholarly practice if it is not the smashing of the disciplinary idols erected by 'court historians' and the corresponding liberation of the subject matter? Nothing but betrayal of progressive knowledge, I think.

NOTES

PREFACE

1 Ibn Sina, 'Mantiq al-mashriqiyyin', in Seyyed Hossein Nasr with Mehdi Aminrazavi, *An Anthology of Philosophy in Persian, Vol. I*, Oxford: Oxford University Press, p. 269. The translation is based on *Mantiq al-mashriqiyyin*, Cairo: Salafiyyah Press, 1910, pp. 2-4.
2 'Islamic Utopian-Romanticism and the Foreign Policy Culture of Iran', *Critique: Critical Middle Eastern Studies*, Vol. 14, No. 3, Fall 2005, pp. 265-92; 'Inventions of the Iran-Iraq War', *Critique: Critical Middle Eastern Studies*, Vol. 16, No. 1, Spring 2007, pp. 63-83.
3 'The Whole Range of Saddam Hussein's War Crimes', *Middle East Report*, Vol. 36, No. 2, Summer 2006, pp. 30-5.
4 'Manufacturing War: Iran in the Neoconservative Imagination', *Third World Quarterly*, Vol. 28, No. 3, 2007, pp. 635-53; 'The Pluralistic Momentum in Iran and the Future of the Reform Movement', *Third World Quarterly*, Vol. 27, No. 4, 2006, pp. 665-74.
5 'Reflections on the Emerging Political Economy of Iran', *International Studies Journal*, Issue 12, Vol. 3, Special Issue, Winter 2007, pp. 23-37.

INTRODUCTION: THE QUESTION OF THE ISLAMIC REPUBLIC

1 On the Iran-Persia 'controversy' see Reza Sheikholeslami, 'Is it Iran or Persia? The Identity Issue in the Islamic Republic', *Journal of South Asian and Middle Eastern Studies*, Vol. 25, No. 1, Fall 2001, pp. 3-12 and Ali Ansari, 'Persia in the Western Imagination', in Vanessa Martin (ed.), *Anglo-Iranian Relations Since 1800*, Royal Asiatic Society Books, London: Routledge, 2006, pp. 8-20.
2 Liz Sidoti, 'McCain Jokes About Bombing Iran', *Associated Press*, 19 April 2007.

3 Eric J. Hobsbawm, *Nations and Nationalism Since 1780: Programme, Myth, Reality*, Cambridge: Cambridge University Press, second edition, 1992, p. 137.
4 For an empirical analysis of 'Western' perceptions of the revolution see Charles Kurzman, 'Historiography of the Iranian Revolutionary Movement, 1977-1979', *Iranian Studies*, Vol. 28, Nos. 1-2, Winter/Spring 1995, pp. 25-38.
5 For the term see Theodor W. Adorno and Max Horkheimer, *Dialectic of Enlightenment*, translated by John Cumming, London: Verso, 1997, especially, pp. 120 ff.
6 Edward Said, *Covering Islam How the Media and the Experts Determine How We See the Rest of the World*, London: Verso, 1997, pp. 6-7.
7 See Farhad Khosrokhavar, Shapour Etemad and Masoud Mehrabi, 'Report on Science in Post-Revolutionary Iran-Part II: The Scientific Community's Problems of Identity', *Critique: Critical Middle Eastern Studies*, Vol. 13, No. 3, Fall 2004, p. 367. There are many other examples of this bias regarding Iranians in general and Muslims in particular, especially after 11 September 2001. The job seekers portal Monster.com, for instance, announced in April 2003 that it had to delete the term 'Iran' from members' résumés because the 'U.S. Department of Treasury's Office of Foreign Assets Control, as well as some states, maintain sanctions which prohibit U.S. companies from conducting certain business activities with organizations located in or residents of the following countries: Burma/Myanmar, Cuba, Iran, Libya, North Korea, Sudan or Syria (the 'Sanctioned Countries')'. See 'No Jobs for Iranians on *Monster.com*', *Pacific News Service*, 15 May 2003. Available at <http://news.pacificnews.org/news/view_article.html?article_id=4f9c3d4b702b1dd3ed1e174079960dd9> [accessed 16 February 2007]. The American Chemical Society has implemented similar measures in April 2007 terminating membership of long-time members living in Iran. See further *Science*, Vol. 315, 30 March 2007.
8 Khosrokhovar *et al.*, 'Report on Science in Post-Revolutionary Iran-Part II' (note 2), pp. 367-8.
9 Ibid., p. 368.
10 Henry Kissinger, *Years of Upheaval*, London: Weidenfeld and Nicolson, 1982, pp. 670-1.
11 See further Edward Said, *Orientalism: Western Conceptions of the Orient*, London: Routledge & Kegan Paul, 1978 and his *Culture and Imperialism*, London: Vintage, 1993.
12 See especially Noam Chomsky, *Deterring Democracy*, London: Verso, 1991 and his *Hegemony or Survival: America's Quest for Global Dominance*, London: Penguin, 2003.

13 For a useful discussion see Stephen Slemon, 'Post-Colonial Critical Theories', in Gregory Castle (ed.), *Postcolonial Discourses: An Anthology*, Oxford: Blackwell, 2001, pp. 99-116.
14 See further Arshin Adib-Moghaddam, *A Metahistory of the Clash of Civilisations* (forthcoming).
15 N. Marbury Efimenco, 'An Experiment with Civilian Dictatorship in Iran; The Case of Mohammad Mossadegh', *The Journal of Politics*, Vol. 17, No. 3, August 1955, p. 390. A recent study by Tim Weiner shows how the CIA rented the allegiance of Iranian soldiers and street mobs, faking violent unrest in order to stage the coup in 1953, which brought back the Shah. See *Legacy of Ashes*, New York: Allen Lane, 2007.
16 The CIA history of the coup was first disclosed by James Risen of *The New York Times* in its editions of 16 April and 18 June 2000. The quoted material is available at <http://www.nytimes.com/library/world/mideast/041600iran-cia-index.html> [accessed 12 February 2007]. For further material see the declassified documents available at the webpage of the National Security Archive at <http://www.gwu.edu/~nsarchiv/NSAEBB/NSAEBB126/index.htm> [accessed 12 February 2007].
17 Roger M. Savory, 'The Principle of Homeostasis Considered in Relation to Political Events in Iran in the 1960's', *International Journal of Middle East Studies (IJMES)*, Vol. 3, No. 3, July 1972, p. 286.
18 Ibid., p. 302.
19 George Lenczowski, 'United States' Support for Iran's Independence and Integrity, 1945-1959', *Annals of the American Academy of Political and Social Science*, Vol. 401, America and the Middle East, May 1972, p. 51.
20 Ibid., p. 55.
21 Other senior US academics, including Bernard Lewis, have not benefited from hindsight and continue to reconfirm the myth that the Shah was reinstated by popular demand. See his *The Crisis of Islam: Holy War and Unholy Terror*, London: Phoenix, 2003, p. 63.
22 Stanford Shaw, 'The Editor's Desk', *International Journal of Middle East Studies (IJMES)*, Vol. 3, No. 3, July 1972, pp. 241-2.
23 See *America: Pathways to the Present*, Englewood Cliffs, NJ: Prentice Hall, 2000, p. 504, line 7, Chapter 16, section 3.
24 'American High School Textbook says Mossadegh was pro-Communist', *Payvand News*, 11 April 2001.
25 For a perceptive discussion of these examples see Stuart Schaar, 'Orientalism at the Service of Imperialism', *Race and Class*, Vol. 21, No. 1, 1979, pp. 67-80.
26 Leonard Binder, *Iran: Political Development in a Changing Society*, Berkeley: University of California Press, 1962, p. 349.

27 James A. Bill and Carl Leiden, *The Middle East: Politics and Power*, Boston: Allyn and Bacon, 1974, p. 143.
28 Marvin Zonis, 'The Political Elite of Iran: a Second Stratum?', in Frank Tachau (ed.), *Political Elites and Political Development in the Middle East*, New York: Halsted Press, 1975, pp. 212-13.
29 'He's back: Nixon Tapes Offer Insights on Shah, World', *Chicago Tribune*, 9 July 2000. Available at <http://www.iranian.com/NEWS/2000/July/nixon.html> [accessed 12 February 2007].
30 'Review', *The Guardian*, 12 November 2005, p. 6.
31 See further Rob Nixon, *London Calling: V.S. Naipaul, Post-colonial Mandarin*, Oxford University Press, 1992.
32 Ryszard Kapuscinski, 'One World, Two Civilisations', in Nathan Gardels (ed.), *The Changing Global Order: World Leaders Reflect*, Oxford: Blackwell, 1997, pp. 7-8.
33 Peter Berger and Stanley Pullberg, 'Reification and the Sociological Critique of Consciousness', *History and Theory*, Vol. 4, No.2, 1965, p. 204.
34 Ibid.
35 Antonio Gramsci, *Selections from the Prison Notebooks*, translated by Quintin Hoare and Geoffrey Nowell Smith, New York: International Publishers, 1971, p. 171.
36 In the aftermath of the most recent Hollywood blockbuster on the Iranian-Greek wars, Warner Brothers' movie '300', produced by Zack Snyder and based on the graphic novel by Frank Miller, some commentators have argued that even that rather more positive image of 'Persia' and 'Persians' has been eroded. See Gary Leupp, 'A Racist and Insulting Film: 300 vs. Iran (and Herodotus)', *Counterpunch*, 1 April 2007.
37 I am drawing on Michel Foucault here. See among other writings his *Power/Knowledge: Selected Interviews and other writings* 1972-1977, edited by C. Gordon, translated by C. Gordon *et al.*, London: Harvester Wheatsheaf, 1980.
38 I am referring to the plethora of think tank papers on the country produced by institutions such as the American Enterprise Institute, the Heritage Foundation, theWashington Institute for Near Policy etc. For an analysis of their influence on the way Iran is portrayed see part 3.
39 See further Arshin Adib-Moghaddam, *The International Politics of the Persian Gulf: A Cultural Genealogy*, London: Routledge, 2006.
40 For a discussion see Fred Halliday, *The Middle East in International Relations: Power Politics and Ideology*, Cambridge University Press, 2005, especially the introduction. See also my *The International Politics of the Persian Gulf*, especially Chapters 1 and 5.
41 On the difference between 'problem-solving theory' and 'critical theory' see Robert Cox, 'Social Forces, States and World Orders: Beyond International

Relations Theory', in Robert Cox, *Approaches to World Order*, Cambridge University Press, 1996, pp. 85-123.

42 A recently published, best-selling book by Michael D. Evans and Jerome Corsi, which argues that Mahmoud Ahmadinejad is driven by a 'messianic' medium to 'destroy Israel' and 'cripple the United States', is a prime example for this. See their *Showdown with Nuclear Iran: Radical Islam's Messianic Mission to Destroy Israel and Cripple the United States*, New York: Nelson Current, 2006. I found one of the many 'reviews' published on Amazon.com illustrative of the targeted audience: 'This book could and will change the way the world see's [sic] things and everyone needs to read it to get the real truth on Iran and how they plan to destroy all of us. But Jesus is our savior and king! Praise God!' [accessed 12 October 2006]. For further examples see Part Three of this book.

43 Consider, for instance, Iran's burgeoning research infrastructure in the 'hard sciences', particularly in astronomy, particle physics and biotechnology. See further Richard Stone, 'Science in Iran: An Islamic Science Revolution?', *Science*, Vol. 309, Issue 5742, 16 September 2005, pp. 1802-4. See also Farhad Khosrokhavar and M. Amin Ghaneirad, 'Iran's New Scientific Community', *Iranian Studies*, Vol. 39, No. 2, June 2006, pp. 253-67.

44 For an analysis of the most commercially successful publications in post-revolutionary Iran see Afshin Matin-Asgari, 'The intellectual Best-sellers of Post-revolutionary Iran: On Backwardness, Elite-Killing, and Western Rationality', *Iranian Studies*, Vol. 37, No. 1, March 2004, pp. 73-88.

45 For an analysis of the Iranian Diaspora in the United States see the special issue of *Iranian Studies*, Vol. 31, No. 1, Winter 1998.

46 On the issue of 'arbitrary rule' in Iran and state-society relations see Homa Katouzian, *State and Society in Iran: The Eclipse of the Qajars and the Emergence of the Pahlavis*, London: I.B. Tauris, 2006.

47 I am referring to the writings of Patrick Clawson, Michael Rubin, Michael Ledeen and other authors who have repeatedly argued for 'regime change' in Iran and/or for military action against the country. See further Part Three.

48 See on this issue Hamid Dabashi, 'Native Informers and the making of the American empire', *Al-Ahram Weekly*, Issue No. 797, 1-7 June 2006. Available at <http://weekly.ahram.org.eg/2006/797/special.htm> [accessed 12 Septe.mber 2006]. For a discussion see 'A Collision of Prose and Politics: A prominent professor's attack on a best-selling memoir sparks debate among Iranian scholars in the U.S.', *The Chronicle of Higher Education*, 13 October 2006. Available at <http://chronicle.com/free/v53/i08/08a01201.htm> [accessed 14 October 2006]. See also Fatemeh Keshavarz, *Jasmine and Stars: Reading More than Lolita in Tehran*, Chapel Hill: University of North Carolina Press, 2007.

49 See Ali Rahnema, *An Islamic Utopian. A Political Biography of Ali Shariati*, London: I.B. Tauris, 2000.
50 See Daryush Shayegan, *Cultural Schizophrenia: Islamic Societies Confronting the West*, translated by John Howe, Syracuse University Press, 1997.
51 See Fariba Adelkhah, *Being Modern in Iran*, translated from the French by Jonathan Derrick, London: Hurst & Company, 1998.
52 See Hamid Enayat, *Modern Islamic Political Thought: The Response of the Shia and Sunni Muslims to the Twentieth Century*, new edition, London: I.B. Tauris, 2005.
53 See Ali Shariati, *On the Sociology of Islam*, Berkeley: Mizan Press, 1979 and Rouhollah Khomeini, *Islam and Revolution: Writings and Declarations of Imam Khomeini*, Berkeley: Mizan Press, 1981. See also his translation of the *Constitution of the Islamic Republic of Iran*, Berkeley: Mizan Press, 1980.
54 See among other writings Seyyed Hossein Nasr, *The Islamic Intellectual Tradition in Persia*, edited by Mehdi Aminrazavi, Surrey: Curzon, 1996. See also his (with Mehdi Aminrazavi) multi-volume *An Anthology of Philosophy in Persia*, Oxford University Press, 1999.
55 There are many more studies with a similar disposition. See, for instance, Ervand Abrahamian, *Khomeinism: Essays on the Islamic Republic*, London: I.B. Tauris, 1993; Mehrzad Boroujerdi, *Iranian Intellectuals and the West: The Tormented Triumph of Nativism*, Syracuse University Press, 1996; Juan R.I. Cole and Nikki R. Keddie (eds), *Shiism and Social Protest*, New Haven: Yale University Press, 1986. With regard to Iran's foreign relations see Kaveh L. Afrasiabi's *After Khomeini: New Directions in Iran's Foreign Policy*, Boulder, CO: Westview, 1994. With *Critique: Critical Middle Eastern Studies* edited by Eric Hooglund, there is even a flagship journal with an explicit emphasis on critical writings on West Asia in general and on Iran in particular.
56 Hans-Georg Gadamer, *Truth and Method*, second revised edition, London: Continuum, 2004, p. 397.
57 Ibid.
58 See Thomas S. Kuhn, *The Structure of Scientific Revolutions*, second edition, University of Chicago Press, 1970.
59 By using the term 'world politics' I am emphasizing the sub-state level of analysis, that is the relevance of transnational actors, NGOs, cultural factors etc. for the conduct and analysis of international affairs. See further Richard Little and Michael Smith (eds), *Perspectives on World Politics*, London: Routledge, 1991.
60 On constructions of Iranian identity see Juan R.I. Cole, 'Marking Boundaries, Marking Time: The Iranian Past and the Construction of the Self by Qajar Thinkers', *Iranian Studies*, Vol. 29, Nos. 1-2, Winter/Spring 1996, pp. 35-56; Mehrzad Boroujerdi, 'Contesting Nationalist Constructions of Iranian Identity', *Critique: Critical Middle Eastern Studies*, Vol. 12, No. 1,

Spring 1998, pp. 43-55; Farideh Farhi, 'Crafting a National Identity amidst Contentious Politics in Contemporary Iran', *Iranian Studies*, Vol. 38, No. 1, March 2005, pp. 7-22.

61 For overviews see Roy Mottahedeh, *The Mantle and the Prophet: Religion and Politics in Iran*, New York: Simon and Schuster, 1985; Hamid Dabashi, *Theology of Discontent: The Ideological Foundation of the Islamic Revolution in Iran*, New York University Press, 1993; Boroujerdi, *Iranian Intellectuals and the West* (note 55); Ali Gheissari, *Iranian Intellectuals in the 20th Century*, Austin: University of Texas Press, 1998; Ali Mirsepassi, *Intellectual Discourse and the Politics of Modernization: Negotiating Modernity in Iran*, Cambridge, MA: Harvard University Press, 2000; Mohammad Tavakoli-Targhi, *Refashioning Iran: Orientalism, Occidentalism and Historiography*, New York: Palgrave, 2001; Farzin Vahdat, *God and Juggernaut: Iran's Intellectual Encounter with Modernity*, Syracuse University Press, 2002; and Negin Nabavi, *Intellectuals and the State in Iran: Politics, Discourse and the Dilemma of Authenticity*, Gainesville: University of Florida Press, 2003.

62 For a review of this book see Afshin Matin-Asgari, 'The Causes of Iran's Backwardness', *Critique: Critical Middle Eastern Studies*, Vol. 13, No. 3, Fall 1998, pp. 103-7. For an analysis linking the formation of national identity to societal development see Davood Gharayagh-Zandi, *Nahadha-ye madani va hoviyat dar Iran* [Civil groupings and identity in Iran], Tehran: Entesharat-e tamadon-e Iran, 1380 (2001).

63 On the emergence of the term intellectual (or *rowshanfekri* in Persian) in Iran see Negin Nabavi, 'The Changing Concept of the "Intellectual" in Iran of the 1960s', *Iranian Studies*, Vol. 32, No. 3, Summer 1999, pp. 333-50.

64 See Ahmad Kasravi, *On Islam and Shi-ism*, translated by M.R. Ghanoonparvar, Costa Mesa: Mazda Publishers, 1990; Jalal Al-e Ahmad, *Plagued by the West (Gharbzadegi)*, translated from the Persian by Paul Sprachman, New York: Caravan, 1982; Ali Shariati, *Man and Islam: Lectures by Ali Shariati*, translated from Persian by Ghulam M. Fayez, Mashhad: University of Mashhad Press, 1982 and his *On the Sociology of Islam* (note 53); Rahnema, *An Islamic Utopian* (note 49); and the material published at <http://www.shariati.com>. For further English translations see Lloyd Ridgeon (ed.), *Religion and Politics in Modern Iran: A Reader*, London: I.B. Tauris, 2005. On Khalil Maleki see Homa Katouzian, *Mussadiq and the Struggle for Power*, London: I.B. Tauris, 1990.

65 Jalal Al-e Ahmad, 'The Ouline of a Disease', in Ridgeon (ed.), *Religion and Politics* (note 59), p. 173.

66 Ali Shariati, 'Civilisation and Modernisation,' in Ridgeon (ed.), *Religion and Politics* (note 59), p. 185.

67 Ibid.

68 See further Nasr, *The Islamic Intellectual Tradition in Persia* (note 49).

69 There is also, of course, systematic cross-fertilization with the canons of European philosophy. See for instance Shahrokh Haghighi, *Gozar az moderniteh? Nicheh, Fuko, Liotar, Derida* [Beyond modernity? Nietzsche, Foucault, Lyotard, Derrida], Tehran: Agah, 2001. See also Niku Sarchosh's and Afshin Jahandideh's recent translation of Michel Foucault's *La Volonté de savoir*, *Eradeh beh danestan: Michel Fuku*, Tehran : Nashreney, 2004. For an overview see Afshin Matin-Asgari, 'Iranian postmodernity: the rhetoric of irrationality?,' *Critique: Critical Middle Eastern Studies*, Vol. 13, No. 1, 1994, pp. 113-23.

70 Michel Foucault, *The Order of Things: An Archaeology of the Human Sciences*, London: Routledge, 1989, pp. 404-5.

71 Abu Nasr Farabi, 'kitab al-jam 'bayn ra'yay al-hakimayn, Aflatun al-ilahi wa Aristu (Reconciliation of the two sages Spiritual Plato and Aristotle)', in Nasr, *An Anthology of Philosophy in Persia, Volume I* (note 49), pp. 113-14.

72 See further the website of Iran' Cultural Heritage Organisation at <http://www.chn.ir>.

73 Friedrich Nietzsche, *The Genealogie of Morals: An Attack*, translated by Francis Golffing, New York: Doubleday & Co., 1956, p. 21.

74 Eshkevari quoted in Ziba Mir-Hosseini & Richard Tapper, *Islam and Democracy in Iran: Eshkevari and the Quest for Reform*, London: I.B. Tauris, 2006, p. 171.

75 See further part 4.

76 See further Ervand Abrahamian, *Iran Between Two Revolutions*, Princeton University Press, 1982.

I. ISLAMIC UTOPIAN ROMANTICISM AND THE FOREIGN POLICY CULTURE OF IRAN

1 Works on Foucault and Iran in English include Didier Eribon, *Michel Foucault*, translated by Betsy Wing, London: Faber and Faber, 1991, p. 281 ff.; James Miller, *The Passion of Michel Foucault*, London: HarperCollins, 1993, p. 306ff; Janet Afary and Kevin B. Anderson, *Foucault and the Iranian Revolution: Gender and the Seductions of Islamism*, University of Chicago Press. See also Foucault's essays 'Open Letter to Mehdi Bazargan' and 'Useless to Revolt?,' in Michel Foucault, *Power: Essential Works of Foucault, 1954-1984*, vol. 3, translated by Robert Hurley *et al.*, London: Penguin, 1997.

2 Sermon delivered on 2 November 1979 and quoted in Farhang Rajaee, *Islamic Values and World View: Khomeyni on Man, the State and International Politics*, vol. XIII, London: University Press of America, 1983, p. 82.

3 Most foreign policy theorists rate ideas as secondary to material factors; see further Judith Goldstein and Robert Keohane (eds), *Ideas and Foreign Policy*, Ithaca, NY: Cornell University Press, 1993.
4 Theodor W. Adorno and Max Horkeimer, *Dialectic of Enlightenment*, translated by John Cumming, London: Verso, 1997, p. 24.
5 Hans-Georg Gadamer, *Truth and Method*, second revised edition, translation revised by Joel Weinsheimer and Donald G. Marshall, London: Continuum, 2004, p. 361.
6 Clifford Geertz, *The Interpretation of Cultures*, New York: Basic Books, 1973, p. 5.
7 According to Hedley Bull, an international system moves to form an international society, because of increasing shared knowledge and softening self-other categorisations. In the absence of the common rules, institutions etc., material factors are dominant and self-help anarchy (systems in a 'Hobbesian' state of war of all against all) prevail. See further Hedley Bull: *The Anarchical Society. A Study of Order in World Politics*, second edition, London: Macmillan, 1995.
8 See, for example, Anoushiravan Ehteshami, *After Khomeini: The Iranian Second Republic*, London: Routledge, 1995; Adam Tarock, *Iran's Foreign Policy since 1990: Pragmatism Supersedes Islamic Ideology*, Commack: Nova Science Press, 1999; and David Menashri, *Post-Revolutionary Politics in Iran: Religion, Society and* Power, London: Frank Cass, 2001, especially Chapter Seven. For a (neo)realist analysis in the Waltzian tradition see A.M. Haji Yousefi, 'The Foreign Policy of the Islamic Republic of Iran: Constraints, Opportunities and Pressures', *The Iranian Journal of International Affairs*, Vol. XVII, Nos. 2 & 3, Summer-Fall 2004, pp. 285-303.
9 See Hans Morgenthau, *Politics among Nations,* New York: Alfred Knopf, 1948.
10 For a comprehensive critique of (neo)realist methodologies and ontology see R.B.J. Walker, *Inside/Outside: International Relations as Political Theory*, Cambridge University Press, 1993, especially Chapter Five, or Robert Cox, *Approaches to World Order*, Cambridge University Press, 1996. For a short critique of (neo)realist interpretations of regional politics in West Asia see Arshin Adib-Moghaddam, 'The Theory of Regional Security Complexes: Exploring the Options', *International Studies Journal*, Issue 9, Vol. 3, No. 1, Summer 2006, pp. 25-37.
11 Peter L. Berger and Thomas Luckmann, *The Social Construction of Reality: A Treatise in the Sociology of Knowledge,* Harmondsworth: Penguin, 1979, pp. 69-70.
12 See further Arshin Adib-Moghaddam, *The International Politics of the Persian Gulf: a Cultural Genealogy,* London: Routledge, 2006.
13 Berger and Luckmann, *The Social Construction of Reality* (note 11), p. 49.

14 Karl Marx, 'The Eighteenth Brumaire of Louis Bonaparte', in Karl Marx, *Survey from Exile*, edited by David Fernbach, Harmondsworth: Penguin, 1973, p. 146.
15 Wilhelm Dilthey, *Selected Writings*, Cambridge University Press, 1976, p. 179.
16 Most contemporary sociological and constructivist analysis, both in international relations and in other disciplines, subscribes to that viewpoint. See further Mlada Bukovansky, *Legitimacy and Power Politics: The American and French Revolutions in International Political Culture*, Princeton University Press, 2002; Alexander Wendt, *Social Theory of International Politics*, Cambridge University Press, 1999, especially Chapter 4; Margaret S. Archer, *Culture and Agency: The Place of Culture in Social Theory*, revised edition, Cambridge University Press, 1996; and Nicholas Onuf, *The Republican Legacy in International Thought*, Cambridge University Press, 1998, Chapter 8.
17 I have drawn on sociological theory here. See Peter Berger and Stanley Pullberg, 'Reification and the Sociological Critique of Consciousness', *History and Theory*, Vol. 4, No. 2, 1965, pp. 196-211; Peter Berger, *The Sacred Canopy*, Garden City: Doubleday, 1966; and Berger and Luckmann, *The Social Construction of Reality* (note 11).
18 Archer, *Culture and Agency* (note 16), p. 107.
19 Herbert Marcuse, *One-dimensional Man: Studies in the Ideology of Advanced Industrial Society*, London: Routledge, 1964, p. 11.
20 The centrality of language is accentuated by the 'semiotic' approach to culture; see, among others, Ferdinand Saussure, *Course in General Linguistics*, New York: McGraw Hill, 1964.
21 For the social construction of legitimacy see Bukovansky, *Legitimacy* (note 16), especially pp. 2-3.
22 Wendt, *Social Theory*, p. 329.
23 Erich Fromm, *To Have or To Be?*, London: Continuum, 1997, p. 64.
24 See George H. Mead, *Mind, Self, and Society*, Chicago University Press, 1934.
25 Wendt, *Social Theory* (note 16), p. 329.
26 Geertz, *The Interpretation of Cultures* (note 6), p. 14.
27 Max Weber, *From Max Weber: Essays in Sociology*, London: Routledge, 1998, p. 176.
28 Antonio Gramsci, *Selections from the Prison Notebooks*, London: Lawrence & Wishart, 1971, p. 12. In lieu with his Marxist inclinations, Gramsci distinguishes between 'organic' intellectuals and 'traditional' intellectuals. Whereas the former are created by dominant social classes to give them homogeneity and awareness of their function, the latter category refers to intellectuals (most notably the clergy, but also administrators, scholars,

philosophers, scientists and theorists) who are already in existence and seem to represent historical continuity.

29 For an examination of this political culture see Mehrzad Boroujerdi, *Iranian Intellectuals and the West: The Tormented Triumph of Nativism*, Syracuse University Press, 1996.

30 I have employed the terminology of Karl Mannheim here; see his *Ideology and Utopia: An Introduction to the Sociology of Knowledge*, New York: Harcourt, Brace & World, 1968 (original edition 1936), p. 174. Here, utopianism is *not* synonymous with ideology as E.H. Carr claimed in *The Twenty Years' Crisis*. Rather, utopianism refers to rationalization of political change (termed 'realism' by Carr). See Edward Hallet Carr, *The Twenty Years' Crisis, 1919-1939: An Introduction to the Study of International Relations*, London: Macmillan, 1961. For an examination of the differing uses of terms common to Carr and Mannheim see Charles Jones, *E.H. Carr and International Relations: A Duty to Lie*, Cambridge University Press, 1998.

31 For a perceptive analysis of Iran's domestic political culture see especially Boroujerdi, *Iranian Intellectuals* (note 29) and Samih K. Farsoun and Mehrdad Mashayekhi, *Iran: Political Culture in the Islamic Republic*, London: Routledge, 1992.

32 Morteza Mottahari, *Islam and Iran*, Beirut: Dar al-Ta'aruf, no date, p. 22, quoted in Wajih Kawtharani, 'Mutual Awareness between Arabs and Iranians,' in Khair el-Din Haseeb (ed.), *Arab-Iranian Relations*, Beirut: Centre for Arab Unity Studies, 1998, p. 74. For a comprehensive analysis of Mottahari's ideas see Mahmood T. Davari, *The Political Thought of Ayatullah Murtaza Mutahhari: An Iranian theoretician of the Islamic state*, London: Routledge, 2005.

33 Indeed, one of the many titles of Mohammad Reza Shah included *Aryamehr*, which means 'light of Aryans' in Persian. His father, Reza Khan, who established the Pahlavi dynasty, promoted the name 'Iran' (or 'Land of Aryans') instead of Persia and supported the elimination of Arabic terms from the Persian language.

34 Golnar Mehran, 'The Presentation of the "Self" and the "Other" in Postrevolutionary Iranian School Textbooks', in Nikki R. Keddie and Rudi Matthee (eds), *Iran and the Surrounding World: Interactions in Culture and Cultural Politics*, Seattle: University of Washington Press, 2002, p. 247, emphasis added.

35 Edward W. Said, *Orientalism*, London: Penguin, 1998, p. 268.

36 See further Mehrdad Kia, 'Persian Nationalism and the Campaign for Language Purification', *Middle Eastern Studies*, Vol. 34, No. 2, April 1998, pp. 9-36.

37 Firoozeh Kashani-Sabet, 'Cultures of Iranianness: The Evolving Polemic of Iranian Nationalism', in Keddie and Matthee (eds), *Iran and the Surrounding World* (note 34), p. 166.

38 'Visit of the Shah of Iran, 11-12 June 1968: Scope Paper', page 2. Available through the Carter Library.

39 Joya Blondel Saad, *The Image of Arabs in Modern Persian Literature*, Lanham, MD: University Press of America, 1996, p. 134.

40 Davari, *The Political Thought of Ayatullah Murtaza Mutahhari* (note 32), p. 56.

41 Ibid., pp. 55-6.

42 Jalal Al-e Ahmad, *Plagued by the West (Gharbzadegi)*, New York: Caravan, 1982, p. 10 ff.

43 See further Arshin Adib-Moghaddam, *A Metahistory of the Clash of Civilisations* (forthcoming).

44 Jalal Al-e Ahmad, 'The Outline of a Disease', in Lloyd Ridgeon (ed.), *Religion and Politics in Modern Iran: A Reader*, London: I.B. Tauris, 2005, p. 168.

45 See Ali Rahnema (2000), *An Islamic Utopian: A Political Biography of Ali Shariati*, London, I.B. Tauris, 2000, pp. 119-28.

46 Ali Shariati, 'Civilisation and Modernisation', in Ridgeon (ed.), *Religion and Politics in Modern Iran* (note 44), pp. 192-3.

47 Rahnema, *An Islamic Utopian* (note 45), p. 159.

48 Mannheim, *Ideology and Utopia* (note 30), p. 173.

49 Ibid., p. 193.

50 Paul Ricoeur, *Lectures on Ideology and Utopia*, edited by George H. Taylor, New York: Columbia University Press, 1986, p. 276.

51 Robert Fisk, *The Great War for Civilisation: The Conquest of the Middle East*, London: Harpers Perennial, 2006, p. 151.

52 Quoted by Margaret Talbot, 'The Agitator: Oriana Fallaci directs her fury toward Islam', *The New Yorker*, 5 June 2006.

53 One of the main tenets of Iran's *Ja'afari* or Twelver Shia school is that the Twelfth Imam went into hiding (*gheiba*) and will return to establish the just rule of God on earth.

54 Mortada [Morteza] Mutahhari [Mottahari], 'Shahid', in M. Abedi and G. Leggenhausen (eds), *Jihad and Shahadat: Struggle and Martyrdom in Islam*, Houston: Institute for Research and Islamic Studies, 1986, p. 126.

55 Ali Shariati, 'Arise and bear witness'. Available at <htttp://www.shariati.com> [accessed 24 March 2003].

56 Ibid., 'A Discussion of Shahid', in Abedi and Leggenhausen (eds), *Jihad* (note 54), p. 233.

57 Ali Shari'ati, *On the Sociology of Islam: Lectures by Ali Shari'ati*, translated by Hamid Algar, Berkeley: Mizan Press, 1979, p. 122.

58 See Roy P. Mottahedeh, 'Shiite Political Thought and the Destiny of the Iranian Revolution', in Jamal S. al-Suwaidi (ed.), *Iran and the Gulf: A Search for Stability*, Abu Dhabi: The Emirates Center for Strategic Studies and Research, 1996, pp. 70-80; and especially Juan R.I. Cole and Nikki R. Keddie (eds), *Shiism and Social Protest*, New Haven: Yale University Press, 1986.

59 See Ervand Abrahamian, *Khomeinism: Essays on the Islamic Republic*, London: I.B. Tauris, 1993.

60 Ayatollah Khomeini, 'The Necessity for Islamic Government', in Ridgeon (ed.), *Religion and Politics in Modern Iran* (note 44), p. 209.

61 Hamid Algar, *Constitution of the Islamic Republic of Iran*, translated by Hamid Algar, Berkeley: Mizan Press, 1980, p. 19.

62 *Bayan,* No. 4, 1990, p. 8. Quoted in Ali Rahnema, *The Constitution of Iran: Politics and the State in the Islamic Republic*, translated by John O' Keane, London: I.B. Tauris, 1997, p. 69.

63 Ayatollah Rouhollah Khomeini, *Sahifey-e nur,* Vol. 18, Tehran: Vezarat-e Ershad, 1364/1985, p. 129.

64 See among others, Rajaee, *Islamic Values and World* View (note 2), pp. 83-4 and R.K. Ramazani, *Revolutionary Iran: Challenge and Response in the Middle-East*, Baltimore: Johns Hopkins University Press, 1986, pp. 26ff. On Iran and Afghanistan see Hafizullah Emadi, 'Exporting Iran's Revolution: The Radicalisation of the Shiite Movement in Afghanistan', *Middle Eastern Studies*, Vol. 31, No. 1, January 1995, pp. 1-12. On Iran and Lebanon see especially Houchang Chehabi (ed.), *Distant Relations: Iran and Lebanon in the Last 500 Years*, London: I.B. Tauris, 2005. For an interesting analysis of Shia transnationalism with a special emphasis on relations between the Amal movement in Lebanon and Iranian Shias see Roschanak Shaery-Eisenlohr, 'Imagining Shiite Iran: Transnationalism and Religious Authenticity in the Muslim World', *Iranian Studies*, Vol. 40, No. 1, February 2007, pp. 17-35.

65 For further analysis see Farhang Rajaee, 'Iranian Ideology and Worldview: The Cultural Export of Revolution,' in John L. Esposito (ed.), *The Iranian Revolution: Its Global Impact*, Miami: Florida International University Press, 1990, pp. 63-80.

66 'Letter from Ayatollah Ruhollah Khomeini to Pope John-Paul II', in Massoumeh Ebtekar, *Takeover in Tehran: The Inside Story of the 1979 U.S. Embassy Capture*, Vancouver: Talonbooks, 2000, p. 246.

67 The occupation occurred about two weeks after the Shah was allowed to go to the United States for medical treatment.

68 Preface to Ebtekar, *Takeover in Tehran* (note 66), p. 26.

69 'Ministry of Foreign Affairs of the Islamic Republic. Extradition Request for Shah in Panama (Tehran, 21 December 1979).' Available through the Carter Library.

70 US Department of State, Incoming Telegram, US Ambassador to Iran Bruce L. Laingen to US Secretary of State, 'Shah's Desire to Reside in the U.S.', Tehran, July 1979. Available through the Carter Library.
71 Fred Halliday, *Revolution and World Politics: The Rise and Fall of the Sixth Great Power*, Durham, NC: Duke University Press, 1999, p. 96.
72 'First Communiqué of the Muslim Students Following the Line of Imam', in Ebtekar, *Takeover in Tehran* (note 66), p. 70.
73 See Fred Halliday, 'Iranian Foreign Policy since 1979: Internationalism and Nationalism in the Islamic Revolution', in Cole and Keddie (eds), *Shiism* (note 58), p. 96.
74 Ebtekar, *Takeover in Tehran* (note 66), pp. 241-2.
75 See David George, 'Pax Islamica: An Alternative New World Order', in Abdel Salam Sidahmed and Anoushiravan Ehteshami (eds), *Islamic Fundamentalism*, Boulder, CO: Westview, 1996, pp. 80ff.
76 *BBC Survey of World Broadcasts*, Part IV (A), The Middle East, 24 November 1979, ME/6280/A/8.
77 Ayatollah Rouhollah Khomeini, Sermon delivered on 5 November 1982 in *Kayhan* (Tehran), 6 November 1982 and quoted in Rajaee, *Islamic Values and World View* (note 2), p. 75.
78 Mehrzad Boroujerdi, 'Iranian Islam and the Faustian Bargain of Western Modernity', *Journal of Peace Research*, Vol. 34, No. 1, February 1997, p. 4.
79 Husein Golchin, *Namazi dar atash va khun* [A prayer in the midst of fire and blood], Tehran: Cultural Centre for Islamic Propaganda, 1372/1993, p. 9.
80 'Martyr Ahmad Sanezadeh', in Majid Zamanpour (ed.), *Jelveha-ye Nur* (The Faces of Light), Tehran: Cultural Centre of the Revolutionary Guards, Spring 1373/1995. Translated and quoted by Nader Nazemi, 'Sacrifice and Authorship: A Compendium of the Will of Iranian War Martyrs', *Iranian Studies*, Vol. 30, Nos. 3-4, Summer-Fall 1997, p. 265.
81 Ibid.
82 'Martyr Bijan Muhammadian', in Zamanpour (ed.), *Jelveha*, pp. 131-2. Translated and quoted by Nader Nazemi, 'Sacrifice and Authorship', p. 266. For translated poems on the death of Ayatollah Khomeini in 1989 see Naser Shakuri, Alireza Emami, Mohammad Ali Bahmani, Fatemeh Rake'i, Parviz Abbasi-Dakani and Reza Esma'ili, 'Elegies for a Lost Leader: Six Poems on the Death of Khomeini', translated by Paul E. Losensky, *Iranian Studies*, Vol. 30, Nos. 3-4, Summer-Fall 1997, pp. 277-89.
83 'Editor's Introduction', in Ricoeur, *Lectures* (note 50), pp. xxviii-xxix.
84 For a conceptualization of 'residual', 'dominant', and 'emergent' culture see Raymond Williams, *Marxism and Literature*, Oxford University Press, 1977, especially pp. 121-7.
85 Ibid., p. 113.
86 See further part 4.

87 Mohammad Khatami, *Islam, Dialogue and Civil Society*, Canberra: Centre for Arab and Islamic Studies, 2000, p. 62. See also Javad Zarif, 'Indispensable Power: Hegemonic Tendencies in a Globalized World," *Harvard International Review* XXIV, No. 4, Winter 2003. Available at <http://www.ceip.org/files/Publications/2003-04-01-brumberg-HIR.asp?from=pubdate> [accessed 13 November 2003]. At the time of writing, Javad Zarif is Ambassador and Permanent Representative of the Islamic Republic of Iran to the United Nations.

88 'Address by His Excellency Dr. Mahmoud Ahmadi-Nejad President of the Islamic Republic of Iran before the 61st Session of the General assembly'. New York, 19 September 2006.

89 Mohammad Javad Zarif and Mohammad Reza Alborzi, 'Weapons of Mass Destruction in Iran's Security Paradigm: The Case of Chemical Weapons', *The Iranian Journal of International Affairs*, Vol. XI, No. 4, Winter 1999-2000, p.513. See further Part Two.

90 See also Fariba Adelkhah (1999), *Being Modern in Iran*, translated by Jonathan Derrick, London: Hurst & Company, 1999.

91 See Mannheim, *Ideology and Utopia* (note 30), esp. chapter IV.

92 Ricoeur, *Lectures* (note 50), p. 278.

93 See further my *A Metahistory* (note 43) and 'Global Intifadah? September 11th and the Struggle Within Islam', *Cambridge Review of International Affairs*, Vol. 15, No. 2, July 2002, pp. 203-16.

94 Abdolkarim Soroush, 'Scientific Development, Political Development', *Kian Monthly Review* 10, No. 54, Oct.-Nov. 2000. Available at <http://www.drsoroush.com/English/By_drsoroush/E-CMB-19990500-Seminar_on_Tradition_and_Modernism_held_in_Beheshti_University.html> [accessed 12 June 2004].

95 Abdolkarim Soroush, *Reason, Freedom, and Democracy in Islam: Essential Writings of 'Abdolkarim Soroush,* translated and edited by Mahmoud Sadri and Ahmad Sadri, Oxford University Press, 2000, p. 156.

96 Ibid., p. 165.

97 For a related argument see Mohammad-Reza Dehshiri, 'The Cycle of Idealism and Realism in the Foreign Policy of the Islamic Republic of Iran', *The Iranian Journal of International Affairs*, Vol. XIII, Nos. 2 & 3, Summer-Fall 2001, pp. 278-300.

98 Tariq Ali, 'Mid-Point in the Middle East?', *New Left Review*, Vol. 38, March-April 2006, p. 17.

99 The emerging "post-Islamic" moment in Iran's foreign relations led in January 2004 to the renaming of the street in Tehran named after Khaled Islambouli, the assassin of former Egyptian President Anwar Sadat, thus opening up the current rapprochement with Egypt. Irish Republicans in January 2001 launched an Internet campaign urging the Iranian Government

not to rename a street in Tehran that was named after the IRA hunger striker Bobby Sands after his death in 1981.

100 Seyed Mohammad Kazem Sajjadpour, 'Iran and September 11: A Conceptual Framework for Understanding Foreign Policy', *The Iranian Journal of International Affairs*, Vol. XIII, No. 4, Winter 2001-2, p. 440.

101 Soroush, *Reason, Freedom, and Democracy in Islam* (note 95), p. 23.

102 Soroush, 'Scientific Development', *Kian Monthly Review* (note 94).

103 A representative survey of public opinion in Iran conducted by 'World Public Opinion' in Washington showed that an 'overwhelming 84 percent of Iranians say it is very important for Iran to have the capacity to enrich uranium. … However, two-thirds of Iranians (66%) endorse Iran's participation in the Nuclear Non-Proliferation Treaty even when reminded that it prohibits Iran from developing nuclear weapons. Only 15 percent want Iran to withdraw from the treaty.' See 'Iranians Want Capacity to Enrich Uranium But Accept NPT Rules Against Developing Nuclear Weapons', *World Public Opinion: Global Public Opinion on International Affairs*, 26 January 2007. Available at <http://www.worldpublicopinion.org/pipa/articles/home_page/307.php?nid=&id=&pnt=307&lb=hmpg1> [accessed 15 February 2007].

104 Edward Rothstein, Herbert Muschkamp and Martin E. Marty, *Visions of Utopia*, Oxford University Press, 2003, p. 16.

105 Jalal Al-e Ahmad, 'The Outline of a Disease', in Ridgeon, *Religion and Politics in Modern Iran* (note 44), p. 170.

106 Richard K. Ashley, 'Foreign Policy as Political Performances', *International Studies Notes*, 1998, p. 53.

107 For the German case see Thomas U. Berger, *Cultures of Antimilitarism: National Security in Germany and Japan*, London: Johns Hopkins University Press, 1998; and John S. Duffield, 'Political Culture and State Behavior: Why Germany Confounds Neorealism', *International Organization*, Vol. 53, No. 4, Autumn 1999, pp. 765-803. For the impact of norms and ideas on French military doctrine see Elizabeth Kier, 'Culture and Military Doctrine: France between the Wars', *International Security*, Vol. 19, No. 4, Spring 1995, pp. 65-93.

108 I am referring to some of the constructive criticism of my *The International Politics of the Persian Gulf*. See among others Gerd Nonneman's review published in *International Affairs*, Vol. 82, No. 5, 2006, pp. 1013-14. See also in German the review by Nadine Scharfenort in *Orient, Deutsche Zeitschrift für Politik und Wirtschaft des Orients*, 47: 3, 2006, pp. 422-4. For an extensive review in Persian see Davoud Gharayagh-Zandi, 'Tabarshenasi-ye farhangi anarshy dar chalij-e fars' [A cultural genealogy of anarchy in the Persian Gulf], *Strategic Studies Quarterly*, Research Institute of Strategic Studies (Iran), Vol. 9, No. 4, Winter 2007, pp. 937-49.

109 See Eric Hobsbawm and Terence Ranger (eds), *The Invention of Tradition*, Cambridge University Press, 2004; and Eric Hobsbawm, *Nations and Nationalism since 1780: Programme, Myth, Reality*, Second Edition, Cambridge University Press, 2004.
110 Max Horkheimer, 'Traditional and Critical Theory', in Max Horkheimer, *Critical Theory: Selected Essays*, New York: Seabury Press, 1972, p. 232.
111 In IR, the return to critical theory has constituted a serious challenge to mainstream portrayals of international relations. For overviews see, among others, Andrew Linklater (ed.), *International Relations: Critical Concepts in Political Science*, especially volumes IV and V, London: Routledge, 2000; and Richard Wyn Jones (ed.), *Critical Theory and World Politics*, London: Lynne Rienner, 2001.

II. INVENTIONS OF THE IRAN-IRAQ WAR AND THE MYTH OF ENDEMIC 'PERSIAN-ARAB' ENMITY

1 With regard to the Iran-Iraq war see, for instance, Shirin Tahir-Kheli and Shaheen Ayubi, *The Iran-Iraq War: New Weapons, Old Conflicts*, London: Praeger, 1983 or Anthony H. Cordesman, *The Iran-Iraq War and Western Security 1984-1987: Strategic Implications and Policy Options*, London: Jane's Publishing Co., 1987.
2 For a review of the core components of realist theory see among others Joseph M. Grieco, 'Realist International Theory and the Study of World Politics', in Michael W. Doyle and G. John Ikenberry (eds), *New Thinking in International Relations Theory*, Oxford: Westview, 1997, pp. 163-201 and Robert O. Keohane (ed.), *Neorealism and its Critics*, New York: Columbia UP, 1986. More recently, realist theory has been adopted by regional experts. See Raymond Hinnebusch and Anoushiravan Ehteshami (eds), *The Foreign Policies of Middle East States*, London: Lynne Rienner, 2002. For a (global) systemic account of regional politics in the Waltzian neo-realist tradition see Birthe Hansen, *Unipolarity and the Middle East*, Richmond, Surrey: Curzon, 2000. For a critique see Arshin Adib-Moghaddam, 'The Theory of Regional Security Complexes: Exploring the Options', *International Studies Journal*, Issue 9, Vol. 3, No.1, Summer 2006, pp. 25-37.
3 'King Abdullah II: "Iraq is the battleground—the West against Iran"', *Middle East Quarterly*, Vol. XII, No. 2, Spring 2005.Available at <http://www.meforum.org/article/688> [accessed 15 February 2007].
4 'Iraqi minister lashes out at Saudi Arabia over rumours', *The Daily Star* (Beirut), 3 October 2005.

5 See also Salah Hemeid, 'The Iranian Iraq', *Al-Ahram Weekly*, 3 January 2007. Available at <http://weekly.ahram.org.eg/2006/826/re121.htm> [accessed 12 February 2007]. For a symbiotic view see Matein Khalid, 'Persian undercurrent in Islamic civilisation', *Khaleej Times*, 29 November 2006.

6 Indeed, Ahmad al-Jarallah, Editor-in-Chief of the *Arab Times,* wrote a strongly worded editorial supporting Saudi collusion with Israel during the war. According to him 'this attitude of Saudi Arabia, which has been doing all it can to protect the Arab world from Israeli aggression, is enough to unmask the adventurers, who have violated the rights of their own countries and tried put their people under the guardianship of foreign countries like Iran and Syria. A battle between supporters and opponents of these adventurers has begun, starting from Palestine to Tehran passing through Syria and Lebanon. This war was inevitable as the Lebanese government couldn't bring Hezbollah within its authority and make it work for the interests of Lebanon. Similarly leader of the Palestinian Authority Mahmoud Abbas has been unable to rein in the Hamas Movement. Unfortunately we must admit that in such a war the only way to get rid of "these irregular phenomena" is what Israel is doing. The operations of Israel in Gaza and Lebanon are in the interest of people of Arab countries and the international community.' Ahmad al-Jarallah, 'No to Syria, Iran agents', *Arab Times*, 17 July 2006.

7 See also Lawrence G. Potter and Gary Sick (eds), *Iran, Iraq and the Legacies of War*, London: Palgrave Macmillan, 2006.

8 See more recently Ali-Reza Barzegar, *Ruzshomar-e jang-e tahmil-ye aragh ba jomhur-ye eslam-ye Iran* [A Chronology of the Iraqi-imposed War against Iran], Tehran: Soroush, 1379/2000, especially the preface. For a translation of the messages and last wills of the Iranian war veterans see Nader Nazemi, 'Sacrifice and Authorship: A Compendium of the Wills of Iranian War Martyrs', *Iranian Studies*, Vol. 30, Nos. 3-4, Summer-Fall 1997, pp. 263-71.

9 In an off the record interview with the author (November 2002), a senior Iranian Foreign Ministry official gave following numbers for those Iranian soldiers affected by chemical weapons: 60,000 dead, 124,000 with over 25 per cent exposure, 200,000 under 25 per cent, 120,000 minimal contamination and 600 with 80 per cent and higher who are close to death. According to Iranian health officials, about 60,000 Iranians were exposed to Iraqi chemical weapon attacks during the war, Agence France Press (AFP), 13 March 2000. Over 15,000 war veterans suffering from chemical weapons syndrome reportedly died in the 12 years after the end of Iran-Iraq war, according to Abbas Khani, the head of the Legal Office for War Veterans, IRNA, 13 November 2000. See also Jean Pascal Zanders, 'Iranian Use of Chemical Weapons: A Critical Analysis of Past Allegations', *SIPRI Chemical and Biological Warfare Project*, 7 March 2001; Farnaz Fassihi, 'In Iran, grim

reminders of Saddam's arsenal', *The Star-Ledger*, 9 December 2002; Paul Hughes, 'Saddam's chemical victims still suffering in Iran', *Reuters*, 20 January 2003 and '40,000 Chemically Wounded Veterans in Iran: Professor', *The Tehran Times*, 28 June 2004.

10 Dilip Hiro stresses the role of the United States, arguing that by 'supplying secret information, which exaggerated Iran's military weakness, to Saudi Arabia for onward transmission to Baghdad, Washington encouraged Iraq to attack Iran'; see his book, *The Longest War: The Iran-Iraq Military Conflict*, London: Grafton Books, 1990, p. 71. See also his *Neighbours Not Friends: Iraq and Iran after the Gulf Wars*, London: Routledge, 2001.

11 This justification was rather more central to the Iraqi efforts to legitimate the invasion: by interfering in the internal affairs of Iraq, it typically was argued, Iran had broken the terms of the Algiers Agreement. See, for example, Majid Khadduri, *The Gulf War. The Origins and Implications of the Iraq-Iran Conflict*, Oxford University Press, 1988, especially Chapter VIII.

12 In terms of international law, the United Nations belatedly settled the question of who started the war its report of 9 December 1991 (S/23273), which—only after Iraq's invasion of Kuwait—referred to 'Iraq's *aggression* against Iran'.

13 See J.S. Bruner, 'Going beyond the Information Given', in University of Colorado, Boulder, Department of Psychology (ed.), *Contemporary Approaches to Cognition*, Cambridge, MA: Harvard University Press, 1957, pp. 218-38.

14 Ying-yi Hong, Michael W. Morris, Chi-yue Chiu and Verónica Benet-Martínez, 'Multicultural Minds: A Dynamic Constructivist Approach to Culture and Cognition', *American Psychologist*, Vol. 55, No. 7, 2000, p. 711.

15 Gordon W. Allport, 'The Role of Expectancy', in Leon Bramson and George W. Goethals (eds), *War Studies from Psychology, Sociology, Anthropology*, London: Basic Books, 1964, p. 179.

16 Michael W. Morris, Tanya Menon and Daniel R. Ames, 'Culturally Conferred Conceptions of Agency: A Key to Social Perception of Persons, Groups, and Other Actors,' *Personality and Social Psychology Review*, Vol. 5, No. 2, 2001, p. 173.

17 Arshin Adib-Moghaddam, *The International Politics of the Persian Gulf: A Cultural Genealogy*, London: Routledge, especially Chapter Two.

18 Quoted in Raymod Williams, *Culture and Society, 1780-1950*, Harmondsworth: Penguin, 1961, p. 270.

19 Consider, for instance, two books published in the early 1980s, *Al-Madaris al-Yahudiyya wa-l-Iraniyya fi-l-'Iraq* (Jewish and Iranian schools in Iraq) by Fadil al-Barrak and *Al-Harb al-sirriyya, khafaya al-dawr al-Isra'ili fi harb al-khalij* (The secret war: The mysterious role of Israel in the [First] Gulf War) by Sa'd al-Bazzaz. The former deals with the 'destructive' and 'dangerous'

impact of Jewish and Iranian schools on Iraqi society. The latter outlines how Israel and Iran conspired to combat Iraq, with special reference to the destruction of the nuclear reactor in Osirak by the Israeli Air Force in June 1981.

20 See Khairallah Talfah, *Three Whom God Should Not Have Created: Persians, Jews and Flies,* or serials entitled *Judhur al-'ada al-Farsi li-l-umma al-'Arabiyya* (The roots of Persian hostility towards the Arab nation), and proverbs such as *Ma hann a'jami 'ala 'Arabi* (An *ajam* or Persian will not have mercy on an Arab).

21 Ofra Bengio, *Saddam's Word: Political Discourse in Iran*, Oxford University Press, 1998, p. 143.

22 Quoted in ibid., p. 143.

23 Bengio, *Saddam's Word* (note 21), pp. 142-3.

24 The phrase, which was to be used in any official Iraqi correspondence, likened the war to the battle of Qadisiyya in 637 AD. During that battle the armies of Sassanian Iran, led by General Roustum, were fighting as a Zoroastrian-Persian force and were defeated by a Muslim army under the command of Saad bin Abi Waqqas. The defeat led to the capture of the Sassanian capital Ctesiphon (its ruins are near Baghdad, itself a Persian term), causing the ending of Sassanian suzerainty in Iraq and opening up ancient Iran for the ensuing process of spreading Islam. After the Second Gulf War, Iraqi-Kurds operating in the semi-autonomous northern 'no-fly zone' forwarded thousands of documents from the Iraqi intelligence's four primary agencies—*al-Amn al-Khas* (Special Security), *al Amn al-'Amn* (General Security), *al-Mukhabarat al-Amma* (General Intelligence) and *al Istikhbarat al-'Askariyya* (Military Intelligence)—to the US government. They are available on the pages of the Iraq Research and Documentation Program at the Center for Middle East Studies, Harvard University, <http://www.fas.harvard.edu/~irdp/ > [accessed 12 March 2004]. The documents show that Saddam Hussein's identification with a comparable historical role and the regime's anti-Iranian disposition were indeed systematic. Whilst most of the documents refer to the Iran-Iraq war as *Qadisiyyat Saddam*, Iranians consistently are referred to in derogatory terms as the 'Zionist Persians', *al-'adu al-ajami* (the illiterate or foreign enemy), *al-'adu al-Irani* (the Iranian enemy) or *majus* (fire worshippers). The official terminology is consistent with other institutional manifestations of anti-Iranianism and its invented linkage with the history of Iraq and the character of Saddam Hussein.

25 See further Adib-Moghaddam, *The International Politics of the Persian Gulf* (note 17), Chapter Two.

26 'Saddam remembers war with Iran', *BBC*, 8 August 1998.

27 Fred Halliday, *The Middle East in International Relations: Power, Politics and Ideology*, Cambridge University Press, 2005, p. 220, emphasis in original.

28 Fred Halliday, *Islam and the Myth of Confrontation. Religion and Politics in the Middle East*, London: I.B. Tauris, 1996, p. 84.
29 Cable from US Embassy Baghdad to US Department of State (DOS), 'Minister of Industry Blasts Senate Action', 13 September 1988, page 2. I am drawing on the set of documents obtained by the National Security Archive (NSA) at George Washington University under the US Freedom on Information Act. See, for example, 'Saddam Hussein: More Secret History', 18 December 2003, <http://www.gwu.edu/~nsarchiv/NSAEBB/NSAEBB107/>[accessed 22 February 2005].
30 Comprehensive Report of the Special Advisor to the DCI on Iraq's WMD, 30 September 2004, <http://www.cia.gov/cia/report/iraq_wmd_2004/transmittal.html> [accessed 21 January 2005]. The report also revealed that Saddam Hussein used the United Nations-managed Oil-for-Food programme to provide millions of dollars in subsidies to an Iranian opposition group, the Mojahedin-e Khalq (MKO), which is listed as a terrorist organization in both the EU and the United States. The MKO is led by Maryam and Massoud Rajavi and has a political wing that operates under the name 'National Council for Resistance in Iran'. The armed military wing, based in Iraq until 2003 but disarmed and confined to one base by the US military since, launched several terrorist attacks inside Iran between 1988 and 2002. See Michael Isikoff and Mark Hosenball, 'Shades of Gray: The Duelfer report alleges that Saddam gave funds to a listed terror group, but the claim does little to advance the White House case for war,' *Newsweek*, 13 October 2004.
31 'Saddam proud of any Iran gas attack', *Gulf Times*, 19 December 2006.
32 See especially Peter L. Berger and Thomas Luckmann, *The Social Construction of Reality: A Treatise in the Sociology of Knowledge*, Harmondsworth: Penguin, 1979; and George Herbert Mead, *Mind, Self, and Society*, Chicago University Press, 1934.
33 Nasir Al-Din Tusi, 'Sayr wa Suluk (Contemplation and Action', in Seyyed Hossein Nasr with Mehdi Aminrazavi, *An Anthology of Philosophy in Persia*, Vol. II, Oxford University Press, p. 350.
34 See Lawrence A. Hirschfeld and Susan A. Gelman (eds), *Mapping the Mind: Domain Specificity in Cognition and Culture*, Cambridge University Press, 1994.
35 Alexander Wendt, *Social Theory of International Politics*, Cambridge University Press, 1999, p. 227.
36 Ibid., p. 372, emphasis in original.
37 David Berreby, *Us and Them: Understanding your Tribal Mind*, London: Hutchinson, 2005, pp. 104ff.
38 Many arguments about the causes of the Iraq war merge on this point, without, however, making explicit the link between Iraqi state identity

(under Saddam Hussein), external confirmation and the decision to launch the invasion. See among others Charles Tripp, *A History of Iraq*, second edition, Cambridge University Press, 2002, p. 231; and Anoushiravan Ehteshami and Gerd Nonneman, *War and Peace in the Gulf: Domestic Politics and Regional Relations into the 1990s*, Reading: Ithaca, 1991, pp. 39ff.

39 The following two sections are revised and extended versions of section 3.2.2 (p. 31 ff.) in my *The International Politics of the Persian Gulf* (note 17) and 'The Whole Range of Saddam Hussein's War Crimes', *Middle East Report*, Vol. 36, No. 2, Summer 2006, pp. 30-5.

40 Ehteshami and Nonneman, *War and Peace in the Gulf* (note 38), pp. 39-43. Responding to Robert Fisk's question about the transfer of CIA intelligence on the Iranian army to the Iraqi government, a German arms dealer stated the obvious: 'Mr. Fisk, I will tell you this. At the very beginning of the war, in September of 1980, I was invited to go to the Pentagon. And there I was handed the very latest US satellite photographs of the Iranian front lines. You could see everything on the pictures. There were the Iranian gun emplacements in Abadan and behind Khorramshahr, the lines of trenches on the eastern side of the Karun river, the tank revetments—thousands of them—all the way up the Iranian side of the border towards Kurdistan. No army could want more than this. And I travelled with these maps from Washington by air to Frankfurt and from Frankfurt on Iraqi Airways straight to Baghdad. The Iraqis were very grateful — *very* grateful.' Robert Fisk, *The Great War for Civilisation: The Conquest of the Middle East*, London: Harper Perennial, 2006, p. 941.

41 Ibid. p. 43; see also Bahman Baktiari, 'Revolutionary Iran's Persian Gulf Policy: The Quest for Regional Supremacy', in Hooshang Amirahmadi and Nader Entessar (eds), *Iran and the Arab World*, London: Macmillan Press, 1998, pp. 74ff.

42 Saideh Lotfian, 'Taking Sides: Regional Powers and the War', in Farhang Rajaee (ed.), *Iranian Perspectives on the Iran-Iraq War*, Gainesville: University Press of Florida, 1997, p. 18.

43 Shahram Chubin and Charles Tripp, *Iran and Iraq at War*, London: I.B. Tauris, 1988, p. 154.

44 Lotfian, 'Taking Sides' (note 42), p. 19.

45 Chubin and Tripp, *Iran and Iraq at War* (note 43), p. 153.

46 US Embassy in Baghdad declassified document number 1985BAGHDA00892, 'Views of the Jordanian and Egyptian Ambassadors on Iraq: The War, The Peace Process and Inter-Arab Relations', March 1985, p. 2, NSA, op. cit.

47 Telegram from British Embassy Baghdad to Foreign and Commonwealth Office, "Saddam Hussein," 20 December 1969, Public Record Office, London, FCO 17/871, p. 4; and NSA, op. cit.

48 "Secretary's Principals and Regionals Staff Meeting," 28 April 1975 (Excerpt), page 22, NSA, op. cit.
49 Cable from US Embassy Amman to DOS, "Hussein on Mubarak's Visit and Their Joint Trip to Iraq", 19 March 1985, p. 3, NSA, op. cit.
50 Cable from US Embassy Baghdad to DOS, "Views of the Jordanian and Egyptian Ambassadors on Iraq: the War, the Peace Process, and Inter-Arab Relations," 28 March 1985, p. 3, NSA, op. cit.
51 See, for instance, Richard Sorabji and David Rodin (eds), *The Ethics of War: Shared Problems in Different Traditions*, Aldershot: Ashgate, 2006.
52 Sir Anthony Parsons, 'Iran and the United Nations, with Particular Reference to the Iran-Iraq War', in Anoushiravan Ehteshami and Manshour Varasteh (eds), *Iran and the International Community*, London: Routledge, 1991, pp. 16 and 18.
53 Julian Perry Robinson and Jozef Goldblat, 'Chemical Warfare in the Iraq-Iran War', *SIPRI Fact Sheet*, Chemical Weapons I. Stockholm International Peace Research Institute (May 1984).
54 Parsons, 'Iran and the United Nations' (note 52), p. 19. The Society for Chemical Weapons Victim Support in Tehran reports further that 'Following many requests by the Iranian Government, three official investigation teams were sent to Iran in March 1984, February/March 1986 and April 1987. The conclusions, based on field inspections, clinical examinations of casualties, and laboratory analysis of samples, were released as three official UN reports (S/16433, S/17911, and S/18852). Based on the UN fact finding team's investigations they confirmed the use of mustard gas as well as nerve agents against Iranian troops.' The NGO further reports four chemical weapons attacks on residential areas in Iran and Iraqi Kurdistan: in Sardasht with mustard gas on 28 June 1987; in villages around the city of Marivan in March 1988; in Halabja on 18 March 1988 (see below) and villages around the cities of Sarpol-e Zahab, Gilan-e-gharb and Oshnavieh between May and June 1988. See Society for Chemical Victims Support (SCWVS), <http//:www.scwvs.org>. See also Kamin Mohammadi (Organization for Defending the Victims of Chemical Weapons in Sardasht), 'The Forgotten Victims of the Iran-Iraq War', *Mail on Sunday*, 26 November 2006.
55 Parsons, 'Iran and the United Nations' (note 52), pp. 19-20.
56 Jean Pascal Zanders, 'Allegations of Iranian CW Use in the 1980-88 Gulf War: A Critical Analysis from Open Sources', Washington DC: SIPRI, 7 March 2001.
57 Talabani was the leader of the Patriotic Union of Kurdistan (PUK), a group that the Iraqis referred to as *Ulama Iran* (agent of Iran) because of its collusion with Iran in the latter periods of the war.
58 Kurdish tribal leaders of paramilitary units officially referred to as *Qiyadet Jahafel al-Difa' al-Watani* (National Defence Battalions) by the Iraqi regime

and derided by other Kurds as *jahsh* or 'donkey foals' because of their alliance with the state.

59 The Ali Hassan al-Majid tapes were obtained by Human Rights Watch (HRW) after the 1991 Persian Gulf War and have been published as Appendix A to HRW's Report, 'Genocide in Iraq. The Anfal Campaign Against the Kurds', <http://www.hrw.org/reports/1993/iraqanfal/> [accessed 23 March 2006].

60 See further Adam Tarock, *The Superpowers' Involvement in the Iran-Iraq War*, Commack: Nova Science Press, 1998, p. 61.

61 See the NSA Electronic Briefing Book No. 82 (25 February 2003), 'Shaking Hands with Saddam Hussein. The US Tilts toward Iraq, 1980-1984', ed. Joyce Battle <http://www.gwu.edu/~nsarchiv/NSAEBB/NSAEBB82/index.htm>[accessed 13 March 2006].

62 US House of Representatives, Speech by Henry B. Gonzalez: 'Bush Administration Had Acute Knowledge of Iraq's Military Industrialisation Plans' (27 July 1992). <http://www.fas.org/spp/starwars/congress/1992/h920727g.htm> [accessed 21 January 2004].

63 US Senate Committee on Banking, Housing, and Urban Affairs (7 October 1994). Committee Staff Report No.3: Chemical Warfare Agent Identification, Chemical Injuries, and Other Findings. Principal Investigator James J Tuite III: 'US Chemical and Biological Exports to Iraq and their Possible Impact on the Health Consequences of the Persian Gulf War', <http://www.chronicillnet.org/PGWS/tuite/chembio.html> [accessed 14 March 2006].

64 For Saddam's international suppliers see Adib-Moghaddam, 'The Whole Range of Saddam Hussein's War Crimes' (note 39) and below.

65 See US Senate, 103rd Congress, Second Session (25 May 1994), a Report of Chairman Donald W. Riegle, Jr. and Ranking Member Alfonse M. D'Amato of the Committee on Banking, Housing and Urban Affairs with Respect to Export Administration: 'The Riegle Report. US Chemical and Biological Warfare-Related Dual Use Exports to Iraq and their Possible Impact on the Health Consequences of the Gulf War', <http://www.gulfweb.org/bigdoc/report/riegle1.html> [accessed 12 February 2005].

66 DOS, Bureau of Near Eastern and South Asian Affairs Information Memorandum, Jonathan T. Howe to Lawrence S. Eagleburger, 'Iran-Iraq War: Analysis of Possible US Shift from Position of Strict Neutrality', 7 October 1983. NSA, op. cit., page 7.

67 This is a reference to a National Security Decision Directive signed by Ronald Reagan in June 1983 and was co-authored by Howard Teicher and another NSC staff member, Geoffrey Kemp. The content of the NSDD and even its identification number remain classified.

68 US District Court (Florida, Southern District) Affidavit. 'United States of America, Plaintiff, v. Carlos Cardoen [et al.]' [Charge that Teledyne Wah Chang Albany Illegally Provided a Proscribed Substance, Zirconium, to Cardoen Industries and to Iraq], 31 January 1995. Teicher also stated that the CIA encouraged Iraq to use cluster bombs against the Iranian 'human wave' attacks. NSA, op. cit., pp. 3, 4 respectively.
69 US Embassy in Italy Cable from Maxwell M. Rabb to the DOS, 'Rumsfeld's Larger Meeting with Iraqi Deputy PM [Prime Minister] and FM [Foreign Minister] Tariz [Tariq] Aziz, 19, 20 December 1983. NSA, op. cit., p. 3.
70 US Embassy in United Kingdom, Cable from Charles H. Price II to the DOS. 'Rumsfeld Mission: December 20 Meeting with Iraqi President Saddam Hussein', 21 December 1983. NSA, op. cit., p. 8.
71 DOS, Bureau of Politico-Military Affairs Information Memorandum from Jonathan T. Howe to George P. Shultz, 'Iraq Use of Chemical Weapons', 1 November 1983. NSA, op. cit., p. 1.
72 DOS, Office of the Assistant Secretary for Near Eastern and South Asian Affairs Action Memorandum from Jonathan T. Howe to Lawrence S. Eagleburger, 'Iraqi Use of Chemical Weapons' [Includes Cables Entitled 'Deterring Iraqi Use of Chemical Weapons' and 'Background of Iraqi Use of Chemical Weapons'], 21 November 1983. NSA, op. cit., page 6, emphasis added.
73 *The Guardian*, 31 December 2002. See also Dilip Hiro, 'When the US Turned a Blind Eye to Poison Gas', *Observer*, 1 September 2002 and Joost Hiltermann, 'Elusive Justice: Trying to Try Saddam', *Middle East Report*, No. 215, Vol. 30, No. 2, 2000, pp. 32-5.
74 *The Guardian*, 31 December 2002.
75 See Alexander Zumach, 'Blühende Geschäfte. In sämtlichen Rüstungsbereichen haben Firmen aus den fünf ständigen Ratsländern Irak unterstützt', *die Tageszeitung (TAZ)*, 19 December 2002, <http://www.taz.de/pt/2002/12/19/a0076.nf/text> [accessed 12 March 2006].
76 The other 11 were: TI Coating, Tektronix, Leybold Vacuum Systems, Finnigan-MAT-US, American Type Culture Collection, Alcolac International, Consarc, Cerberus, International Computer Systems, Canberra Industries and Axel Electronics. In addition, ten companies were listed as sponsors of Iraq's rocket and/or conventional weapons programmes (Bechtel, Honeywell, Spectra Physics, Semetex, Sperry, Rockwell, Eastman Kodak, Carl Zeiss, Electronic Associates and EZ Logic Data Systems). Other reports have implicated Nu Kraft Mercantile (affiliated with United Steel and Strip), Celery, Matrix-Churchill (regarded as a front for the Iraqi government, according to Gonzalez, who quoted US intelligence documents to this effect in his 1992 speech on the House floor), Mouse Master, Lilburn, Sullaire, Pure Aire, Posi Seal, Evapco and Gorman-Rupp. Additionally,

several other companies were sued in connection with their activities providing Iraq with chemical or biological supplies: subsidiaries or branches of Fisher Controls International, Rhone-Poulenc, Bechtel and Lummus Crest, which built one chemical plant in Iraq and, before the Iraqi invasion of Kuwait in August 1990, was building an ethylene facility. See also William Blum, 'Anthrax for Export: US Companies Sold Iraq the Ingredients for a Witch's Brew,' *The Progressive*, April 1998.

77 The Möllemann report also revealed that toxics such as botulinus A und B were exported from Germany, without, however, naming the perpetrating parties. See Hans Branscheid, 'Der deutsche Exportweltmeister als Todeshändler: Dokumentation über den deutschen Rüstungs- und Giftgas-Transfer: Die Akte Möllemann' (Medico International), available at <http://www.fdj.de/irak/wirtschaft_brd_irak.pdf#search='Hans%20Branscheid%20akte> and Ronald Ofteringer, ‚Irakische Vernichtungswaffen und industriestaatliche Proliferation: Die UN Kommission für Irak und die Bundesrepublik'. Available at <http://www.nadir.org/nadir/initiativ/kurdi-almani-kassel/aktuell/2001/dez2001/irakwaff.htm> [accessed 22 March 2006].

78 *The Guardian*, 6 March 2003.

79 Ibid.

80 Ibid. The *Tageszeitung* investigation cited above further revealed that ten British companies were directly involved in Iraq's atomic research programme and that International Military Services, owned by the British Ministry of Defence, was a sponsor of the country's rocket programme. The companies named in the report are Euromac, C. Plath-Nuclear, Endshire Export Marketing, International Computer Systems, MEED International, International Computer, Matrix Churchill, Ali Ashour Daghir, XYY Options and Inwako.

81 On Rumsfeld's role in the negotiations, see also Joost R. Hilterman, 'The Men Who Helped the Man Who Gassed His Own People,' in Micah L. Sifry and Christopher Cerf (eds), *The Iraq War Reader. History, Documents, Opinions*, London: Touchstone, 2003, pp. 41-4.

82 DOS, Bureau of Near Eastern and South Asian Affairs Memorandum from James A. Placke to James M. Ealum [et al.]. ['US Condemnation of Iraqi Chemical Weapons Use'], 4 March 1984. NSA, op. cit., p. 2.

83 Ibid., p. 3, emphasis added.

84 See Zumach, 'Blühende Geschäfte' (note 75).

85 US Interests Section in Iraq, Cable from William L. Eagleton, Jr. to the DOS, 'Iraqi Warning re Iranian Offensive', 22 February 1984. NSA, op. cit., page 1.

86 DOS Cable from George P. Shultz to the United States Embassy in Lebanon [et al.]. 'Department Press Briefing, March 30, 1984', 31 March 1984. NSA, op. cit., page 3.

87 DOS, Bureau of Near Eastern and South Asian Affairs Cover Memorandum from Allen Overmyer to James A. Placke [United Nations Security Council Response to Iranian Chemical Weapons Complaint; Includes Revised Working Paper], 30 March 1984. NSA, op. cit., p. 1.

88 It was later established that the Iranian allegation that the US cruiser was in Iranian territorial waters was accurate. The captain of the USS *Vincennes*, Will Rogers, and even more surprisingly the Air Warfare Co-ordinator, Scott Lustig, would subsequently receive medals for their engagements in the Persian Gulf. The latter even achieved the Navy Commendation Medal with Combat V authorisation for what was summarized as his 'heroic achievements'.

89 The USS *Stark* was hit by Exocet missiles that Iraq had acquired from France in a deal that was backed by the United States. In his speech to the US House of Representative, the late Texas Democrat Henry Gonzales touched on that point: 'I ask you how could we be supplying Iraq with everything from intelligence—because we had an intelligence-gathering agreement all during that war with Iraq—supplied them with everything else, even backed up foreign countries like France to make sure they supplied military things all the way from Mirages to Exocet missiles, one of which, incidentally, was the one that killed 37 of our sailors in the Persian Gulf', op. cit.

90 See further Joel Brinkley (ed.), *Report of the Congressional Committee Investigating the Iran-Contra* Affair, New York: Times Book, 1988. For a discussion of the Iran-Contra Affair and its impact on the Iran-Iraq war see Tarock, *The Superpowers' Involvement* (note 60), pp. 91-122.

91 White House, John M. Poindexter Memorandum to President Reagan, 'Covert Action Finding Regarding Iran,' (with attached presidential finding), 17 January 1986. Available through the National Security Archive at George Washington University. <http://216.239.59.104/search?q=cache:_6OuPIR7QvwJ:www.gwu.edu/~nsarchiv/NSAEBB/NSAEBB210/index.htm+White+House,+John+M.+Poindexter+Memorandum+to+President+Reagan,+%E2%80%98Covert+Action+Finding+Regarding+Iran,%E2%80%99+(with+attached+presidential+finding),+17+January+1986&hl=en&ct=clnk&cd=1&gl=uk> [accessed 14 February 2007]. The documents also show that apart from Elliott Abrams, Michael Ledeen, John Bolton, the former US Secretary of State Colin Powell and the current US Secretary of Defense Robert Gates were also involved in the process. See also Noam Chomsky, *Fateful Triangle: The United States, Israel, and the Palestinians*, updated edition, London: Pluto, 1999, pp. 457 ff.

92 'Covert Action Finding Regarding Iran' (with attached presidential finding), 17 January 1986, op. cit.

93 'The Glaspie Transcript: Saddam meets the US Ambassador (25 July 1990)', in Micah L. Sifry and Christopher Cerf (eds), *The Gulf War Reader: History, Documents, Opinions*, New York: Times Books, 1991, p. 125.

94 See 'Saddam Hussein's Iraq'. Prepared by the US Department of State, September 1999. Available at <http://www.fas.org/news/iraq/2000/02/iraq99.htm> [accessed 12 August 2006] In recent years, investigative journalists have provided further evidence for the aid to Saddam. See David Leigh and John Hooper, 'Britain's dirty secret', *The Guardian*, 6 March 2003, <http://www.guardian.co.uk/Iraq/Story/0%2C2763%2C908426%2C00.html> [accessed 13 March 2004]; Babak Dehghanpisheh, 'Grim Legacy', *Newsweek*, 19 March 2003 <http://msnbc.msn.com/id/3068535/> [accessed 6 March 2006]; Christopher Dickey and Evan Thomas, 'How Saddam Happened', *Newsweek*, 23 September 2002, <http://foi.missouri.edu/terrorbkgd/howsaddam.html> [accessed 13 January 2006]; Michael Dobbs, 'U.S. had key role in Iraq buildup, trade in chemical arms allowed despite their use on Iranians, Kurds', *The Washington Post*, 30 December 2002, <http://www.washingtonpost.com/ac2/wp-dyn/A52241-2002Dec29?language=printer> [accessed 13 March 2004] ; and Blum, 'Anthrax for export', *The Progressive*, April 1998, <http://www.progressive.org/0901/anth0498.html> [accessed 13 June 2001].

95 Margaret Mead, 'Warfare is only an invention—Not a Biological Necessity', in Leon Bramson and George W. Goethals (eds), *War: Studies from Psychology, Sociology, Anthropology*, London: Basic Books, 1964, pp. 269-74.

96 John Mueller, *Retreat from Doomsday: The Obsolescence of Major War*, London: Basic Books, 1990, p. 13.

97 See further 'Ahmadinejad rolls out red carpet for Maliki, vows to help restore security', *The Daily Star* (Beirut), 13 September 2006; 'Iran, Iraq agree to establish joint security committee in charge of Arvandroud', IRNA, 14 August 2006; 'Iran, Iraq ink deal to remove landmines', IRNA, 12 December 2005; 'Iran to aid Iraq with $1 billion loan to help tackle insecurity', *The Daily Star* (Beirut), 24 November 2005; 'Iran, Iraq ink letter of understanding to boost cooperation', IRNA, 19 November 2003.

98 See further 'Baghdad works to free Iranians detained in US raid: "Very annoying ... they have been working under the approval of the government",' *The Daily Star* (Beirut), 13 January 2007; James Glanz and Sabrina Tavernise, "US detains Iranians in Iraq', *The International Herald Tribune*, 25 December 2006.

99 Full text available at <http://www.jihadunspun.com/intheatre_internal.php?article=106739&list=/home.php%20> [accessed 20 November 2006].

100 'Sunni leader appeals for help against what he calls Iranian-supported death squads and militias', *Associated Press*, 12 August 2007.

101 See further *The International Politics of the Persian Gulf* (note 17), p. 16ff.
102 For a theoretical case for inter-state cooperation between Muslim states see Amr G.E. Sabet, 'The Islamic Paradigm of Nations: Toward a Neo-Classical Approach', *Peace and Conflict Studies*, Vol. 8, No. 2, November 2001, pp. 23-50.
103 Fouad Ajami, *The Foreigner's Gift: The Americans, the Arabs, and the Iraqis in Iraq*, New York: Free Press, 2007; Vali Nasri, *The Shia Revival: How Conflicts within Islam will Shape the Future*, New York: W.W. Norton, 2007. See also the latter's 'Prepared testimony before the Senate Committee on Foreign Relations', 17 January 2007.
104 Herbert Marcuse, *Towards A Critical Theory of Society: Collected Papers of Herbert Marcuse*, Vol. 2, ed. Douglas Kellner, London: Routledge, 2001, p. 173.
105 Marcuse, *Towards a Critical Theory of Society* (note 104), p. 54.
106 Robert W. Cox, 'Towards a Posthegemonic Conceptualisation of World Order: Reflections on the Relevancy of Ibn Khaldun', in Robert W. Cox, *Approaches to World Order*, Cambridge University Press, 1996, p. 163.
107 See further Adib-Moghadam, *The International Politics of the Persian Gulf* (note 17), chapters 1 and 5.

III. IRANIAN-AMERICAN ENCOUNTERS: THE ISLAMIC REPUBLIC IN THE NEOCONSERVATIVE MIND

1 Hans.Georg Gadamer, *Truth and Method*, second revised edition, London: Continuum, 2004, p. 203.
2 Abu Nasr Farabi, 'Kitab al-burhan [Paraphrase of Aristotle's *Analytica Posteriora*]', in *An Anthology of Philosophy in Persia, Vol. I*, eds. Seyyed Hossein Nasr with Mehdi Aminrazavi, Oxford University Press, 1999, pp. 98-9.
3 I am drawing on the sociological theory of Peter L. Berger and Thomas Luckmann here. See *The Social Construction of Reality*, New York: Anchor Books, 1966.
4 For such 'realist' approaches to the international politics of West Asia see Raymond Hinnebusch and Anoushiravan Ehteshami (eds), *The Foreign Policies of Middle East States*, London: Lynne Rienner, 2002); Shibley Telhami, *Power and Leadership in International Bargaining: The Path to the Camp David Accords*, New York: Columbia University Press, 1990; Barry Buzan and Ole Waever, *Regions and Powers: The Structure of International Security*, Cambridge University Press, 2003. For a study in the neo-realist, Waltzian tradition see Birthe Hansen, *Unipolarity and the Middle East*, Richmond, Surrey: Curzon, 2000. For a discussion of the various

approaches see Raymond Hinnebusch, *The International Politics of the Middle East*, Manchester University Press, 2003 and Arshin Adib-Moghaddam, *The International Politics of the Persian Gulf: A Cultural Genealogy*, London: Routledge, 2006.

5 See Eric Hobsbawm and Terence Ranger (eds), *The Invention of Tradition*, Cambridge University Press, 1983.

6 See further Adib-Moghaddam, *The International Politics of the Persian Gulf* (note 4), especially chapters 1 and 5.

7 The necessarily imperfect term 'neoconservative' denotes those functionaries, bureaucrats, decision-makers and academics who advocate an aggressive foreign policy posture for the United States. The most prominent proponents are Paul Wolfowitz, Richard Perle, Elliott Abrams, Douglas Feith, Michael Ledeen, Charles Krauthammer, Jeane J. Kirkpatrick and William Kristol. See Julie Kosterlitz, 'The Neoconservative Moment', *National Journal*, Vol. 35, No. 20, 17 May 2003, pp. 1540-6. In the 7 April 2002 issue of the *New Statesmen*, Michael Lind describes the emergence of US neoconservatism as follows: 'How did they get the name? Many of them started off as anti-Stalinist leftists or liberals. They are products of the largely Jewish-American Trotskyist movement of the 1930s and 1940s, which morphed into anti-communist liberalism between the 1950s and 1970s and finally into a kind of militaristic and imperial right with no precedents in American culture or political history. They call their revolutionary ideology "Wilsonianism" (after President Woodrow Wilson), but it is really Trotsky's theory of the permanent revolution mingled with the far-right Likud strain of Zionism.' For a history of US neoconservatism see Peter Steinfels, *The Neoconservatives: The Men Who Are Changing America's Politics*, New York: Simon and Schuster, 1979 and Herbert von Borch, *Amerika-Dekadenz und Größe*, Munich: R. Piper & Co., 1981, especially p. 121 ff. For a recent analysis of neoconservative grand strategy see among others Andrew J. Bacevich, *The New American Militarism: How Americans Are Seduced by War*, Oxford University Press, 2005 and John Bellamy Foster, 'Naked Imperialism', *Monthly Review*, Vol. 57, No. 4, September 2005. Available at <http://www.monthlyreview.org/nakedimperialism.htm> [accessed 12 May 2006]. For the ideological linkages between the Zionist ideal and US American idealism see Lawrence Davidson, 'Christian Zionism as a Representation of American Manifest Destiny', *Critique: Critical Middle Eastern Studies*, Vol. 14, No. 2, Summer 2005, pp. 157-69.

8 For the term 'international society' see Hedley Bull, *The Anarchical Society: A Study of Order in World Politics*, second edition London: Macmillan, 1995.

9 On discursive formations see Michel Foucault, *The Archaeology of Knowledge*, translated by A.M. Sheridan Smith, London: Routledge, 1989. See also

Edward W. Said, *Orientalism: Western Conceptions of the Orient*, London: Routledge & Kegan Paul, 1978.

10 See on this point John Mearsheimer and Stephen Walt, 'The Israel Lobby', *London Review of Books*, Vol. 28, No. 6, 23 March 2006. Available at <http://www.lrb.co.uk/v28/n06/mear01_.html> [accessed 23 May 2006].

11 See further Adib-Moghaddam, *The International Politics of the Persian Gulf* (note 4), Chapters Three and Four.

12 The phrase 'Anyone can go to Baghdad. Real men go to Tehran' has been attributed to a senior Bush administration official in May 2003.

13 See Leon T. Hadar, 'The "Neocons": From the Cold War to the "Global Initifada"', *Washington Report on Middle East Affairs*, April 1991, pp. 27-46. Available at < http://www.washington-report.org/backissues/0491/9104027.htm> [accessed 23 August 2006]; Michael Lind, 'A Tragedy of Errors', *The Nation*, 23 February 2004. Available at <http://www.thenation.com/doc/20040223/lind> [accessed 28 August 2006]; Leila Hudson, 'Lessons From Wal-Mart and the *Wehrmacht*: Team Wolfowitz on Administration in the Information Age,' *Middle East Policy*, Vol. XI, No. 2, Summer 2004. Available at <http://www.mepc.org/journal_vol11/0406_hudson.asp> [accessed 1 September 2006].

14 The authors accurately observe that the lobby, while predominantly Jewish, also includes prominent Christian evangelicals and non-Jewish neoconservatives such as former CIA Director James Woolsey and former Education Secretary William Bennett. Mearsheimer and Walt, 'Israel Lobby' (note 10).

15 See amongst others Joel Beinin, 'Pro-Israel Hawks and the Second Gulf War', *Middle East Online*, 6 April 2006. Available at <http://www.merip.org/mero/mero040603.html> [accessed 4 September 2006]; Karen Kwiatkowski, 'The New Pentagon Papers', *Salon*, 10 March 2004. Available at <http://dir.salon.com/story/opinion/feature/2004/03/10/osp_moveon/index.html> [accessed 2 September 2006].

16 See Brian Whitaker 'US think tanks give lessons in foreign policy', *The Guardian*, 19 August 2002. See also his 'Selective Memri', *The Guardian*, 12 August 2002.

17 All material pertaining to the Project is quoted from documents accessible at <http://www.newamericancentury.org/> [accessed 12 August 2005].

18 In that capacity Abrams also invited Iranian exiles and separatists to a meeting at the White House on July 2006.

19 See also Arshin Adib-Moghaddam, 'The Neo-Conservative *asabiyya*', *State of Nature*, No. 4 (Summer 2006). Available at <http://www.stateofnature.org/neoconservativeAsabiyya.html> [accessed 12 August 2006].

20 See also part 2.

21 See Footnote 12.

22 Those readers who are familiar with Fox News and its propensity for ready-made, formulaic analysis by former members of the US armed forces will recognize some of the supporters of the IPC: Lt. Col. Bill Cowan, USMC (ret.); Lt. Gen. Thomas McInerney USAF (ret.); Maj. Gen. Paul E. Valley, US Army (ret.); Capt. Charles T. Nash, USN (ret.); and Lt. Gen. Edward Rowny, US Army (ret.). Other IPC members are also familiar faces: the aforementioned Raymond Tanter; Clare Lopez, a former CIA analyst; and Jim Atkins, US ambassador to Saudi Arabia during the presidency of Richard Nixon.

23 Quoted from the Institute's webpage at <www.religionandpolicy.org> [accessed 12 July 2006].

24 See Golnaz Yazdchi, 'Santorum portrays Iran as top source of "Islamic Fascism", calls for regime change', National Iranian-American Council (NIAC), 21 July 2006.

25 Brian Bennett, Elaine Shannon and Adam Zagorin, 'A web of intrigue: Inside the Israel espionage investigation', *Time Magazine*, 5 September 2004.

26 'Pentagon man jailed over spying', BBC, 20 January 2006. The District court found Franklin guilty of count 1 'Conspiracy to communicate national defence information to persons not entitled to receive it, 18 U.S.C. §§ 793 (d), (e) and (g) count 2-4 'Communication of national defense information to persons not entitled to receive it', 18 USC § 793 (d) and count 5 'Conspiracy to communicate classified information to agent of foreign government', 50 U.S.C. § 783, 18 U.S.C. § 371. Rosen was found guilty on counts 1-3 and Weissman on count 1. The full indictment is available at <http://fl1.findlaw.com/news.findlaw.com/nytimes/docs/dod/usfrnklin80205ind.pdf> [accessed 12 February 2007].

27 The Chairman of the Senate Armed Services Committee, Senator Carl Levin, released the declassified 'Pentagon Inspector General Report on Intelligence Assessment Activities of the Office of Under Secretary of Defense Doug Feith' in April 2007. It was stated that Feith concluded incorrectly that 'intelligence indicates cooperation [between the regime of Saddam Hussein and al-Qaeda] in all categories' and that he asserted wrongly that an alleged meeting in April 2001 in Prague between an Iraqi intelligence officer and the lead 9/11 hijacker Mohammed Atta was a 'known' contact. The full declassified report is available at <http://www.fas.org/irp/agency/dod/ig020907-decl.pdf> [accessed 14 April 2007].

28 See <http://www.onejerusalem.org> [accessed 12 August 2006]. The organization is chaired by Natan Sharansky.

29 Available at <http://www.nationalreview.com/ledeen/ledeen200506160752.asp> [accessed 11 July 2006].

30 Available at <http://www.washingtontimes.com/commentary/20050616-100858-6525r.htm> [accessed 5 July 2006].
31 Available at <http://www.aei.org/publications/filter.allpubID.22685.pub_detail.asp> [accessed 8 July 2006].
32 For a commentary see Behrooz Ghamari-Tabrizi, 'The World Isn't Florida and the US isn't Its Supreme Leader: Iran's Elections', *Counterpunch*, 18 December 2006.
33 John Simpson, 'Iran's New Leader, A Familiar Face?', *BBC*, 28 June 2005.
34 See further part 4.
35 For a perceptive critique see Farid Marjai, 'konferanc-e holokast va diplomac-ye Irani' [The Holocaust Conference and Iranian diplomacy], *Etemad-e Melli*, No. 259, p. 11, 29 Azar 1385 [20 December 2006].
36 Available at <http://www.danielpipes.org/article/2814 > [accessed 25 July 2005].
37 Available at <http://weeklystandard.com/Content/Public/Articles/000/000/006/617pwzlq.asp> [accessed 25 July 2005].
38 <http://weeklystandard.com/comment/berman200601190821.asp> [accessed 27 July 2005].
39 This is another similarity to the build-up of the invasion of Iraq when the US media played a key role in reproducing, and thereby disseminating, both the 'Hitler-Hussein' and 'US-New World Order'analogies. In a study ofthe number of stories citing Saddam Hussein and Adolf Hitler, and the New World Order, in *The Washington Post* before, during and after the Second Gulf War, Shaw and Martin found a direct correlation between the intensity of conflict and the employment of the phrases by the *Post*'s reporters. In the pre-war period between 30 June 1990 and 1 August 1990, Hussein and Hitler were mentioned twice (an average of 0.06 news stories per day) and the New World Order phrase not at all (obviously because the phrase had not yet entered the jargon of US policy-makers and Iraq had not yet invaded Kuwait). In the build-up to the US offensive between 2 August 1990 and 15 January 1991, the Hussein-Hitler analogy was used 118 times (an average of 0.71 news stories per day) and the New World Order phrase fifty times (an average of 0.30 stories per day). During the air war from 16 January 1991 to 22 February 1991, the Hussein-Hitler comparison was referred to 39 times (an average of 1.03 times per day) and the New World Order phrase was mentioned 45 times (an average of 1.18 numbers of stories per day). During the US offensive on the ground, that is in a period of four days between 23 February and 27 February 1991, the Hussein-Hitler analogy was mentioned seven times (an average of 1.40 number of stories per day) and the New World Order norm five times (an average of one story per day). The employment of both phrases decreased in the post-war period between 28 February 1991 and 30 March 1991; the Hitler-Hussein comparison was

made seven times (an average of 0.23 stories per day) and the New World Order phrase was used 21 times (an average of 0.68 news stories per day). See Donald L. Shaw and Shannon E. Martin, 'The Natural, and Inevitable, Phases of War Reporting: Historical Shadows, New Communication in the Persian Gulf', in Robert E. Denton Jr. (ed.), *The Media and the Persian Gulf War*, Westport, CT: Praeger, 1993, p. 53.

40 Available at <http://www.ivanyi-consultants.com/articles/aboutiran.html> [accessed 29 July 2005].

41 Charles Krauthammer, 'In Iran, arming for Armageddon', *The Washington Post*, 16 December 2005, emphasis added.

42 Bernard Lewis, 'August 22: Does Iran have something in store', *The Wall Street Journal*, 8 August 2006.

43 Kenneth R. Timmerman, 'Is Iran's Ahmadinejad a messianic medium?', *The Daily Star*, 30 December 2005.

44 See further Ron Jacobs, 'Kenneth Timmerman's Iranian "Democracy" and the "Intelligence" Summit', *Monthly Review Webzine*, 1 February 2006. Available at <http://mrzine.monthlyreview.org/jacobs010206.html> [accessed 12 May 2006].

45 Marc Perelman, 'US Probes Diplomacy on Iran Nukes', *The Forward*, 27 January 2006.

46 See as another example William Kristol, 'Unacceptable? Is the America of 2006 more willing to thwart the unacceptable than the France of 1936?', *The Weekly Standard* 11, Issue 30 (24 April 2006).

47 Before the Islamic revolution, between 1972 and 1979, Taheri was executive editor-in-chief of *Kayhan*, one of Iran's main daily newspapers.

48 Amir Taheri, 'A colour code for Iran's infidels', *National Post*, 19 May 2006.

49 Ibid.

50 Jim Lobe, 'Iran the target of disinformation campaign', *Inter Press Service*, 23 May 2006.

51 Larry Cohler-Essess, 'Bunkum from Benador', *The Nation*, 3 July 2006. Available at <http://www.thenation.com/doc/20060703/cohleresses> [accessed 3 September 2006].

52 Guy Dinmore, 'Bush and Blair meet Iranian opposition', *Financial Times*, 31 May 2006.

53 Tehran's Jewish cemetery is online at <http://www.beheshtieh.com> [accessed 12 May 2007].

54 The webpage of the hospital can be found at <http://www.iranjewish.com/English.htm> [accessed 12 May 2007].

55 I am not suggesting that Iranian-Jews, do not face discrimination, of course. What I have intended to show is that the reality of life as an Iranian-Jew in

the Islamic Republic lies beyond the narratives engendered by Ahmadinejad, Taheri and others.

56 Jim Lobe, 'Iran showdown tests power of "Israel Lobby"', Inter Press Service, 12 April 2006.

57 Jay Solomon and Andrew Higgins, 'Exiled Iranian has another run as U.S. informant', *The Wall Street Journal*, 13 July 2006.

58 CIA, Memorandum, 'Subject: Fabricator Notice - Manuchehr ((Gorbanifar)),' SECRET, 25 July, 1984. Available through the National Security Archive at <http://216.239.59.104/search?q=cache:_6OuPIR7QvwJ:www.gwu.edu/~nsarchiv/NSAEBB/NSAEBB210/index.htm+White+House,+John+M.+Poindexter+Memorandum+to+President+Reagan,+%E2%80%98Covert+Action+Finding+Regarding+Iran,%E2%80%99+(with+attached+presidential+finding),+17+January+1986&hl=en&ct=clnk&cd=1&gl=uk> [accessed 16 February 2007].

59 Shervin Boloorian, 'Fakhravar stands with neoconservatives, calls for US sponsored regime change in Iran', NIAC, 24 July 2006.

60 Toby Harnden, 'Ex-student hailed as Iran's hope', *The Sunday Telegraph*, 2 July 2006.

61 Quoted in Ibid.

62 Jim Lobe, 'The demagogue neocons love to hate', Inter Press Service, 25 January 2006.

63 Peter Konradi, 'Iran as bad as Nazis: Merkel', *The Sunday Times*, 5 February 2006. Available at <http://www.timesonline.co.uk/article/0,,2089-2025730,00.html> [2 September 2006].

64 Quoted in ibid.

65 See further Dilip Hiro, 'Tehranophobia', *The Guardian*, 10 August 2007.

66 Joseph Farah, 'Gingrich sees Iran threat to US like Nazi Germany: Ex-Speaker latest official to raise alarm on threat of nuclear EMP attack by Tehran', *WorldNetDaily*, 20 November 2005. Available at <http://www.worldnetdaily.com/news/article.asp?ARTICLE_ID=47501>[accessed 12 July 2006].

67 This is expressed from a neoconservative perspective in Irwin Stelzer (ed.), *Neoconservatism*, London: Atlantic, 2004.

68 See further Adib-Moghaddam, *The International Politics of the Persian Gulf*, especially section 4.3.1.1. For the new militarism in US foreign policy see Chalmers Johnson, *The Sorrows of Empire: Militarism, Secrecy, and the End of the Republic*, New York: Metropolitan, 2004; Noam Chomsky, *Hegemony or Survival: America's Quest for Global Dominance*, New York: Metropolitan, 2003; Carl Boggs (ed.), *Masters of War: Militarism and Blowback in the Era of American Empire*, London: Routledge, 2003; Clyde Prestowitz, *Rogue Nation: American Unilateralism and the Failure of Good Intentions*, New York: Basic Books, 2004; Michael Mann, *Incoherent Empire*, London: Verso,

2003; John Bellamy Foster, *Naked Imperialism: The U.S. Pursuit of Global Dominance*, New York: Monthly Review Press, 2006 and Bacevich, *New American Militarism* (note 7).

69 The 'global war on terror' narrative also served the purpose of escalating US military spending. Ismael Hossein-Zadeh has noted that the budget of the Pentagon for the fiscal year 2007 is about US$456 billion. President Bush has proposed an increase of 10% for 2008, bringing the budget to US$501.6 billion. This degree of military spending would be larger than military spending by all of the other nations in the world combined. Moreover, a pending supplemental appropriation to pay for the wars in Afghanistan and Iraq 'brings proposed military spending for FY 2008 to $647.2 billion, the highest level of military spending since the end of World War II—higher than Vietnam, higher than Korea, higher than the peak of the Reagan buildup.' See William D. Hartung, 'Bush Military Budget Highest Since WW II', *Common Dreams*, 10 February 2007. Available at <http://www.commondreams.org/views07/0210-26.htm> [accessed 27 April 2007]. For a comprehensive analysis see Ismael Hossein-Zadeh, *The Political Economy of U.S. Militarism*, London: Palgrave-Macmillan, 2006.

70 <http://www.commentarymagazine.com/Summaries/V113I2P21-1.htm> [accessed 24 July 2006].

71 'Bush's United States Military Academy Graduation Speech', *The Washington Post*, 2 June 2002.

72 Available at <http://www. whitehouse.gov/nsc/nss.html> [accessed 24 July 2006].

73 See especially Seymour Hersh, 'The Iran Plans: Would President Bush go to war to stop Tehran from getting the bomb?', *The New Yorker*, 17 July 2006, and his 'The next act: Is a damaged Administration less likely to attack Iran, or more?', *The New Yorker*, 27 November 2006. See also Dan Plesch, 'Next Target Tehran: All the signs are that Bush is planning for a neocon-inspired military assault on Iran', *The Guardian*, 15 January 2007.

74 Available at <http://www.business.timesonline.co.uk/article/0,,2089-2125207,00.html> [accessed 2 July 2006].

75 Available at <http://www.fas.org/irp/offdocs/nspd/nspd-17.html> [accessed 10 July 2006].

76 Mike Allen and Barton Gellman, 'Preemptive strikes part of US strategic doctrine: "All options" open for countering unconventional arms', *The Washington Post*, 11 December 2002.

77 Available at <http://www.law.cornell.edu/background/warpower/sj23.pdf#search=%22US%20Senate%20Joint%20Resolution%2023%20%22 > [accessed 12 August 2006].

78 Alan Dershowitz, 'Amend International Law To Allow Preemptive Strike on Iran', *Forward*, 20 August 2004.

79 Available at <http://www.whitehouse.gov/nsc/nss/2006/nss2006.pdf> [accessed 4 July 2006].

80 Ibid.

81 Available at <http://www.washingtonpost.com/wp-dyn/content/article/2006/03/12/AR2006031201016.html> [accessed 4 July 2006].

82 Farah Stockman, 'US unit works quietly to counter Iran's sway, backs dissidents, nearby nations', *The Boston Globe*, 2 January 2007.

83 Guy Dinmore, 'US marines probe tensions among Iran's minorities', *Financial Times*, 23 February 2006.

84 Jack Wheeler, 'Eliminate Iraq and Iran', *Freedom Research Foundation*, 2 December 2002.

85 Michael Rubin, 'Domestic Threats to Iranian Stability: Khuzistan and Baluchistan', *JCPA Jerusalem Issue Brief*, 13 November 2005.

86 Edward N. Luttwak, 'Would Iranians rally 'round the flag'?', *Los Angeles Times*, 10 February 2006. Luttwak is a senior senior fellow at the Center for Strategic and International Studies in Washington.

87 See Joseph S. Nye, *Soft Power: The Means to Success in World Politics*, New York: PublicAffairs, 2004.

88 Raymond Williams, *Culture and Society, 1780-1950*, London: Penguin, 1961, p. 324.

89 For a neoconservative justification of imperial dominance see Irving Kristol, 'The Neoconservative Persuasion: What it Was, and What it Is', in Irwin Stelzer (ed.), *Neoconservatism*, London: Atlantic, 2004, p. 36.

90 See Jim Lobe, 'Energised neo-cons say Israel's fight is Washington's', Inter Press Service, 17 July 2006.

91 Michael Ledeen, 'The same war: Hezbollah, natch', *National Review Online*, 13 July 2006.

92 Larry Kudlow, 'Israel's moment, the free world's gain': We are all Israelis now', *National Review Online*, 17 July 2006. Available at <http://article.nationalreview.com/q=ZjM1OGMxZWU0YzQ4MTQwZGU5NGRkMzQzM2MzNzdiNDc=> [accessed 7 September 2006].

93 Ibid.

94 William Kristol, 'Why Bush should go to Tel Aviv - and confront Iran', *Financial Times*, 16 July 2006. For A a similar view see Joshua Muravchik, 'Bombing Iran may buy time until democrats win', *The Daily Star*, 1 May 2006.

95 For an analysis of media misrepresentations of Iran see also Foad Izadi and Hakimeh Saghaye-Biria, 'A Discourse Analysis of Elite American Newspaper Editorials: The Case of Iran's Nuclear Program', *Journal of Communication Inquiry*, Vol. 31, No. 2 (April 2007), pp. 140-65.

96 Paul Ricoeur, *Time and Narrative, Volume I*, translated by Kathleen McLaughlin and David Pellauer, University of Chicago Press, 1984, pp. 176-7.

97 Graham E. Fuller, 'Repairing U.S.-Iranian Relations', *Middle East Policy*, Vol. VI, No. 2, 1998, pp. 140-4.

98 Mearsheimer and Walt, 'Israel Lobby' (note 10).

99 Zbigniew Brzezinski, 'Terrorised by "War on Terror": How a three-word mantra has undermined America', *The Washington Post*, 25 March 2007, p. B01.

100 'Remarks of Senator Barack Obama to the Chicago Council on Global Affairs', 23 April 2007. Available at <http://my.barackobama.com/page/content/fpccga> [accessed 26 April 2007].

101 See further Michael Crowley, 'The Real Reason She Won't Apologise: Hillary's War', *The New Republic*, 2 April 2007.

102 I have paraphrased Gadamer here, *Truth and Method* (note 1), p. 148.

103 It shouldn't come as a surprse that there have also been concerted efforts to blame the violence in Iraq on Iran (not entirely successful). See Kim Sengupta, Ben Russell and Terri Judd, 'Anger as Britain admits it was wrong to blame Iran for deaths in Iraq', *The Independent*, 5 January 2006. Available at <http://news.independent.co.uk/uk/politics/article336567.ece> [accessed 10 February 2007]; Ellen Knickmeyer, 'British find no evidence of arms traffic from Iran: Troops in Southeast Iraq test U.S. claim of aid for Militias', *The Washington Post*, 4 October 2006, A21; Greg Harkin, Francis Elliott and Raymond Whitaker, 'IRA bombs killed eight British soldiers in Iraq: Terror devices used by the IRA in a vicious murder campaign in Ulster blew up British servicemen as the world blamed Iran', *The Independent*, 16 October 2006. Available at <http://news.independent.co.uk/uk/ulster/article320004.ece> [accessed, 2 February 2007]; Alexandra Zavis and Greg Miller, 'Scant Evidence Found of Iran-Iraq Arms Link: U.S. warnings of advanced weaponry crossing the border are overstated, critics say ', *Los Angeles Times*, 23 January 2007. Available at <http://www.latimes.com/news/nationworld/world/la-fg-iraniraq23jan23,1,2522871.story?coll=la-headlines-world&ctrack=1&cset=true> [accessed, 7 February 2007]; and Emile Tyyep, 'Another U.S. Attempt to severe Iran/Iraq ties', *Al Jazeera Magazine*, 25 January 2007. Available at <http://www.aljazeera.com/me.asp?service_ID=13245> [accessed, 9 February 2007].

104 Joshua Muravchik, 'The *FP* Memo: Urgent: Operation Comaback,' ('Neoconservatives have the president's ear, but they also have lots of baggage. To stay relevant, they must admit mistakes, embrace public diplomacy, and start making the case for bombing Iran'), *Foreign Policy*, November/December 2006.

105 A recent report published by CASMII reveals, for instance, that Con Coughlin, 'who broke the story of Iraq's 45 minute WMD capacity', is the author of numerous articles 'containing unsubstantiated allegations against Iran' based on 'unnamed or untraceable sources'. The appendix of the report

lists sixteen articles by Coughlin between October 2005 and October 2006. None of them named a source. See <http://www.campaigniran.org/casmii/> [accessed 21 January 2007].

106 See further Adib-Moghaddam, *The International Politics of the Persian Gulf* (note 4), especially chapter 5.

107 A transcript of the symposium is available at <http://www.danielpipes.org/article/2814> [accessed 7 September 2006].

IV. IRAN'S PLURALISTIC MOMENTUM AND THE FUTURE OF IRANIAN DEMOCRACY

1 Islamic Republic News Agency (IRNA), 11 November 2003.

2 See further Dilip Hiro, *The Iranian Labyrinth: Journeys Through Theocratic Iran and its Furies*, New York: Nation Books, 2005, especially Chapter Two.

3 Agence France Press (AFP), 1 February 2004.

4 IRNA, 4 February 2005.

5 For a critique of this strategy see Akbar Ganji, 'The Struggle Against Sultanism', *Journal of Democracy*, Vol. 16, No. 4, October 2004, pp. 38-51.

6 See Morad Saghafi, 'The New Landscape of Iranian Politics', translated from French by Kaveh Ehsani, *Middle East Report*. Available at <http://www.merip.org/mer/mer233/saghafi.html> [accessed 10 Decmber 2005].

7 At the time of writing, leading members of the IFM such as Reza Alijani, Hoda Saber and Taghi Rahmani are in prison where they have been since 2003.

8 The results of the first round of votes were announced on 18 June 2005. Rafsanjani won with 21 per cent of the votes, hence failing to secure an absolute majority (above 50 per cent) required according to the electoral law in Iran. Moin came in fourth, securing only 14 per cent of the vote.

9 For an analysis of the ascendancy of Khatami and the Islamic-democratic movement in Iran see Ray Takeyh, 'God's Will: Iranian Democracy and the Islamic Context', *Middle East Policy*, Vol. VII, No. 4, October 2000, pp. 41-49. Available at <http://www.mepc.org/public_asp/journal_vol7/0010_takeyh.asp> [accessed 4 May 2002].

10 'Khatami justifies years in office', *BBC*, 3 May 2004. Available at <http://news.bbc.co.uk/go/pr/fr/-/1/hi/world/middle_east/3681153.stm> [accessed 8 December 2005].

11 The campaign themes of Mahmoud Ahmadinejad—social equality, cracking down on elite corruption, redistributing Iran's oil and gas income and returning to the spiritual ideals of the Islamic revolution—were

especially effective in the working-class districts of Iran's major cities. He did not primarily 'market' himself in the radio and television like the other candidates (reformers and conservatives alike). Rather than solely relying on official media outlets, he used recorded messages which were transmitted to the streets of Tehran and other major cities through loudspeakers.

12 Ahmadinejad secured a landslide victory, winning 62 per cent of the vote, with Rafsanjani taking only 36 per cent. For a balanced analysis of Ahmadinejad's election victory see Kamal Nazer Yasin, 'Iran: New Direction?,' *Middle East International*, 3 August 2005. Available at <http://meionline.com/features/390.shtml> [accessed 1 Decmber 2005]. Also Mark Gasiorowski, 'The Causes and Consequences of Iran's June 2005 Presidential Election,' *Strategic Insights*, Vol. IV, Issue 8, August 2005. Available at <http://www.ccc.nps.navy.mil/si/2005/Aug/gasiorowskiAug05.pdf> [accessed 21 November 2005]. For complementing views see Doug Lorimer, 'Iran: A vote against neo-liberalism,' *Green Left Weekly*, 6 July 2005. Available at <http://www.greenleft.org.au/back/2005/632/632p14.htm> [accessed 11 December 2005] and Patrick Seale, 'Iran's election may provide an Islamic role model', *The Daily Star*, Beirut, 11 July 2005. Available at <http://www.dailystar.com.lb/article.asp?edition_id=10&categ_id=5&article_id=16645> [accessed 11 November 2005].

13 For a comprehensive analysis of Iran's Internet Surveillance Regime see 'A Country Study: Internet Filtering in Iran 2004-2005,' published by Opennetinitiative *<http://www.opennetinitiative.net/Iran>* [accessed 21 November 2005].

14 'Ebadi protests Iran human rights violations', *AFP*, 31 December 2005.

15 'Iranian Women Make Headway in Municipal Politics', *The Daily Star* (Beirut), 5 January 2007.

16 Nayereh Tohidi, 'Iran's Women's Rights Movement and the One Million Signatures Campaign', translated by Taraneh Amin and edited by Sussan Tahmasebi and Nayereh Tohidi. Available at <http://www.we-change.org> [accessed 12 April 2007].

17 See among others Ali Gheissari and Vali Nasri, *Democracy in Iran: History and the Quest for Liberty*, Oxford University Press, 2006; Ali M. Ansari, 'Continuous Regime Change from within', *The Washington Quarterly*, Vol. 26, No. 4, Autumn 2003, pp. 53-67. Available at <http://www.twq.com/03autumn/docs/03autumn_ansari.pdf#search='Continuous%20regime%20change%20from%20within> [accessed 15 December 2005]; Ali M. Ansari, *Iran, Islam and Democracy: The Politics of Managing Change*, London: Royal Institute of International Affairs, 2000; Ali R. Abootalebi, 'Civil Society and Iran's quest for democracy,' *Iran Analysis Quarterly*, Vol. 1, No. 1, June-August 2003, pp. 2-5. Available at <http://web.mit.edu/isg/IAQ/IAQSUMMER.pdf#search='Civil%20Society%20and%20Iran%E2%80%9

9s%20quest%20for%20democracy> [accessed 12 November 2005] and Reza Sheikholeslami, 'The Transformation of Iran's Political Culture', *Critique: Critical Middle Eastern Studies*, Vol. 9, No. 3, 2000, pp. 105-134.

18 For Khatami's political philosophy see his *Az 'donyay-e shahr' ta 'shahr-e donya'* [From the 'city world' to the 'global city'], 9th edition, Tehran: Nashr-e Ney, 1379 (2000). For an interpretation of his political agenda see Massoud Laali, *Khatami az che myguyad?* [What is Mr. Khatami talking about? Logic of talks, freedom of though, law and its enforcement], 2nd edition, Tehran: Entesharat-e Azady-e Andishe, 1378 (1999), especially the introduction by Sadegh Zibakalam. For his ideas in English see *Hope and Challenge*, Binghamton: State University of New York, 1998 or his *Islam, Dialogue and Civil Society*, Canberra: Centre for Arab and Islamic Studies, 2000. For English analyses of his political ascendancy see among others Matthew C. Wells, 'Thermidor in the Islamic Republic of Iran: the rise of Muhammad Khatami', *British Journal of Middle Eastern Studies*, Vol. 26, No. 1, Winter 1999, pp. 27-39; Said Amir Arjomand, 'Civil Society and the Rule of Law in the Constitutional Politics of Iran under Khatami', *Social Research*, Vol. 67, No. 2, Spring 2000, pp. 283-301.

19 Reza Shakeri, *Andish-e siasy Shariati va naghd-e Shariatism* [The political thought of Ali Shariati and the exploration of Shariatiism], Tehran: Pejuheshgah-e Olum-e Ensani-ye va Eshtemahi-ye Jahad-e Daneshgahi, 1382 (2003), especially pp. 169 ff. and Hamidreza Jalaeipour, 'Religious Intellectuals and Political Action in the Reform Movement', Paper prepared for delivery at the conference in 'Intellectual Trends in 20th Century Iran' at Princeton University, 21 October 2000. Available at <http://www.drsoroush.com/PDF/E-CMO-20001021-Religious_Intellectuals_and_Political_Action_in_the_Reform_Movement.pdf> [accessed 12 February 2007]. See also Behrooz Ghamari-Tabrizi, 'Contentious public religion. Two conceptions of Islam in revolutionary Iran: Ali Shari'ati and Abdolkarim Soroush', *International Sociology*, Vol. 19, No. 4, Winter 2004, pp. 504-523. For Soroush's view on the link between him and the reform movement see 'Soroush: pedar chande-ye eslah talaban nistam [Soroush: I am not the godfather of the reform movement], *Shargh*, 29 Mordad 1385, (20 August 2006).

20 Quoted in Nayereh Tohidi, 'International Connections of the Iranian Women's Movement', in Nikki R. Keddie and Rudi Matthee (eds), *Iran and the Surrounding World: Interactions in Culture and Cultural Politics*, Seattle: University of Washington Press, 2002, p. 226.

21 See Abdolkarim Soroush, *Reason, Freedom and Democracy. Essential Writings of Abdolkarim Soroush,* translated and edited by Mahmoud Sadri and Ahmad Sadri, Oxford University Press, 2000. For a comparative analysis of Soroush's thoughts within an Islamic context see Bernhard J. Trautner, 'The Clash

Within Civilisations: Islam and the Accommodation of Plurality,' InIIS-Working Paper No. 13/99, Institut für Interkulturelle und Internationale Studien, Universität Bremen. Available at <http://www-user.uni-bremen.de/~bjtraut/clash/clash.pdf> [accessed 12 November 2001]. See also Charles Kurzman, *Liberal Islam: A Sourcebook*, Oxford University Press, 1998 and idem, 'Critics Within: Islamic Scholars' Protests Against the Islamic State in Iran', *International Journal of Politics, Culture and Society*, Vol. 15, No.2, Winter 2001, pp. 341-59; Robin B. Wright, 'Two Visions of Reformation,' *Journal of Democracy,* Vol. 7, No. 2 (1996), pp. 64-75. Available at <http://muse.jhu.edu/journals/journal_of_democracy/v007/7.2wright01.html> [accessed 23 February 2000]; Valla Vakilli, *Debating Religion and Politics: The Political Thought of Abdol Karim* Soroush, New York: Council on Foreign Relations, 1997; and Laura Secor, 'The democrat: Iran's leading reformist intellectual tries to reconcile religious duties and human rights,' *Boston Globe,* 14 March 2004. Available at <http://www.boston.com/news/globe/ideas/articles/2004/03/14/the_democrat/> [accessed 15 March 2004]. For Mohsen Kadivar's philosophical and political ideas see especially his *Daftar-e aql: majmueh-ye maqalat-e falsafi-alami* [The book of reason: collection of philosophical-theological articles], Tehran: Entesharat-e Ettela'at, 1377 (1998) and his *Andishe-ye Siyasi dar Eslam*, Vol. 3 *Hokumat-e Entesabi* [Government by Appointment], Tehran: Nashr-e Ney, 1382 (2002). For comparative approaches in English see Farzin Vahdat, 'Post-revolutionary Discourses of Mohammad Mojtahed Shabestari and Mohsen Kadivar: reconciling the Terms of Mediated Subjectivity.' Available at <http://www.kadivar.com/Htm/English/Reviews/Paper-01.htm> [accessed 14 November 2005] and his *God and Juggernaut: Iran's Intellectual Encounter with Modernity*, Syracuse University Press, 2002; Chapter 16 in Asghar Schirazi, *The Constitution of Iran: Politics and the State in the Islamic Republic*, translated by John O' Kane, London: I.B. Tauris, 1998; and Mahmoud Sadri, 'Sacral Defence of Secularism: the Political Theologies of Soroush, Shabestari, and Kadivar', *International Journal of Politics, Culture and Society*, Vol. 15, No. 2, pp. 257-70.

22 On the topic of Islam and gender see Lois Beck and Nikki Keddie (eds), *Women in the Muslim World*, Cambridge, MA: Harvard University Press, 1978; Leila Ahmed, *Women and Gender in Islam: Historical Roots of a Modern Debate*, New Haven: Yale University Press, 1992; Mai Yamani (ed.), *Feminism and Islam: Legal and Literary Perspectives*, London: Ithaca Press, 1996; Ziba Mir-Hosseini, *Islam and Gender: The Religious Debate in Contemporary Iran*, Princeton University Press, 1999; Herbert L. Bodman and Nayereh Tohidi (eds), *Women in Muslim Societies: Diversity within Unity*, Boulder, CO: Lynne Rienner, 1998; Yvonne Y. Haddad and John L. Esposito (eds), *Islam, Gender, and Social Change*, Oxford University Press,

1998; Qudsia Mirza (ed.), *Islamic Feminism and Law*, London: Cavendish House, 2005. For a progressive religious view within the Shia-Iranian context see Morteza Mottahari, *The Rights of Women in Islam*, Tehran: World Organization for Islamic Service, 1974. On the history of the women's movement in Iran see among others Haideh Moghissi, *Populism and Feminism in Iran*, London: Macmillan, 1994; Parvin Paidar, *Women and the Political Process in Twentieth-Century Iran*, Cambridge University Press, 1995; Haleh Esfandiari, *Reconstructed Lives: Women and Iran's Islamic Revolution*, Baltimore: Johns Hopkins University, 1997; Azadeh Kian, 'Women and Politics in Post-Islamist Iran', *British Journal of Middle Eastern Studies*, Vol. 24, No. 1, 1997, pp. 75-96; and Nikki R. Keddie, 'Women in Iran since 1979', *Social Research*, Vol. 67, No. 2, 2000, pp. 407-438.

23 On the treatment of political prisoners in Iran both before and after the revolution see Ervand Abrahamian, *Tortured Confessions: Prison and Public Recantations in Modern Iran*, Berkeley: University of California Press, 1999; Reza Afshari, *Human Rights in Iran: The Abuse of Cultural Relativism*, Philadelphia: University of Pennsylvania Press, 2001; Afshin Matin-Asgari, *Iranian Student Opposition to the Shah*, Costa Mesa: Mazda, 2001; and Darius M. Rejali, *Torture and Modernity: Self, Society, and State in Modern Iran*, Boulder, CO: Westview, 1994.

24 For a list of Iranian NGOs including websites see Syma Sayyah, 'A short note on NGOs in Iran.' Available at <http://www.payvand.com/news/03/jan/1114.html > [accessed 14 November 2005].There are also constructive efforts to link the work of NGOs operating within Iran with Iranians living abroad. Iranian Alliances Across Borders (IAAB) and the Iranian Studies Group (ISG), for instance, have recently launched a project aimed at attracting Iranians in the Diaspora 'who are looking for opportunities to intern/ volunteer in the service of Iranian civil society.' See <http://www.project-connection.org>

25 I am employing sociological theory here. See Peter L. Berger, *The Sacred Canopy: Elements of a Sociological Theory of Religion*, London: Anchor Books, 1967 and idem, *A Rumour of Angels. Modern Society and the Rediscovery of the Supernatural*, London: Anchor Books, 1969.

26 Leon Trotsky, *The Revolution Betrayed: What is the Soviet Union and where is it Going?*, New York: Pathfinder, 1937, p. 9.

27 'According to the republican view,' Jürgen Habermas argues, 'the political opinion- and will-formation occurring in the public sphere and in parliament obeys not the structures of market processes but the obstinate structures of a public communication oriented to mutual understanding. ... This dialog conception imagines politics as contestation over questions of value and not simply questions of preference.' Jürgen Habermas, 'Three Normative Models

of Democracy', in Ronald J. Terchek and Thomas C. Conte (eds), *Theories of Democracy: A Reader*, Oxford: Rowman & Littlefield, 2001, p. 238.

28 For an analysis of the dialectics between the state and society in Iran see Davood Gharayagh-Zandi, *Nahadha-ye madani va hoviyat dar Iran* [Civil groupings and identity in Iran], Tehran: Entesharat-e tamadon-e Iran, 1380 (2001).

29 For a discussion of some of the sociological indicators mentioned see *Critique's* special issue in collaboration with the University of Tehran: *Critique: Critical Middle Eastern Studies*, Vol. 14, No. 1, Spring 2005.

30 Indeed, with an estimated 100,000 active Iranian blogs, Persian is now (together with French) the second most common 'blogging language' after English. See *Time* Magazine, 9 May 2005.

31 I have discussed the impact of these changes in my *The International Politics of the Persian Gulf: A Cultural Genealogy*, London: Routledge, 2006, especially Chapters 3 and 4.

32 Fariba Adelkhah, *Being Modern in Iran*, translated by Jonathan Derrick, London: Hurst & Company, 1998, p. 177.

33 It should be noted that the post-revolutionary generation in Iran comprises both reformist groups who have contributed to the election victories of the Khatami Presidencies *and* (neo)conservative forces who have contributed to the election of Mahmoud Ahmadinejad. For our line of argument it is important to note that in both instances the electorate voted for the 'outsider', that is for the candidate who was perceived to act in opposition to the establishment.

34 Karl Marx, *The Eighteenth Brumaire of Louis Bonaparte*, translated by Daniel de Leon, London: Labour News, 1898, p. 24.

35 Friedrich Engels, 'Letter to J. Bloch', 21 September 1890, in Engels, *Selected Correspondence*, London: Lawrence & Wishart, 1934, p. 475, emphasis in original.

36 Robert Gilpin, *The Political Economy of International Relations*, Princeton University Press, 1987, p. 34.

37 See also G. John Ikenberry, 'The International Spread of Privatisation Policies: Inducements, Learning, and "Policy Bandwagoning",' in Ezra N. Suleiman and John Waterbury (eds), *The Political Economy of Public Sector Reform and Privatisation*, Boulder, CO: Westview, 1990, pp. 95-6.

38 'Iran: Supreme Leader issues guidelines for privatisation drive', IRNA, 2 July 2006.

39 See also Paul Starr, 'The New Life of the Liberal State: Privatisation and the Restructuring of State-Society Relations', in Suleiman and Waterbury (eds), *The Political Economy of Public Sector Reform* (note 37), pp. 39 ff.

40 Ayatollah Mahmud Taleghani, 'The Characteristics of Islamic Economics', in John J. Donohue and John L. Esposito (eds), *Islam in Transition: Muslim*

Perspectives, 2nd edition, Oxford University Press, 2007, p. 234. His *Islam wa Malekiyat* (Islam and ownership) has been translated by William Darrow, Houston: Islamic Distribution Center, n.d..

41 Mohammad Bagher al-Sadr, 'The Psychological Role of Islam in Economic Development' in Donohue and Esposito (eds), *Islam in Transition* (note 40), p. 257.

42 See among others Abbas Alnasrawi, *Arab Nationalism, Oil and the Political Economy of Dependency*, London: Greenwood, 1991; Michel Chatelus, 'From the Mirage of Rent to the Burden of Debt: Adjustment and Insecurity in Arab Economies', in Bahgat Korany, Paul Noble and Rex Brynen (eds), *The Many Faces of National Security in the Middle East*, New York: Macmillan, 1993, pp. 145-68, or Jaqueline Ismael, *Kuwait: Dependency and Class in a Rentier State*, Gainesville: University Press of Florida, 1993.

43 See Raymond Hinnebusch, *The International Politics of the Middle East*, Manchester University Press, 2003, p. 45 ff.

44 For a critical analysis see '20 Year Vision: Opportunities and challenges', *Iran Daily*, 29 November 2006, p. 6.

45 See Robert Dahl, Dilemmas of Pluralist Democracy: Autonomy vs. Control, New Haven: Yale University Press, 1982, p. 5.

46 'Iran report says rights violations common in prison', *Reuters*, 23 July 2005; 'Iran to hold jury trials for press offences', *AFP*, 5 October 2005.

47 See Michel Foucault, *The Will to Knowledge: The History of Sexuality Volume 1*, translated by Robert Hurley, London: Penguin, 1981, p. 92 ff. and idem, 'Two Lectures,' in Michael Kelly (ed.), *Critique and Power: Recasting the Foucault/Habermas Debate*, Cambridge, MA: MIT Press, 1998, pp. 17-46.

48 Ibid., p. 40.

49 Edward Said, *Reflections on Exile: and other Essays*, Cambridge, MA: Harvard University Press, 2000, p. 580.

50 Ervand Abrahamian, 'The Islamic Left: From Radicalism to Liberalism', in Stephanie Cronin (ed.), *Reformers and Revolutionaries in Modern Iran: New Perspectives on the Iranian Left*, London: Routledge, 2004, p. 268.

51 Others disagree. See for instance Charles Kurzman, 'Critics within: Islamic Scholars Protest against the Islamic State in Iran', *International Journal of Politics, Culture and Society*, Vol. 15, No. 2, Winter 2001, pp. 341-59.

52 Ganji, 'The Struggle Against Sultanism' (note 5), p. 51.

53 Hasan Yousefi Eshkevari, 'Iran after the elections', in Ziba Mir-Hosseini and Richard Tapper, *Islam and Democracy in Iran: Eshkevari and the Quest for Reform*, London: I.B. Tauris, 2006, pp. 150-1.

54 Kurt Schock, *Unarmed Insurrections: People Power Movements in Nondemocracies*, London: University of Minnesota Press, 2005, p. 3. See also John Foran, 'The Iranian Revolution of 1977-79: A Challenge for Social

Theory', in John Foran (ed.), *A Century of Revolution: Social Movements in Iran*, London: University of Minnesota Press, 1994, Chapter 7.

55 Ibid., p. 6. See also Gene Sharp, *The Politics of Nonviolent Action*, Boston: Porter Sargent, 1973.

56 See further Mehrzad Boroujerdi, 'The Paradoxes of Politics in Post-Revolutionary Iran', in John L. Esposito and R. K. Ramazani (eds), *Iran at the Crossroads*, Basingstoke: Palgrave, 2001, pp. 13-27. For analyses in German see Katajun Amirpur, 'Gibt es in Iran noch einen Reformprozess?,' *Aus Politik und Zeitgeschichte*, 23 February 2004, pp. 18-24; Mehdi Parvizi Amineh, 'Demokratisierung und ihre Feinde in Iran,' *Aus Politik und Zeitgeschichte*, 23 February 2004, pp. 25-8.

57 See further Mohammad Maljoo, 'Worker Protest in the Age of Ahmadinejad', *Middle East Report*, No. 241, Vol. 36, No. 4, Winter 2006, pp. 30-3.

58 For a history of Iranian cinema see Mohammad Ali Issari, *Cinema in Iran, 1900-1979*, Metuchen, NJ: Scarecrow, 1989. For the post-revolutionary cinema see Richard Tapper (ed.), *The New Iranian Cinema: Politics, Representation and* Identity, London: I.B. Tauris, 2002 and Hamid Naficy 'Cinematic Exchange Relations: Iran and the West', in Nikki R. Keddie and Rudi Matthee (eds), *Iran and the Surrounding World: Interactions in Culture and Cultural Politics*, Seattle: University of Washington Press, pp. 254-78. For a review of modern Persian poetry with a special emphasis on Abbas Kiarostami see Khatereh Sheibani, 'Kiarostami and the Aesthetics of Modern Persian Poetry', *Iranian Studies*, Vol. 39, No. 4, December 2006, pp. 509-37.

59 The differentiation and competition in the political sphere are not confined to the reformist camp, as the recent controversies between 'orthodox traditionalists' and 'neoconservatives' indicate. Publicly, the conservative factions continue to show unity despite their poor results in the latest Municipal Council and Assembly of Experts elections. In a statement to ISNA on 3 January 2007, Mohammad Nabi Habibi who leads the 'Islamic Coalition Society' (a member of the 'Front of Followers of the Path of the Imam and Leadership') denied that there was a generation gap between the traditional 'Right' and 'neoconservatives' organized around President Ahmadinejad. The daily *Etemad-e Melli*, on the other side, noted on 11 January 2007 that Habibi's party is a central actor within the conservative camp and that his 'Front of Followers' did not support the pro-Ahmadinejad list in December's elections, speculating that some traditionalists were increasingly critical of the government's failure to contain inflation. See also Scott Peterson's commentary in the *Christian Science Monitor* (18 December 2006): 'What Iran vote says about Ahmadinejad's support: The president's supporters hailed Friday's high turnout as a sign of satisfaction; reformers pointed to discontent'.

V. IN PLACE OF A CONLUSION: TOWARDS CRITICAL IRANIAN STUDIES

1 Olivier Roy, *The Failure of Political Islam*, translated by Carol Volk, London: I.B. Tauris, 1999. Roy has refined his thesis in *Globalised Islam: The Search for a New Ummah*, London: Hurst & Company, 2004. See also specifically on the success and failures of the Iranian revolution Hamidreza Jalaeipour, 'Iran's Islamic Revolution: Achievements and Failures', *Critique: Critical Middle Eastern Studies*, Vol. 15, No. 3, Fall 2006, pp. 207-15.

2 Hans-Georg Gadamer, *Truth and Method*, second revised edition, London: Continuum, p. 59.

3 Hayden White, *Metahistory: The Historical Imagination in Nineteenth-Century Europe*, Baltimore: Johns Hopkins University Press, 1973, p. 21, emphases in original.

4 I have adopted this example from David Berreby, *Us and Them: Understanding your Tribal Mind*, London: Hutchinson, 2005, p. 127.

5 Theodor W. Adorno and Max Horkheimer, *Dialectic of Enlightenment*, translated by John Cumming, London: Verso, 1997, pp. 188-9.

6 Peter L. Berger, *The Sacred Canopy. Elements of a Sociological Theory of Religion*, New York: Anchor, 1967, pp. 5-6, emphasis in original.

7 Edward Said, 'Travelling Theory', in Moustafa Bayoumi and Andrew Rubin (eds), *The Edward Said Reader*, London: Granta, 2001, p. 211.

8 For an analysis of the Iranian Left see Afshin Matin-asgari, 'From Social Democracy to Social Democracy: The twentieth-century Odyssey of the Iranian Left', in Stephanie Cronin (ed.), *Reformers and Revolutionaries in Modern Iran: New Perspectives on the Iranian Left*, London: Routledge, 2004, pp. 37-64.

9 On these ancient Iranian gymnasiums see D.H. Luijendijk, *Zoor Khane: History and Techniques of the Ancient Martial Art of Iran*, Boulder, CO: Paladin, 2006 or Philippe Rochard, 'The Identities of the Iranian *Zurkhanah*', translated by H.E. Chehabi, *Iranian Studies*, Vol. 35, No. 4, Fall 2002, pp. 313-40.

10 Adorno and Horkheimer, *Dialectic of Enlightenment*, pp. 154-5.

11 For the shifts in Iran's literary tradition and a selection of poems by Ahmad Shamlu, Mohammad Hossein Shahriyar and Ayatollah Khomeini, see the special issue of *Iranian Studies*, Vol. 30, Nos. 3-4, Summer/Fall 1997.

BIBLIOGRAPHY

Abootalebi, Ali R., 'Civil Society and Iran's Quest for Democracy,' *Iran Analysis Quarterly*, Vol. 1, No. 1, June-August 2003, pp. 2-5.

Abrahamian, Ervand, 'The Islamic Left: From Radicalism to Liberalism', in Stephanie Cronin (ed.), *Reformers and Revolutionaries in Modern Iran: New Perspectives on the Iranian Left*, London: Routledge, 2004, pp. 268-79.

Abrahamian, Ervand, *Tortured Confessions: Prison and Public Recantations in Modern Iran*, Berkeley: University of California Press, 1999.

Abrahamian, Ervand, *Khomeinism: Essays on the Islamic Republic*, London: I.B. Tauris, 1993.

Abrahamian, Ervand, *Iran between Two Revolutions*, Princeton University Press, 1982.

Adelkhah, Fariba, *Being Modern in Iran*, translated from the French by Jonathan Derrick, London: Hurst & Company, 1998.

Adib-Moghaddam, Arshin, *A Metahistory of the Clash of Civilisations* (forthcoming).

Adib-Moghaddam, Arshin, 'Manufacturing War: Iran in the neoconservative Imagination', *Third World Quarterly*, Vol. 28, No. 3, 2007, pp. 635-53.

Adib-Moghaddam, Arshin, 'Reflections on the Emerging Political Economy of Iran', *International Studies Journal*, Issue 12, Vol. 3, Special Issue, Winter 2007, pp. 23-37.

Adib-Moghaddam, Arshin, 'Inventions of the Iran-Iraq War', *Critique: Critical Middle Eastern Studies*, Vol. 16, No. 1, Spring 2007, pp. 63-83.

Adib-Moghaddam, Arshin, *The International Politics of the Persian Gulf: A Cultural Genealogy*, London: Routledge, 2006.

Adib-Moghaddam, Arshin, 'The Pluralistic Momentum in Iran and the Future of the Reform Movement', *Third World Quarterly*, Vol. 27, No. 4, 2006, pp. 665-74.

Adib-Moghaddam, Arshin, 'The Theory of Regional Security Complexes: Exploring the Options', *International Studies Journal*, Issue 9, Vol. 3, No. 1, Summer 2006, pp. 25-37.

Adib-Moghaddam, Arshin, 'The Whole Range of Saddam Hussein's War Crimes', *Middle East Report*, Vol. 36, No. 2, Summer 2006, pp. 30-5.

Adib-Moghaddam, Arshin, 'Islamic Utopian-Romanticism and the Foreign Policy Culture of Iran', *Critique: Critical Middle Eastern Studies*, Vol. 14, No. 3, Fall 2005, pp. 265-92.

Adib-Moghaddam, Arshin, 'Global Intifadah? September 11th and the Struggle Within Islam', *Cambridge Review of International Affairs*, Vol. 15, No. 2, July 2002, pp. 203-16.

Adorno, Theodor W. and Max Horkheimer, *Dialectic of Enlightenment*, translated by John Cumming, London: Verso, 1997.

Afary, Janet and Kevin B. Anderson, *Foucault and the Iranian Revolution: Gender and the Seductions of Islamism*, University of Chicago Press.

Afrasiabi, Kaveh L., *After Khomeini: New Directions in Iran's Foreign Policy*, Boulder, CO: Westview, 1994.

Afshari, Reza, *Human Rights in Iran: The Abuse of Cultural Relativism*, Philadelphia: University of Pennsylvania Press, 2001.

Ahmed, Leila, *Women and Gender in Islam: Historical Roots of a Modern Debate*, New Haven: Yale University Press, 1992.

Ajami, Fouad, *The Foreigner's Gift: The Americans, the Arabs, and the Iraqis in Iraq*, New York: Free Press, 2007.

Algar, Hamid, *Constitution of the Islamic Republic of Iran*, translated by Hamid Algar, Berkeley: Mizan Press, 1980.

Al-e Ahmad, Jalal, *Plagued by the West (Gharbzadegi)*, translated from the Persian by Paul Sprachman, New York: Caravan, 1982.

Ali, Tariq, 'Mid-Point in the Middle East?', *New Left Review*, Vol. 38, March-April 2006, pp. 5-19.

Allport, Gordon W., 'The Role of Expectancy', in Leon Bramson and George W. Goethals (eds), *War Studies from Psychology, Sociology, Anthropology*, London: Basic Books, 1964, pp. 177-94.

Alnasrawi, Abbas, *Arab Nationalism, Oil and the Political Economy of Dependency*, London: Greenwood, 1991.

Amineh, Mehdi Parvizi 'Demokratisierung und ihre Feinde in Iran ', *Aus Politik und Zeitgeschichte*, 23 February 2004, pp. 25-28.

Amirpur, Katajun, 'Gibt es in Iran noch einen Reformprozess?', *Aus Politik und Zeitgeschichte*, 23 February 2004, pp. 18-24.

Ansari, Ali, 'Persia in the Western Imagination', in Vanessa Martin (ed.), *Anglo-Iranian Relations since 1800, Royal Asiatic Society Books*, London: Routledge, 2006, pp. 8-20.

Ansari, Ali M., 'Continuous Regime Change from within', *The Washington Quarterly*, Vol. 26, No. 4, Autumn 2003, pp. 53-67.

Ansari, Ali M., *Iran, Islam and Democracy: The Politics of Managing Change*, London: Royal Institute of International Affairs, 2000.

Archer, Margaret S., *Culture and Agency: The Place of Culture in Social Theory*, revised edition, Cambridge University Press, 1996.

Arjomand, Said Amir, 'Civil Society and the Rule of Law in the Constitutional Politics of Iran under Khatami', *Social Research*, Vol. 67, No. 2, Spring 2000, pp. 283-301.

Ashley, Richard K., 'Foreign Policy as Political Performances', *International Studies Notes*, 1998, pp. 51-4.

Bacevich, Andrew J., *The New American Militarism: How Americans Are Seduced by War*, Oxford University Press, 2005.

Baktiari, Bahman, 'Revolutionary Iran's Persian Gulf Policy: The Quest for Regional Supremacy', in Hooshang Amirahmadi and Nader Entessar (eds), *Iran and the Arab World*, London: Macmillan Press, 1998, pp. 69-93.

Bayoumi, Moustafa and Andrew Rubin (eds), *The Edward Said Reader*, London: Granta, 2001.

Barzegar, Ali-Reza, *Ruzshomar-e jang-e tahmil-ye aragh ba jomhur-ye eslam-ye Iran* [A Chronology of the Iraqi-imposed War against Iran], Tehran: Soroush, 1379/2000.

Beck, Lois and Nikki Keddie (eds.), *Women in the Muslim World*, Cambridge, MA: Harvard University Press, 1978.

Bengio, Ofra, *Saddam's Word: Political Discourse in Iran*, Oxford University Press, 1998.

Berger, Peter L. and Thomas Luckmann, *The Social Construction of Reality: A Treatise in the Sociology of Knowledge*, Harmondsworth: Penguin, 1979.

Berger, Peter, *A Rumour of Angels. Modern Society and the Rediscovery of the Supernatural*, London: Anchor Books, 1969.

Berger, Peter, *The Sacred Canopy*, Garden City: Doubleday, 1966.

Berger, Peter and Stanley Pullberg, 'Reification and the Sociological Critique of Consciousness', *History and Theory*, Vol. 4, No.2, 1965, pp. 196-211.

Berger, Thomas U., *Cultures of Antimilitarism: National Security in Germany and Japan*, London: Johns Hopkins University Press, 1998.

Berreby, David, *Us and Them: Understanding your Tribal Mind*, London: Hutchinson, 2005.

Bill, James A. and Carl Leiden, *The Middle East: Politics and Power*, Boston: Allyn and Bacon, 1974.

Binder, Leonard, *Iran: Political Development in a Changing Society*, Berkeley: University of California Press, 1962.

Bodman, Herbert L. and Nayereh Tohidi (eds), *Women in Muslim Societies: Diversity within Unity*, Boulder, CO: Lynne Rienner, 1998.

Boggs, Carl (ed.), *Masters of War: Militarism and Blowback in the Era of American Empire*, London: Routledge, 2003.

Borch, Herbert von, *Amerika-Dekadenz und Größe*, Munich: R. Piper & Co., 1981.

Boroujerdi, Mehrzad, 'The Paradoxes of Politics in Post-Revolutionary Iran', in John L. Esposito and R.K. Ramazani (eds), *Iran at the Crossroads*, Basingstoke: Palgrave, 2001, pp. 13-27.

Boroujerdi, Mehrzad, 'Contesting Nationalist Constructions of Iranian Identity', *Critique: Critical Middle Eastern Studies*, Vol. 12, No. 1, Spring 1998, pp. 43-55.

Boroujerdi, Mehrzad, 'Iranian Islam and the Faustian Bargain of Western Modernity', *Journal of Peace Research*, Vol. 34, No. 1, February 1997, pp. 1-5.

Boroujerdi, Mehrzad, *Iranian Intellectuals and the West: The Tormented Triumph of Nativism*, Syracuse University Press, 1996.

Bramson, Leon and George W. Goethals (eds), *War Studies from Psychology, Sociology, Anthropology*, London: Basic Books, 1964.

Brinkley, Joel (ed.), *Report of the Congressional Committee: Investigating the Iran-Contra* Affair, New York: Times Book, 1988.

Bruner, J.S., 'Going beyond the Information Given', in University of Colorado, Boulder, Department of Psychology (ed.), *Contemporary Approaches to Cognition*, Cambridge, MA: Harvard University Press, 1957, pp. 218-38.

Bukovansky, Mlada, *Legitimacy and Power Politics: The American and French Revolutions in International Political Culture*, Princeton University Press, 2002.

Bull, Hedley, *The Anarchical Society: A Study of Order in World Politics*, second edition, London: Macmillan, 1995.

Buzan, Barry and Ole Waever, *Regions and Powers: The Structure of International Security*, Cambridge University Press, 2003.

Carr, Edward Hallet, *The Twenty Years' Crisis, 1919-1939: An Introduction to the Study of International Relations*, London: Macmillan, 1961.

Castle, Gregory (ed.), *Postcolonial Discourses: An Anthology*, Oxford: Blackwell, 2001, pp. 99-116.

Chatelus, Michel, 'From the Mirage of Rent to the Burden of Debt: Adjustment and Insecurity in Arab Economies', in Bahgat Korany, Paul Noble and Rex Brynen (eds), *The Many Faces of National Security in the Middle East*, New York: Macmillan, 1993, pp. 145-168.

Chehabi, Houchang (ed.), *Distant Relations: Iran and Lebanon in the Last 500 Years*, London: I.B. Tauris, 2005.

Chomsky, Noam, *Hegemony or Survival: America's Quest for Global Dominance*, London: Penguin, 2003.

Chomsky, Noam, *Fateful Triangle: The United States, Israel, and the Palestinians*, updated edition, London: Pluto, 1999.

Chomsky, Noam, *Deterring Democracy*, London: Verso, 1991.

Chubin, Shahram and Charles Tripp, *Iran and Iraq at War*, London: I.B. Tauris, 1988.

Cole, Juan R.I., 'Marking Boundaries, Marking Time: The Iranian Past and the Construction of the Self by Qajar Thinkers', *Iranian Studies*, Vol. 29, Nos. 1-2, Winter/Spring 1996, pp. 35-56.

Cole, Juan R.I. and Nikki R. Keddie (eds), *Shiism and Social Protest*, New Haven: Yale University Press, 1986.

Cordesman, Anthony H., *The Iran-Iraq War and Western Security 1984-1987: Strategic Implications and Policy Options*, London: Jane's Publishing Co., 1987.

Cox, Robert, *Approaches to World Order*, Cambridge University Press, 1996.

Cox, Robert W., 'Towards a Posthegemonic Conceptualisation of World Order: Reflections on the Relevancy of Ibn Khaldun', in Robert W. Cox, *Approaches to World Order*, Cambridge University Press, 1996, pp. 144-73.

Cox, Robert, 'Social Forces, States and World Orders: Beyond International Relations Theory', in Robert Cox, *Approaches to World Order*, Cambridge University Press, 1996, pp. 85-123.

Cronin, Stephanie (ed.), *Reformers and Revolutionaries in Modern Iran: New Perspectives on the Iranian Left*, London: Routledge, 2004.

Dabashi, Hamid, *Theology of Discontent: The Ideological Foundation of the Islamic Revolution in Iran*, New York University Press, 1993.

Dahl, Robert, *Dilemmas of Pluralist Democracy: Autonomy vs. Control*, New Haven: Yale University Press, 1982.

Davari, Mahmood T., *The Political Thought of Ayatullah Murtaza Mutahhari: An Iranian Theoretician of the Islamic State*, London: Routledge, 2005.

Davidson, Lawrence, 'Christian Zionism as a Representation of American Manifest Destiny', *Critique: Critical Middle Eastern Studies*, Vol. 14, No. 2, Summer 2005, pp. 157-69.

Dehshiri, Mohammad-Reza, 'The Cycle of Idealism and Realism in the Foreign Policy of the Islamic Republic of Iran', *The Iranian Journal of International Affairs*, Vol. XIII, Nos. 2 & 3, Summer-Fall 2001, pp. 278-300.

Dilthey, Wilhelm, *Selected Writings*, Cambridge University Press, 1976.

Doyle, Michael W. and G. John Ikenberry (eds), *New Thinking in International Relations Theory*, Oxford: Westview, 1997.

Duffield, John S., 'Political Culture and State Behavior: Why Germany Confounds Neorealism', *International Organization*, Vol. 53, No. 4, Autumn 1999, pp. 765-803.

Ebtekar, Massoumeh, *Takeover in Tehran: The Inside Story of the 1979 U.S. Embassy Capture*, Vancouver: Talonbooks, 2000.

Efimenco, N. Marbury, 'An Experiment with Civilian Dictatorship in Iran; The Case of Mohammad Mossadegh', *The Journal of Politics*, Vol. 17, No. 3, August 1955, pp. 390-406.

Ehteshami, Anoushiravan and Gerd Nonneman, *War and Peace in the Gulf: Domestic Politics and Regional Relations into the 1990s*, Reading: Ithaca, 1991.

Ehteshami, Anoushiravan, *After Khomeini: The Iranian Second Republic*, London: Routledge, 1995.

Emadi, Hafizullah, 'Exporting Iran's Revolution: The Radicalisation of the Shiite Movement in Afghanistan', *Middle Eastern Studies*, Vol. 31, No. 1, January 1995, pp. 1-12.

Enayat, Hamid, *Modern Islamic Political Thought: The Response of the Shia and Sunni Muslims to the Twentieth Century*, new edition, London: I.B. Tauris, 2005.

Engels, Friedrich, *Selected Correspondence*, London: Lawrence & Wishart, 1934.

Eribon, Didier, *Michel Foucault*, translated by Betsy Wing, London: Faber and Faber, 1991.

Esfandiari, Haleh, *Reconstructed Lives: Women and Iran's Islamic Revolution*, Baltimore: Johns Hopkins University, 1997.

Eshkevari, Hasan Yousefi, 'Iran after the Elections', in Ziba Mir-Hosseini and Richard Tapper, *Islam and Democracy in Iran: Eshkevari and the Quest for Reform*, London: I.B. Tauris, 2006, pp. 150-5.

Farabi, Abu Nasr, 'kitab al-jam 'bayn ra'yay al-hakimayn, Aflatun al-ilahi wa Aristu (Reconciliation of the two sages Spiritual Plato and Aristotle)', in Hossein Nasr with Mehdi Aminrazavi, *An Anthology of Philosophy in Persia, Volume I*, Oxford University Press, 1999, pp. 110-18.

Farhi, Farideh, 'Crafting a National Identity amidst Contentious Politics in Contemporary Iran', *Iranian Studies*, Vol. 38, No. 1, March 2005, pp. 7-22.

Farsoun, Samih K. and Mehrdad Mashayekhi, *Iran: Political Culture in the Islamic Republic*, London: Routledge, 1992.

Fisk, Robert, *The Great War for Civilisation: The Conquest of the Middle East*, London: Harpers Perennial, 2006.

Foran, John, 'The Iranian Revolution of 1977-79: A Challenge for Social Theory', in John Foran (ed.), *A Century of Revolution: Social Movements in Iran*, London: University of Minnesota Press, 1994.

Foster, John Bellamy, *Naked Imperialism: The U.S. Pursuit of Global Dominance*, New York: Monthly Review Press, 2006.

Foster, John Bellamy, 'Naked Imperialism', *Monthly Review*, Vol. 57, No.4, September 2005. Available at <http://www.monthlyreview.org/naked-imperialism.htm> [accessed 12 May 2006].

Foucault, Michel, *Power: Essential Works of Foucault, 1954-1984*, vol. 3, translated by Robert Hurley *et al.*, London: Penguin, 1997.

Foucault, Michel, *The Archaeology of Knowledge*, translated by A.M. Sheridan Smith, London: Routledge, 1989.

Foucault, Michel, *The Order of Things: An Archaeology of the Human Sciences*, London: Routledge, 1989.

Foucault, Michel, *The Will to Knowledge: The History of Sexuality Volume 1*, translated by Robert Hurley, London: Penguin, 1981.

Foucault, Michel, *Power/Knowledge: Selected Interviews and Other Writings* 1972-1977, edited by C. Gordon, translated by C. Gordon *et al.*, London: Harvester Wheatsheaf, 1980.

Fromm, Erich, *To Have or To Be?*, London: Continuum, 1997.

Fuller, Graham E., 'Repairing U.S.-Iranian Relations', *Middle East Policy*, Vol. VI, No.2, 1998, pp. 140-4.

Gadamer, Hans-Georg, *Truth and Method*, second revised edition, London: `continuum, 2004.

Ganji, Akbar, 'The Struggle Against Sultanism,' *Journal of Democracy*, Vol. 16, No. 4, October 2004, pp. 38-51.

Gasiorowski, Mark, 'The Causes and Consequences of Iran's June 2005 Presidential Election,' *Strategic Insights*, Vol. IV, Issue 8, August 2005. Available at <http://www.ccc.nps.navy.mil/si/2005/Aug/gasiorowskiAug05.pdf> [accessed 21 November 2005].

Geertz, Clifford, *The Interpretation of Cultures*, New York: Basic Books, 1973.

George, David, 'Pax Islamica: An Alternative New World Order', in Abdel Salam Sidahmed and Anoushiravan Ehteshami (eds), *Islamic Fundamentalism*, Boulder, CO: Westview, 1996, pp. 71-90.

Ghamari-Tabrizi, Behrooz, 'Contentious Public Religion. Two Conceptions of Islam in Revolutionary Iran: Ali Shari'ati and Abdolkarim Soroush', *International Sociology*, Vol. 19, No. 4, Winter 2004, pp. 504-23.

Gharayagh-Zandi, Davood *et al.*, *Nahadha-ye madani va hoviyat dar Iran* [Civil groupings and identity in Iran], Tehran: Entesharat-e tamadon-e Iran, 1380 (2001).

Gheissari, Ali and Vali Nasri, *Democracy in Iran: History and the Quest for Liberty*, Oxford University Press, 2006.

Gilpin, Robert, *The Political Economy of International Relations*, Princeton University Press, 1987.

Goldstein, Judith and Robert Keohane (eds), *Ideas and Foreign Policy*, Ithaca, NY: Cornell University Press, 1993.

Gramsci, Antonio, *Selections from the Prison Notebooks*, translated by Quintin Hoare and Geoffrey Nowell Smith, New York: International Publishers, 1971.

Grieco, Joseph M., 'Realist International Theory and the Study of World Politics', in Michael W. Doyle and G. John Ikenberry (eds), *New Thinking in International Relations Theory*, Oxford: Westview, 1997, pp. 163-201.

Golchin, Husein, *Namazi dar atash va khun* [A prayer in the midst of fire and blood], Tehran: Cultural Centre for Islamic Propaganda, 1372/1993.

Habermas, Jürgen, 'Three Normative Models of Democracy', in Ronald J. Terchek and Thomas C. Conte (eds), *Theories of Democracy: A Reader*, Oxford: Rowman & Littlefield, 2001, pp. 236-43.

Hadar, Leon T., 'The "Neocons": From the Cold War to the "Global Initifada"', *Washington Report on Middle East Affairs*, April 1991, pp. 27-46.

Haddad, Yvonne Y. and John L. Esposito (eds.), *Islam, Gender, and Social Change*, Oxford University Press, 1998.

Haghighi, Shahrokh, *Gozar az moderniteh? Nicheh, Fuko, Liotar, Derida* [Beyond modernity? Nietzsche, Foucault, Lyotard, Derrida], Tehran: Agah, 1380/2001.

Halliday, Fred, *The Middle East in International Relations: Power Politics and Ideology*, Cambridge University Press, 2005.

Halliday, Fred, *Revolution and World Politics: The Rise and Fall of the Sixth Great Power*, Durham, NC: Duke University Press, 1999.

Halliday, Fred, *Islam and the Myth of Confrontation. Religion and Politics in the Middle East*, London: I.B. Tauris, 1996.

Halliday, Fred, 'Iranian Foreign Policy since 1979: Internationalism and Nationalism in the Islamic Revolution', in Juan R.I. Cole and Nikki R. Keddie (eds), *Shiism and Social Protest*, New Haven: Yale University Press, 1986, pp. 88-107.

Hansen, Birthe, *Unipolarity and the Middle East*, Richmond, Surrey: Curzon, 2000.

Haseeb, Khair el-Din (ed.), *Arab-Iranian Relations*, Beirut: Centre for Arab Unity Studies, 1998.

Hinnebusch, Raymond, *The International Politics of the Middle East*, Manchester University Press, 2003.

Hinnebusch, Raymond and Anoushiravan Ehteshami (eds), *The Foreign Policies of Middle East States*, London: Lynne Rienner, 2002.

Hiro, Dilip, *The Iranian Labyrinth: Journeys Through Theocratic Iran and its Furies*, New York: Nation Books, 2005.

Hiro, Dilip, *Neighbours Not Friends: Iraq and Iran after the Gulf Wars*, London: Routledge, 2001.

Hiro, Dilip, *The Longest War: The Iran-Iraq Military Conflict*, London: Grafton Books, 1990.

Hirschfeld, Lawrence A. and Susan A. Gelman (eds), *Mapping the Mind: Domain Specificity in Cognition and Culture*, Cambridge University Press, 1994.

Hilterman, Joost R., 'The Men Who Helped the Man Who Gassed His Own People', in Micah L. Sifry and Christopher Cerf (eds), *The Iraq War*

Reader. History, Documents, Opinions, London: Touchstone, 2003, pp. 41-4.

Hiltermann, Joost R., 'Elusive Justice: Trying to Try Saddam,' *Middle East Report*, No. 215, Vol. 30, No. 2, 2000, pp. 32-5.

Hobsbawm, Eric and Terence Ranger (eds), *The Invention of Tradition*, Cambridge University Press, 2004.

Hobsbawm, Eric J., *Nations and Nationalism since 1780: Programme, Myth, Reality*, Cambridge University Press, second edition, 1992.

Hong, Ying-yi, Michael W. Morris, Chi-yue Chiu and Verónica Benet-Martínez, 'Multicultural Minds: A Dynamic Constructivist Approach to Culture and Cognition', *American Psychologist*, Vol. 55, No. 7, 2000, pp. 709-20.

Horkheimer, Max, *Critical Theory: Selected Essays*, New York: Seabury Press, 1972.

Hossein-Zadeh, Ismael, *The Political Economy of U.S. Militarism*, London: Palgrave-Macmillan, 2006.

Hudson, Leila, 'Lessons From Wal-Mart and the *Wehrmacht*: Team Wolfowitz on Administration in the Information Age,' *Middle East Policy*, Vol. XI, No. 2, Summer 2004. Available at <http://www.mepc.org/journal_vol11/0406_hudson.asp> [accessed 1 September 2006].

Ikenberry, G. John, 'The International Spread of Privatisation Policies: Inducements, Learning, and 'Policy Bandwagoning",' in Ezra N. Suleiman and John Waterbury (eds), *The Political Economy of Public Sector Reform and Privatisation*, Boulder, CO: Westview, 1990, pp. 88-113.

Ismael, Jaqueline, *Kuwait: Dependency and Class in a Rentier State*, Gaineswille: University Press of Florida, 1993.

Issari, Mohammad Ali, *Cinema in Iran, 1900-1979*, Metuchen, NJ: Scarecrow, 1989.

Izadi, Foad and Hakimeh Saghaye-Biria, 'A Discourse Analysis of Elite American Newspaper Editorials: The Case of Iran's Nuclear Program', *Journal of Communication Inquiry*, Vol. 31, No. 2 (April 2007), pp. 140-65.

Jalaeipour, Hamidreza, 'Iran's Islamic Revolution: Achievements and Failures', *Critique: Critical Middle Eastern Studies*, Vol. 15, No. 3, Fall 2006, pp. 207-15.

Jalaeipour, Hamidreza, 'Religious Intellectuals and Political Action in the Reform Movement', Paper prepared for delivery at the conference in 'Intellectual Trends in 20th Century Iran' at Princeton University, 21 October 2000. Available at <http://www.drsoroush.com/PDF/E-CMO-20001021Religious_Intellectuals_and_Political_Action_in_the_Reform_Movement.pdf> [accessed 12 February 2007].

Jones, Charles, *E.H. Carr and International Relations: A Duty to Lie*, Cambridge University Press, 1998.

Jones, Richard Wyn (ed.), *Critical Theory and World Politics*, London: Lynne Rienner, 2001.

Johnson, Chalmers, *The Sorrows of Empire: Militarism, Secrecy, and the End of the Republic*, New York: Metropolitan, 2004.

Kadivar, Mohsen, *Andishe-ye Siyasi dar Eslam*, Vol. 3 *Hokumat-e Entesabi* [Government by Appointment], Tehran: Nashr-e Ney, 1382 (2002).

Kadivar, Mohsen, *Daftar-e aql: majmueh-ye maqalat-e falsafi-alami* [The book of reason: collection of philosophical-theological articles], Tehran: Entesharat-e Ettela'at, 1377 (1998).

Kapuscinski, Ryszard, 'One World, Two Civilisations', in Nathan Gardels (ed.), *The Changing Global Order: World Leaders Reflect*, Oxford: Blackwell, 1997, pp. 3-8.

Kashani-Sabet, Firoozeh, 'Cultures of Iranianness: The Evolving Polemic of Iranian Nationalism', in Nikki R. Keddie and Rudi Matthee (eds), *Iran and the Surrounding World: Interactions in Culture and Cultural Politics*, Seattle: University of Washington Press, 2002, pp. 162-81.

Kasravi, Ahmad, *On Islam and Shi-ism*, translated by M.R. Ghanoonparvar, Costa Mesa: Mazda Publishers, 1990.

Katouzian, Homa, *Mussadiq and the Struggle for Power*, London: I.B. Tauris, 1990.

Katouzian, Homa, *State and Society in Iran: The Eclipse of the Qajars and the Emergence of the Pahlavis*, London: I.B. Tauris, 2006.

Kawtharani, Wajih, 'Mutual Awareness between Arabs and Iranians,' in Khair el-Din Haseeb (ed.), *Arab-Iranian Relations*, Beirut: Centre for Arab Unity Studies, 1998, pp. 73-102.

Keddie, Nikki R. and Rudi Matthee (eds), *Iran and the Surrounding World: Interactions in Culture and Cultural Politics*, Seattle: University of Washington Press, 2002.

Keddie, Nikki R., 'Women in Iran since 1979', *Social Research*, Vol. 67, No. 2, 2000, pp. 407-38.

Keohane, Robert O. (ed.), *Neorealism and its Critics*, New York: Columbia University Press, 1986.

Keshavarz, Fatemeh, *Jasmine and Stars: Reading more than Lolita in Tehran*, Chapel Hill: University of North Carolina Press, 2007.

Khadduri, Majid, *The Gulf War. The Origins and Implications of the Iraq-Iran Conflict*, Oxford University Press, 1988.

Khatami, Mohammad, *Islam, Dialogue and Civil Society*, Canberra: Centre for Arab and Islamic Studies, 2000.

Khatami, Mohammad, *Az 'donyay-e shahr' ta 'shahr-e donya'* [From the 'city world' to the 'global city'], 9th edition, Tehran: Nashr-e Ney, 1379 (2000).

Khatami, Mohammad, *Hope and Challenge*, Binghamton: State University of New York, 1998.

Khomeini, Rouhollah, *Sahifey-e nur,* Vol. 18, Tehran: Vezarat-e Ershad, 1364 (1985).

Khosrokhavar, Farhad and M. Amin Ghaneirad, 'Iran's New Scientific Community', *Iranian Studies*, Vol. 39, No. 2, June 2006, pp. 53-267.

Khosrokhavar, Farhad Shapour Etemad and Masoud Mehrabi 'Report on Science in Post-Revolutionary Iran-Part II: The Scientific Community's Problems of Identity', *Critique: Critical Middle Eastern Studies*, Vol. 13, No. 3, Fall 2004, pp. 363-82.

Kia, Mehrdad, 'Persian Nationalism and the Campaign for Language Purification', *Middle Eastern Studies*, Vol. 34, No. 2, April 1998, pp. 9-36.

Kian, Azadeh, 'Women and Politics in Post-Islamist Iran', *British Journal of Middle Eastern Studies*, Vol. 24, No. 1, 1997, pp. 75-96.

Kier, Elizabeth, 'Culture and Military Doctrine: France between the Wars', *International Security*, Vol. 19, No. 4, Spring 1995, pp. 65-93.

Kissinger, Henry, *Years of Upheaval,* London: Weidenfeld and Nicolson, 1982.

Kristol, Irving, 'The Neoconservative Persuasion: What it Was, and What it Is', in Irwin Stelzer (ed.), *Neoconservatism*, London: Atlantic, 2004, pp. 31-7.

Kuhn, Thomas S., *The Structure of Scientific Revolutions*, second edition, University of Chicago Press, 1970.

Kurzman, Charles, 'Critics Within: Islamic Scholars' Protests Against the Islamic State in Iran', *International Journal of Politics, Culture and Society*, Vol. 15, No.2, Winter 2001, pp. 341-59.

Kurzman, Charles, *Liberal Islam: A Sourcebook*, Oxford University Press, 1998.

Kurzman, Charles, 'Historiography of the Iranian Revolutionary Movement, 1977-1979', *Iranian Studies*, Vol. 28, Nos. 1-2, Winter/Spring 1995, pp. 25-38.

Laali, Massoud, *Khatami az che myguyad*? [What is Mr. Khatami talking about? Logic of talks, freedom of thought, law and its enforcement], 2nd edition, Tehran: Entesharat-e Azady-e Andishe, 1378 (1999).

Lenczowski, George, 'United States' Support for Iran's Independence and Integrity', 1945-1959', *Annals of the American Academy of Political and Social Science*, Vol. 401, America and the Middle East, May 1972, pp. 45-55.

Little, Richard and Michael Smith (eds), *Perspectives on World Politics*, London: Routledge, 1991.

Linklater, Andrew (ed.), *International Relations: Critical Concepts in Political Science,* especially volumes IV and V, London: Routledge, 2000.

Lotfian, Saideh, 'Taking Sides: Regional Powers and the War', in Farhang Rajaee (ed.), *Iranian Perspectives on the Iran-Iraq War*, Gainesville: University Press of Florida, 1997, pp. 13-28.

Luijendijk, D.H., *Zoor Khane: History and Techniques of the Ancient Martial Art of Iran*, Boulder, CO: Paladin, 2006.

Maljoo, Mohammad, 'Worker Protest in the Age of Ahmadinejad', *Middle East Report*, No. 241, Vol. 36, No. 4, Winter 2006, pp. 30-3.
Mann, Michael, *Incoherent Empire*, London: Verso, 2003.
Marcuse, Herbert, *Towards A Critical Theory of Society: Collected Papers of Herbert Marcuse*, Vol. 2, edited by Douglas Kellner, London: Routledge, 2001.
Marcuse, Herbert, *One-dimensional Man: Studies in the Ideology of Advanced Industrial Society*, London: Routledge, 1964.
Marx, Karl, *Survey from Exile*, edited by David Fernbach, Harmondsworth: Penguin, 1973.
Marx, Karl, *The Eighteenth Brumaire of Louis Bonaparte*, translated by Daniel de Leon, London: Labour News, 1898.
Matin-Asgari, Afshin, 'From Social Democracy to Social Democracy: The Twentieth-Century Odyssey of the Iranian Left', in Stephanie Cronin (ed.), *Reformers and Revolutionaries in Modern Iran: New Perspectives on the Iranian Left*, London: Routledge, 2004, pp. 37-64.
Matin-Asgari, Afshin, 'The Intellectual Best-sellers of Post-revolutionary Iran: On Backwardness, Elite-Killing, and Western Rationality', *Iranian Studies*, Vol. 37, No. 1, March 2004, pp. 73-88.
Matin-Asgari, Afshin, *Iranian Student Opposition to the Shah*, Costa Mesa: Mazda, 2001.
Matin-Asgari, Afshin, 'The Causes of Iran's Backwardness', *Critique: Critical Middle Eastern Studies*, Vol. 13, No. 3, Fall 1998, pp. 103-7.
Matin-Asgari, Afshin, 'Iranian Postmodernity: the Rhetoric of Irrationality?', *Critique: Critical Middle Eastern Studies*, Vol. 13, No. 1, 1994, pp. 113-23.
Mead, George H., *Mind, Self, and Society*, Chicago University Press, 1934.
Mead, Margaret, 'Warfare is only an Invention—Not a Biological Necessity', in Leon Bramson and George W. Goethals (eds), *War: Studies from Psychology, Sociology, Anthropology*, London: Basic Books, 1964, pp. 269-74.
Mearsheimer, John and Stephen Walt, 'The Israel Lobby', *London Review of Books*, Vol. 28, No. 6, 23 March 2006. Available at <http://www.lrb.co.uk/v28/n06/mear01_.html> [accessed 23 May 2006].
Menashri, David, *Post-Revolutionary Politics in Iran: Religion, Society and Power*, London: Frank Cass, 2001.
Mehran, Golnar, 'The Presentation of the "Self" and the "Other" in Postrevolutionary Iranian School Textbooks', in Nikki R. Keddie and Rudi Matthee (eds), *Iran and the Surrounding World: Interactions in Culture and Cultural Politics*, Seattle: University of Washington Press, 2002, pp. 232-53.
Miller, James, *The Passion of Michel Foucault*, London: HarperCollins, 1993.
Mir-Hosseini, Ziba and Richard Tapper, *Islam and Democracy in Iran: Eshkevari and the Quest for Reform*, London: I.B. Tauris, 2006.

Mir-Hosseini, Ziba, *Islam and Gender: The Religious Debate in Contemporary Iran*, Princeton University Press, 1999.

Mirsepassi, Ali, *Intellectual Discourse and the Politics of Modernization: Negotiating Modernity in Iran*, Cambridge, MA: Harvard University Press, 2000.

Mirza, Qudsia (ed.), *Islamic Feminism and Law*, London: Cavendish House, 2005.

Moghissi, Haideh, *Populism and Feminism in Iran*, London: Macmillan, 1994.

Morgenthau, Hans, *Politics among Nations*, New York: Alfred Knopf, 1948.

Morris, Michael W., Tanya Menon and Daniel R. Ames, 'Culturally Conferred Conceptions of Agency: A Key to Social Perception of Persons, Groups, and Other Actors', *Personality and Social Psychology Review*, Vol. 5, No. 2, 2001, pp. 169-82.

Mottahedeh, Roy P., 'Shiite Political Thought and the Destiny of the Iranian Revolution', in Jamal S. al-Suwaidi (ed.), *Iran and the Gulf: A Search for Stability*, Abu Dhabi: The Emirates Center for Strategic Studies and Research, 1996, pp. 70-80.

Mottahedeh, Roy, *The Mantle and the Prophet: Religion and Politics in Iran*, New York: Simon and Schuster, 1985.

Mutahhari [Mottahari], Mortada [Morteza], 'Shahid', in M. Abedi and G. Leggenhausen (eds), *Jihad and Shahadat: Struggle and Martyrdom in Islam*, Houston: Institute for Research and Islamic Studies, 1986.

Mottahari, Morteza, *The Rights of Women in Islam*, Tehran: World Organization for Islamic Service, 1974.

Mottahari, Morteza, *Islam and Iran*, Beirut: Dar al-Ta'aruf, no date.

Mueller, John, *Retreat from Doomsday: The Obsolescence of Major War*, London: Basic Books, 1990.

Nabavi, Negin, *Intellectuals and the State in Iran: Politics, Discourse and the Dilemma of Authenticity*, Gainesville: University of Florida Press, 2003.

Nabavi, Negin, 'The Changing Concept of the "Intellectual" in Iran of the 1960s', *Iranian Studies*, Vol. 32, No. 3, Summer 1999, pp. 333-50.

Naficy, Hamid, 'Cinematic Exchange Relations: Iran and the West', in Nikki R. Keddie and Rudi Matthee (eds), *Iran and the Surrounding World: Interactions in Culture and Cultural Politics*, Seattle: University of Washington Press, pp. 254-78.

Nasr, Hossein with Mehdi Aminrazavi, *An Anthology of Philosophy in Persia*, Volumes I and II, Oxford University Press, 1999.

Nasr, Hossein *The Islamic Intellectual Tradition in Persia*, edited by Mehdi Aminrazavi, Surrey: Curzon, 1996.

Nasri, Vali, *The Shia Revival: How Conflicts within Islam will Shape the Future*, New York: W.W. Norton, 2007.

Nazemi, Nader, 'Sacrifice and Authorship: A Compendium of the Will of Iranian War Martyrs', *Iranian Studies*, Vol. 30, Nos. 3-4, Summer-Fall 1997, pp. 263-71.

Nietzsche, Friedrich, *The Genealogie of Morals: An Attack*, translated by Francis Golffing, New York: Doubleday & Co., 1956.

Nixon, Rob, *London Calling: V.S. Naipaul, Post-colonial Mandarin*, Oxford University Press, 1992.

Nye, Joseph S., *Soft Power: The Means to Success in World Politics*, New York: PublicAffairs, 2004.

Onuf, Nicholas, *The Republican Legacy in International Thought*, Cambridge University Press, 1998.

Paidar, Parvin, *Women and the Political Process in Twentieth-Century Iran*, Cambridge University Press, 1995.

Parsons, Anthony, 'Iran and the United Nations, with Particular Reference to the Iran-Iraq War', in Anoushiravan Ehteshami and Manshour Varasteh (eds), *Iran and the International Community*, London: Routledge, 1991.

Prestowitz, Clyde, *Rogue Nation: American Unilateralism and the Failure of Good Intentions,* New York: Basic, 2004.

Rajaee, Farhang (ed.), *Iranian Perspectives on the Iran-Iraq War*, Gainesville: University Press of Florida, 1997.

Rajaee, Farhang, 'Iranian Ideology and Worldview: The Cultural Export of Revolution,' in John L. Esposito (ed.), *The Iranian Revolution: Its Global Impact*, Miami: Florida International University Press, 1990, pp. 63-80.

Rajaee, Farhang, *Islamic Values and World View: Khomeyni on Man, the State and International Politics*, vol. XIII, London: University Press of America, 1983.

Rahnema, Ali, *An Islamic Utopian. A Political Biography of Ali Shariati*, London: I.B. Tauris, 2000.

Rahnema, Ali, *The Constitution of Iran: Politics and the State in the Islamic Republic*, translated by John O' Keane, London: I.B. Tauris, 1997.

Ramazani, R.K., *Revolutionary Iran: Challenge and Response in the Middle-East*, Baltimore: Johns Hopkins University Press, 1986.

Rejali, Darius M., *Torture and Modernity: Self, Society, and State in Modern Iran*, Boulder, CO: Westview, 1994.

Ricoeur, Paul, *Time and Narrative, Volume I*, translated by Kathleen McLaughlin and David Pellauer, University of Chicago Press, 1984.

Ricoeur, Paul, *Lectures on Ideology and Utopia,* edited by George H. Taylor, New York: Columbia University Press, 1986.

Ridgeon, Lloyd (ed.), *Religion and Politics in Modern Iran: A Reader*, London: I.B. Tauris, 2005.

Robinson, Julian Perry and Jozef Goldblat, 'Chemical Warfare in the Iraq-Iran War', *SIPRI Fact Sheet*, Chemical Weapons I. Stockholm International Peace Research Institute (May 1984).

Rochard, Philippe, 'The Identities of the Iranian *Zurkhanah*', translated by H.E. Chehabi, *Iranian Studies*, Vol. 35, No. 4, Fall 2002, pp. 313-40.

Rothstein, Edward, Herbert Muschkamp and Martin E. Marty, *Visions of Utopia*, Oxford University Press, 2003.

Roy, Olivier, *Globalised Islam: The Search for a New Ummah*, London: Hurst & Company, 2004.

Roy, Olivier, *The Failure of Political Islam*, translated by Carol Volk, London: I.B. Tauris, 1999.

Saad, Joya Blondel, *The Image of Arabs in Modern Persian Literature*, Lanham: University Press of America, 1996.

al-Sadr, Mohammad Bagher, 'The Psychological Role of Islam in Economic Development' in John J. Donohue and John L. Esposito (eds), *Islam in Transition: Muslim Perspectives*, 2nd edition, Oxford University Press, 2007, pp. 249-259.

Sadri, Mahmoud, 'Sacral Defence of Secularism: the Political Theologies of Soroush, Shabestari, and Kadivar', *International Journal of Politics, Culture and Society*, Vol. 15, No. 2, pp. 257-70.

Said, Edward, *Reflections on Exile: and other Essays*, Cambridge, MA: Harvard University Press, 2000.

Said, Edward, *Covering Islam How the Media and the Experts Determine How We See the Rest of the World*, London: Verso, 1997.

Said, Edward, *Culture and Imperialism*, London: Vintage, 1993.

Said, Edward, *Orientalism: Western Conceptions of the Orient*, London: Routledge & Kegan Paul, 1978.

Sajjadpour, Mohammad Kazem, 'Iran and September 11: A Conceptual Framework for Understanding Foreign Policy', *The Iranian Journal of International Affairs*, Vol. XIII, No. 4, Winter 2001-2002, pp. 421-43.

Sarchosh, Niku and Afshin Jahandideh, *Eradeh beh danestan : Michel Fuku*, Tehran: Nashreney, 2004.

Savory, Roger M., 'The Principle of Homeostasis Considered in Relation to Political Events in Iran in the 1960's', *International Journal of Middle East Studies (IJMES)*, Vol. 3, No. 3, July 1972, pp. 282-302.

Saussure, Ferdinand, *Course in General Linguistics*, New York: McGraw Hill, 1964.

Schaar, Stuart, 'Orientalism at the Service of Imperialism', *Race and Class*, Vol. 21, No. 1, 1979, pp. 67-80.

Schirazi, Asghar, *The Constitution of Iran: Politics and the State in the Islamic Republic*, translated by John O' Kane, London: I.B. Tauris, 1998.

Schock, Kurt, *Unarmed Insurrections: People Power Movements in Nondemocracies*, London: University of Minnesota Press, 2005.

Shaery-Eisenlohr, Roschanak, 'Imagining Shiite Iran: Transnationalism and Religious Authenticity in the Muslim World', *Iranian Studies*, Vol. 40, No. 1, February 2007, pp. 17-35.

Shakeri, Reza, *Andish-e siasy Shariati va naghd-e Shariatism* [The political thought of Ali Shariati and the exploration of Shariatiism], Tehran: Pejuheshgah-e Olum-e Ensani-ye va Eshtemahi-ye Jahad-e Daneshgahi, 1382 (2003).

Shakuri, Naser Alireza Emami, Mohammad Ali Bahmani, Fatemeh Rake'i, Parviz Abbasi-Dakani and Reza Esma'ili, 'Elegies for a Lost Leader: Six Poems on the Death of Khomeini', translated by Paul E. Losensky, *Iranian Studies*, Vol. 30, Nos. 3-4, Summer-Fall 1997, pp. 277-89.

Shariati, Ali, *Man and Islam: Lectures by Ali Shariati*, translated from Persian by Ghulam M. Fayez, Mashhad: University of Mashhad Press, 1982.

Sharp, Gene, *The Politics of Nonviolent Action*, Boston: Porter Sargent, 1973.

Shaw, Donald L. and Shannon E. Martin, 'The Natural, and Inevitable, Phases of War Reporting: Historical Shadows, New Communication in the Persian Gulf', in Robert E. Denton Jr. (ed.), *The Media and the Persian Gulf War*, Westport, CT: Praeger, 1993, pp. 43-70.

Shaw, Stanford, 'The Editor's Desk', *International Journal of Middle East Studies (IJMES)*, Vol. 3, No. 3, July 1972, pp. 241-2.

Shayegan, Daryush, *Cultural Schizophrenia: Islamic Societies Confronting the West*, translated by John Howe, Syracuse University Press, 1997.

Sheibani, Khatereh, 'Kiarostami and the Aesthetics of Modern Persian Poetry', *Iranian Studies*, Vol. 39, No. 4, December 2006, pp. 509-37.

Sheikholeslami, Reza, 'The Transformation of Iran's Political Culture', *Critique: Critical Middle Eastern Studies*, Vol. 9, No. 3, 2000, pp. 105-34.

Sheikholeslami, Reza, 'Is it Iran or Persia? The Identity Issue in the Islamic Republic', *Journal of South Asian and Middle Eastern Studies*, Vol. 25, No. 1, Fall 2001, pp. 3-12.

Sifry, Micah L. and Christopher Cerf (eds), *The Iraq War Reader. History, Documents, Opinions*, London: Touchstone, 2003.

Sina, Ibn, *Mantiq al-mashriqiyyin* [The Logic of Orientals], Cairo: Salafiyyah Press, 1910.

'Soroush: pedar chande-ye eslah talaban nistam [Soroush: I am not the godfather of the reform movement], *Shargh*, 29 Mordad 1385, (20 August 2006).

Soroush, Abdolkarim, *Reason, Freedom and Democracy in Islam: Essential Writings of 'Abdolkarim Soroush,* Mahmoud Sadri and Ahmad Sadri, translators and editors, Oxford University Press, 2000.

Soroush, Abdolkarim, 'Scientific Development, Political Development', *Kian Monthly Review* 10, No. 54, Oct.-Nov. 2000. Available at <http://www.

drsoroush.com/English/By_drsoroush/E-CMB-19990500-Seminar_on_Tradition_and_Modernism_held_in_Beheshti_University.html> [accessed 12 June 2004].

Starr, Paul, 'The New Life of the Liberal State: Privatisation and the Restructuring of State-Society Relations', in Ezra N. Suleiman and John Waterbury (eds), *The Political Economy of Public Sector Reform and Privatisation*, Boulder, CO: Westview, 1990, pp. 22-54.

Steinfels, Peter, *The Neoconservatives: The Men Who Are Changing America's Politics,* New York: Simon and Schuster, 1979.

Stelzer, Irwin (ed.), *Neoconservatism*, London: Atlantic, 2004.

Stone, Richard, 'Science in Iran: An Islamic Science Revolution?', *Science*, Vol. 309, Issue 5742, 16 September 2005, pp. 1802-4.

Slemon, Stephen, 'Post-Colonial Critical Theories', in Gregory Castle (ed.), *Postcolonial Discourses: An Anthology*, Oxford: Blackwell, 2001, pp. 99-116.

Tahir-Kheli, Shirin and Shaheen Ayubi, *The Iran-Iraq War: New Weapons, Old Conflicts*, London: Praeger, 1983.

Takeyh, Ray, 'God's Will: Iranian Democracy and the Islamic Context', *Middle East Policy*, Vol. VII, No. 4, October 2000, pp. 41-9.

Taleghani, Mahmud [Mahmoud], 'The Characteristics of Islamic Economics', in John J. Donohue and John L. Esposito (eds), *Islam in Transition: Muslim Perspectives*, 2nd edition, Oxford University Press, 2007, pp. 229-35.

Taleghani, Mahmoud, *Islam and Ownership* (Islam wa malekiyat), translated by William Darrow, Houston: Islamic Distribution Center, n.d.

Tapper, Richard (ed.), *The New Iranian Cinema: Politics, Representation and* Identity, London: I.B. Tauris, 2002.

Tarock, Adam, *Iran's Foreign Policy since 1990: Pragmatism Supersedes Islamic Ideology*, Commack: Nova Science Press, 1999.

Tarock, Adam, *The Superpowers' Involvement in the Iran-Iraq War*, Commack: Nova Science Press, 1998.

Tavakoli-Targhi, Mohammad, *Refashioning Iran: Orientalism, Occidentalism and Historiography*, New York: Palgrave, 2001.

Telhami, Shibley, *Power and Leadership in International Bargaining: The Path to the Camp David Accords*, New York: Columbia University Press, 1990.

Tohidi, Nayereh, 'International Connections of the Iranian Women's Movement', in Nikki R. Keddie and Rudi Matthee (eds), *Iran and the Surrounding World: Interactions in Culture and Cultural Politics*, Seattle: University of Washington Press, 2002, pp. 205-31.

Trautner, Bernhard J., 'The Clash *Within* Civilisations: Islam and the Accommodation of Plurality,' InIIS-Working Paper No. 13/99, Institut für Interkulturelle und Internationale Studien, Universität Bremen. Available at <http://www-user.uni-bremen.de/~bjtraut/clash/clash.pdf> [accessed 12 November 2001].

Tripp, Charles, *A History of Iraq*, second edition, Cambridge University Press, 2002.

Trotsky, Leon, *The Revolution Betrayed: What is the Soviet Union and where is it Going?*, New York: Pathfinder, 1937.

Tusi, Nasir Al-Din 'Sayr wa Suluk' (Contemplation and Action), in Seyyed Hossein Nasr with Mehdi Aminrazavi, *An Anthology of Philosophy in Persia*, Vol. II, Oxford: Oxford University Press, pp. 344-56.

Vahdat, Farzin, *God and Juggernaut: Iran's Intellectual Encounter with Modernity*, Syracuse University Press, 2002.

Vakilli, Valla, *Debating Religion and Politics: The Political Thought of Abdol Karim Soroush*, New York: Council on Foreign Relations, 1997.

Walker, R.B.J., *Inside/Outside: International Relations as Political Theory*, Cambridge: Cambridge University Press, 1993.

Weber, Max, *From Max Weber: Essays in Sociology*, London: Routledge, 1998.

Wells, Matthew C., 'Thermidor in the Islamic Republic of Iran: the rise of Muhammad Khatami', *British Journal of Middle Eastern Studies*, Vol. 26, No. 1, Winter 1999, pp. 27-39.

Wendt, Alexander, *Social Theory of International Politics*, Cambridge: Cambridge University Press, 1999.

White, Hayden, *Metahistory: The Historical Imagination in Nineteenth-Century Europe*, Baltimore: The Johns Hopkins University Press, 1973.

Williams, Raymond, *Marxism and Literature*, Oxford: Oxford University Press, 1977.

Williams, Raymond, *Culture and Society, 1780-1950*, Harmondsworth: Penguin, 1961.

Wright, Robin B., 'Two Visions of Reformation,' *Journal of Democracy*, Vol. 7, No. 2 (1996), pp. 64-75.

Yamani, Mai (ed.), *Feminism and Islam: Legal and Literary Perspectives*, London: Ithaca Press, 1996.

Yasin, Kamal Nazer, 'Iran: New Direction?,' *Middle East International*, 3 August 2005. Available at <http://meionline.com/features/390.shtml> [accessed 1 Decmber 2005].

Yousefi, A.M. Haji, 'The Foreign Policy of the Islamic Republic of Iran: Constraints, Opportunities and Pressures', *The Iranian Journal of International Affairs*, Vol. XVII, Nos. 2 & 3, Summer Fall 2004, pp. 205-303.

Zamanpour, Majid (ed.), *Jelveha-ye Nur* (The Faces of Light), Tehran: Cultural Centre of the Revolutionary Guards, Spring 1373 (1995).

Zanders, Jean Pascal, 'Allegations of Iranian CW use in the 1980-88 Gulf War: A critical analysis from open sources', Washington DC: SIPRI, 7 March 2001.

Zarif, Javad, 'Indispensable Power: Hegemonic Tendencies in a Globalized World," *Harvard International Review* XXIV, No. 4, Winter 2003. Available at <http://www.ceip.org/files/Publications/2003-04-01-brumberg-HIR.asp?from=pubdate> [accessed 13 November 2003].

Zarif, Mohammad Javad and Mohammad Reza Alborzi, 'Weapons of mass destruction in Iran's Security Paradigm: The Case of Chemical Weapons', *The Iranian Journal of International Affairs*, Vol. XI, No. 4, Winter 1999-2000, pp. 511-523.

Zonis, Marvin, 'The Political Elite of Iran: a second stratum?', in Frank Tachau (ed.), *Political elites and political development in the Middle East*, New York, Halsted Press, 1975.

Zumach, Alexander, 'Blühende Geschäfte. In sämtlichen Rüstungsbereichen haben Firmen aus den fünf ständigen Ratsländern Irak unterstützt', *die Tageszeitung (TAZ)*, 19 December 2002, <http://www.taz.de/pt/2002/12/19/a0076.nf/text> [accessed 12 March 2006].

NEWSPAPERS, E-NEWSLETTERS, AGENCIES, JOURNALS, PERIODICALS ETC.

Agence France Press (AFP)
Al-Ahram
American Psycholigist
Annals of the American Academy of Political and Social Science
Aus Politik und Zeitgeschichte
Bayan
BBC Summary of World Broadcasts
BBC Survey of World Broadcasts
bitterlemons-international.org
Boston Globe
British Journal of Middle Eastern Studies
Cambridge Review of International Affairs
Christian Science Monitor
Common Dreams
Counterpunch
Critique: Critical Middle Eastern Studies
die Tageszeitung (TAZ)
Etemad-e Melli
Financial Times
Foreign Affairs

Foreign Policy
Green Left Weekly
Gulf Times
History and Theory
International Affairs
International Journal of Middle East Studies
International Journal of Politics, Culture and Society
International Organisation
International Security
International Sociology
International Studies Journal
International Studies Notes
Inter Press Service (IPS)
Iran Analysis Quarterly
Iran Daily
Iranian Studies
Islamic Republic News Agency (IRNA)
Journal of Communication Inquiry
Journal of Democracy
Journal of Peace Research
Kayhan (Tehran)
Kian Monthly Review
London Review of Books
Los Angeles Times
Middle East International
Middle East Online
Middle East Policy
Middle East Quarterly
Middle East Report
Middle Eastern Studies
Monthly Review
Monthly Review Webzine
National Journal
New Left Review
New Statesmen
Newsweek
Orient, Deutsche Zeitschrift für Politik und Wirtschaft des Orients
Personality and Social Psychology Review
The Progressive
Race and Class
Reuters
Safedemocracy.org

Salon
Science
Shargh
Social Research
State of Nature
Strategic Insights
Strategic Studies Quarterly
Tehran Times
The Chronicle of Higher Education
The Daily Star (Beirut)
The Guardian
The Independent
The International Herald Tribune
The Iranian Journal of International Affairs
The Journal of Politics
The Nation
The New Republic
The New York Times
The New Yorker
The Observer
The Star-Ledger
The Sunday Times
The Wall Street Journal
The Washington Post
The Washington Quarterly
Time Magazine
Washington Report on Middle East Affairs

SELECTED INTERNET SOURCES

'Comprehensive Report of the Special Advisor to the DCI on Iraq's WMD', 30 September 2004, <http://www.cia.gov/cia/report/iraq wmd 2004/transmittal.html> [accessed 21 January 2005].

Human Rights Watch, 'Genocide in Iraq. The Anfal Campaign Against the Kurds', <http://www.hrw.org/reports/1993/iraqanfal/> [accessed 23 March 2006].

'Iran Cultural Heritage Organisation' <http://www.chn.ir> [accessed 21 January 2007].

Iraq Research and Documentation Program at the Center for Middle East Studies, Harvard University, <http://www.fas.harvard.edu/~irdp/ > [accessed 12 February 2005].

National Security Archive (NSA), George Washington University. 'Saddam Hussein: More Secret History', 18 December 2003, <http://www.gwu.edu/~nsarchiv/NSAEBB/NSAEBB107/> [accessed 14 March 2006].

NSA Electronic Briefing Book No. 82 (25 February 2003), 'Shaking Hands with Saddam Hussein. The US Tilts toward Iraq, 1980-1984', Joyce Battle, ed., <http://www.gwu.edu/~nsarchiv/NSAEBB/NSAEBB82/index.htm> [accessed 13 March 2006].

'Pentagon Inspector General Report on Intelligence Assessment Activities of the Office of Under Secretary of Defense Doug Feith' (April 2007). <http://www.fas.org/irp/agency/dod/ig020907-decl.pdf> [accessed 14 April 2007].

Society for Chemical Victims Support (SCWVS), <http//:www.scwvs.org> [accessed 14 February 2007].

US Department of State, Foreign Relations, 1969-1976, Volume E-4, Documents on Iran and Iaq, 1969-1972, <http://www.state.gov/r/pa/ho/frus/nixon/e4/> [accessed 21 April 2007].

US House of Representatives, Speech by Henry B. Gonzalez: 'Bush Administration Had Acute Knowledge of Iraq's Military Industrialisation Plans' (27 July 1992). <http://www.fas.org/spp/starwars/congress/1992/h920727g.htm> [accessed 21 January 2004].

US Senate, 103rd Congress, Second Session (25 May 1994) a Report of Chairman Donald W. Riegle, Jr. and Ranking Member Alfonse M. D'Amato of the Committee on Banking, Housing and Urban Affairs with Respect to Export Administration: 'The Riegle Report. US Chemical and Biological Warfare-Related Dual Use Exports to Iraq and their Possible Impact on the Health Consequences of the Gulf War', <http://www.gulfweb.org/bigdoc/report/riegle1.html> [accessed 12 February 2005].

US Senate Committee on Banking, Housing, and Urban Affairs (7 October 1994). Committee Staff Report No.3: Chemical Warfare Agent Identification, Chemical Injuries, and Other Findings. Principal Investigator James J Tuite III: 'US Chemical and Biological Exports to Iraq and their Possible Impact on the Health Consequences of the Persian Gulf War', <http://www.chronicillnet.org/PGWS/tuite/chembio.html> [accessed 14 March 2006].

World Public Opinion: Global Public Opinion on International Affairs, 26 January 2007. <http://www.worldpublicopinion.org/pipa/articles/home_page/307.php?nid=&id=&pnt=307&lb=hmpg1> [accessed 15 February 2007].

Jimmy Carter Library and Museum, 'The Hostage Crisis in Iran', <http://www.jimmycarterlibrary.org/documents/hostages.phtml> [accessed 18 April 2007].

INDEX